VALUING LANGUAGE STUDY

Valuing Language Study

Inquiry into Language for Elementary and Middle Schools

YETTA M. GOODMAN
University of Arizona

National Council of Teachers of English
1111 W. Kenyon Road, Urbana, Illinois 61801-1096

Staff Editor: Bonny Graham
Interior Design: Jenny Jensen Greenleaf
Cover Design: Pat Mayer
Cover and Interior Photographs: Joel Brown

NCTE Stock Number: 56266-3050

Library of Congress Cataloging-in-Publication Data

Goodman, Yetta M., 1931–
    Valuing language study : inquiry into language for elementary and middle schools / Yetta M. Goodman.
        p. cm.
Includes bibliographical references and index.
    ISBN 0-8141-5626-6 (pbk.)
    1. Language arts (Elementary). 2. Language arts (Middle school) I. National Council of Teachers of English. II. Title
    LB1576 .G7195 2003
    372.6—dc21
                                                                2002151992

To my daughters, Debi, Karen, and Wendy, who continue to show me how to value language and language development. As children they intrigued and inspired me with their love of talk and books and their language inventions. As adolescents they introduced me to the flexible ranges of urban dialects and registers as they communicated with friends, teachers, and other adults in their lives. Their reading and written expressions revealed their personalities and understandings. As adults they continue to reveal the concept of lifelong language learning as I interact with them, as they add new languages and new ways of using language, and as they develop as authors. As professionals they continue to heighten my understanding of the importance of trusting and respecting learners of all ages. As mothers they have provided a second generation of language informants. So I also dedicate this to Eli, Reuben, Aaron, Shoshana, Joshua, Noah, and Rachel.

CONTENTS

PREFACE

I have been researching, teaching, and writing about language and literacy all of my professional life. Language study provides me with many opportunities to consider the role of language in relation to the human condition and to support the rights of students and their teachers to use their own language and thinking to understand the world—to express what they know and believe freely and to be able to make sense of what others say and write.

I have been writing this book on language study in elementary and middle school classrooms for more than a decade. I have read work by others regarding language study that supported my continual rethinking and aided in organizing language study possibilities. I have used this work to reflect on what I think is valuable about language study for kids in school. As a former teacher of both children and adolescents, I knew that kids could get excited about language issues that affected their daily lives. My interest in language study for students built on my own teaching and was extended through dynamic discussions with colleagues, including teachers who hold similar beliefs about the importance of language study experiences that energize and excite elementary and middle school students. The teachers in my classes responded enthusiastically to these ideas. Most of them hadn't considered the possibilities of a whole language inquiry curriculum focused on studying language through their own and their students' questions and concerns.

A number of years ago I began to write these ideas for possible publication and shared my writing with colleagues and graduate students. Their responses and our interactions have enriched the ideas in this book and helped me continuously revise and adapt my writing. I never revisit this book without finding something new to add or remembering something more that I want to share.

I continue to wonder why K–12 curricula do not focus more on language as an object of study—language and linguistic study. As an educational community, colleagues, students, and teachers love to think and talk about language. We wonder about language use and its power, we contemplate how people use language to control others, and we marvel at how children manipulate language and reveal their own knowledge of its system and use. We observe with awe children's inventions as they explore speaking, listening, reading, and writing for their own purposes. At the same time, we are concerned about the myths expressed in the popular press and by self-styled language purists. Parents and the general public often use folk linguistic notions to make voting and policy decisions about language issues and schooling. Considering this interest in language use in school and society, it is curious that we aren't doing more to teach *about* language—to bring our excitement, our interests, and concerns to our students. We need to find innovative ways to generate the excitement of learning about language and linguistics among children and adolescents. This book is my attempt to help raise the consciousness of teachers and the language arts profession as a whole to consider the importance of treating language as a matter for serious inquiry by young people.

Therefore, I invite the readers of this book to explore the power of teaching and learning about language, to share your ideas with me, and also to present your ideas to the world. We all have language stories within us that help us and others learn lessons about the power of language. Emily Dickinson declares her passion in a poem: "This is my letter to the world." This book is my attempt to expand that simple but powerful statement to teachers and students, encouraging them to find multiple ways to send their letters to the world. As a reader of this book, you also can support my continuous adventure into the study of language by e-mailing or writing me to make suggestions and ask tough questions that will help me reconsider the directions in which I'm traveling. Please e-mail ygoodman@ u.arizona.edu; write University of Arizona, College of Education,

Department of Language, Reading and Culture, Room 504, Tucson, Arizona 85721; or interact with me at conferences (come up and say hello). Although I am interested in your responses to my ideas, I expect you to add to my thinking and let me know what you've done in relation to language study.

As we share the continuous and ever-growing knowledge about language, we contribute to one another's growth. With such knowledge, teachers at all levels of education develop the insights that support their students in discovering the possibilities in language study. As a result, students come to understand that conscious awareness (as opposed to intuitive awareness) of their language use and the form it takes greatly influences the language they use and the lives they live.

With a book so long in development, I must thank the many people who have often pushed me toward disequilibrium and influenced my thinking in response to this manuscript. And I'm sure there are many more whose names I have missed. In any case, I want to make sure that this group, at least, knows how grateful I am for their thoughtful consideration and help: Sumru Akcan, Wendy Black, Betsy Brown, Joel Brown, Carole Edelsky, Ann Freeman, David Freeman, Lauren Freedman, Peter Fries, Debra Goodman, Kenneth Goodman, Debra Jacobson, Sandy Kaser, Koomi Kim, Marge Knox, Judith Lindfors, Sapargul Mirseitova, Sharon Murphy, Sheila Nicholas, Carol Porter, Marie Ruiz, Tracy Smiles, Cathy Wallace, Wen-Yun Lin, Sandra Wilde, and Andy Young. Also, thanks to my support system at NCTE: Peter Feely, Kurt Austin, and Bonny Graham who helped me bring this work to fruition.

INTRODUCTION

Parents, teachers, and language researchers amuse themselves and others with wonderful stories about children's comments about language. Ruqaiya Hasan (1973, p. 13), a language development researcher, recorded the following conversations with young school-age children:

> INTERVIEWER: . . . [W]hen you have a small baby in the house, do you call it "it" or do you call it "she" or "he"?
>
> CHILD 1: Well, if you don't know what it is, I think you ought to call it "it," because you don't know whether you're calling it a boy or a girl, and if it gets on, and if you start calling it "she" then you find out it's a boy, you can't stop yourself, 'cause you've got used to calling it "she."
>
> CHILD 2: Well, if it's in your family, I think you should call it either "he" or "she" or else the poor thing when it grows up won't know what it is.

Stephanie Youngerman, a first-grade teacher from Boise, Idaho, tells a language story about one of her first graders. Her class fell in love with Pete Seeger's (1986) story/song "Abiyoyo." The boy in the story likes to pluck on his guitar while his father plays annoying tricks on the townspeople. They are both ostracized for disturbing members of the community, and it is obvious in the story that being ostracized means they have to live on the edge of town. One day while Stephanie and her class were rearranging desks, one of her first graders said to her, "Oh, no! I'm being ostracized." Stephanie asked, "What do you mean?" The six-year-old replied, "My desk is at the edge of the room!"

Students also provide commentary about language use. When Kenneth Goodman taught eighth grade, he decided to discuss metaphors with his kids after an experience he had with them while on a field trip. As they passed a cemetery, Mark, who was looking out the bus window, called out, "Hey, there's Marlbor-ough Country," echoing the words of a current cigarette com-mercial. When Ken asked what that meant, the kids looked at one another as if they couldn't believe their ears, and Shelly said, "You don't know that? Cemeteries are Marlborough Country because cigarettes cause death."

Children explore and talk about written language as well as oral language. Ander's mother, a graduate student, told me that when he was three years old, he looked at a Safeway bag, pointed to the first *a* in *Safeway,* and said, "That's mine." Parents with inquisitive three- or four-year-olds often hear them ask, "What does this say?" as the child points to a written sign or name. The child is using language to talk about language using the word *say* as a metaphor for *read.* These language stories are lessons that reveal to teachers and language researchers that students within a range of ages talk and think about language (Harste, Wood-ward, & Burke, 1984, p. xv).

Talking about Language: A Folk Process

People in different communities, adults as well as children, also talk and explore language and language issues. In the Jewish com-munity, folks tell a story about a Jewish man named Shawn Ferguson. He got his Irish-sounding name because he was told by a friend on the boat coming to the United States from Europe that he should not tell the immigration officials that his name was Itzik Ladishkov. Immigration officials, according to his friend, simply change the names of immigrants on their official entry documents whenever they find them too difficult to pronounce or spell. "Tell them your name is Cohen or Levy," the friend said. "The officials can handle those names because they are easy to spell and you'll still have a Jewish name." But when the man came before the official, he forgot the names his friend had sug-gested, and he said in Yiddish, "Oy Shoin Fargessen" (which means, Oh my! I forgot already). The official, thinking the phrase *shoin fargessen* was a name, wrote "Shawn Ferguson" on the official document. I've heard similar stories from other ethnic groups. My Swedish American professor, for example, liked to tell her classes about one of her countrymen who had a Chinese-sounding name. She explained that he was standing in a very long line waiting for his turn to be interviewed and officially admitted to the United States. He overheard a number of his countrymen in line immediately in front of him say to the immigration officer, "My name is Ole Olson." When the immigrant came before the official, he decided to save time and said, "The same thing." But once again, through ignorance, the official heard a name rather than an English phrase, and he wrote "Sam Ting" on the man's entry documents.

Immigrant communities circulate many jokes poking fun at government officials who misinterpret names and other language forms they are not familiar with. Of course, this kind of humor passes on the accepted ethnic folklore that bureaucrats are insensitive to immigrants and their languages and that such officials are not very bright and thus easily hoodwinked. The talk of immigrants reveals that they not only talk about language but also are well aware of its power in society. Jokes that focus on the ways in which immigrants' first language gets distorted in the English-speaking culture and the ridiculous ways that English speakers attempt to pronounce and understand languages other than English abound in multilingual communities. I get hearty applause when I ask a bilingual audience:

QUESTION: What do you call someone who speaks two languages?

ANSWER: Bilingual.

QUESTION: And what do you call someone who speaks three languages?

ANSWER: Trilingual.

QUESTION: And someone who speaks one language?

ANSWER: Monolingual?

RESPONSE: No! American!

The term *folk linguistics* is often used to refer to the comments made by the public about language that represents a mix of scholarly insights and superstition. In everyday life, as people try to understand the meanings of others and to ensure that their own messages are clear, it is common to hear, "I didn't understand that"; "What do you mean, you don't know what I'm saying?"; "I hate it when she calls me 'cutie'!"; "Boy, does he sound uppity"; "Is that clear?!" Folk linguistics reflects people's beliefs about language and what they know about how people talk or change their talk. Their comments indicate a general awareness that language is used to establish an "outsider" category for some, whereas other language use provides entrée to a specific community.

Children in Detroit, Michigan, chant a jump rope rhyme, which I have also heard from children growing up in the South, that goes:

> She went away to college,
> She went away to school,
> And when she came back,
> She was an educated fool.

This commentary about language represents local people's suspicions about the differences they observe when a person leaves a community and eventually returns showing influences from other cultures. Ken Johnson, who studies dialect variation, tells a story about his great aunt whom he visited on a regular basis in Chicago. Once she asked him some questions about her income tax. He shifted to legalese English as he tried to represent the complexity of the tax system. She responded quickly, asserting her matriarchal role: "If you can't talk right, then just hush up."

Politicians also talk about language and often use it to assert power. William Safire, a self-styled word maven who writes editorials about language issues, reported being in a meeting with the U.S. president in which "mouth-filling words like multilateral and multinational [were] flying around." An unidentified senator "wondered if they weren't losing touch with the words that real people use in everyday life" (2002, p. 12). In fact, the Doublespeak Award given annually by the National Council of Teachers of English (see Chapter 7) addresses directly the issue of powerful people in society who use language purposely to mislead.

Talk about language leads to all kinds of debate: how language is used to influence public opinion; what language is appropriate for job interviews or school settings; and the inappropriate use of slang or profanity. Recent controversies about national language policy in Quebec, Canada, and in Latvia, as well as in the United States, have led to debates such as which language to use for instruction in schools; which languages deserve translation in courts and on ballots; and which language will appear on official signs. In defining the differences between a language and a dialect, language scholars often say that a language is a dialect with an army and a navy. Activists concerned with race, gender, and ethnic issues cite language use as a prime factor in prejudice and discrimination. Such controversies suggest that language is interesting to study and think about, not just something to be studied didactically in school.

Metalinguistics and Metalanguage

The examples I have provided emphasize that language is a powerful issue, and when people have reason to comment on language, they find many ways to talk and write about the ways in which language affects their lives. This overt talk about language is called *metalanguage* or *metalinguistic awareness* by academics. Metalanguage is the language people use when they talk about the objects of language study or terms about language use such as *read, write, name, talk, say, word, sentence, letter, book,* and so forth. The ability to talk about and reflect on language as an object of study is referred to as *metalinguistic knowledge* (Bruner, 1966).

Some researchers believe that metalinguistic knowledge or awareness is a prerequisite to learning to read and write. These educators often call for explicit teaching of grammar, phonics, or vocabulary before students begin reading and writing. I disagree with such a stance because my research on the language processes of children and adolescents makes it abundantly clear that students talk about language in a comprehensible way when they have a reason and opportunity to do so. Since talking about language is a function of all language use, I see no reason to consider metalinguistics a special ability of only some students. I address this issue because the language study lessons and theme cycles suggested in this book involve language use that fits the definition of metalinguistics. Students are encouraged to explore language by talking and thinking about it as they use it. Since terms such as *meta-arithmetic* and *metachemistry* are not used in response to students' talk about number or science concepts, I tend not to use the term *metalinguistics*. Rather, I prefer to say, "talking about language."

Language users not only talk about language, but they also think about language simultaneously as they read and write about it and when they hear others talk and write about it. The term *megacognition* describes the activity of humans thinking about their own language or thought processes. All humans, including the young, use language to talk and think about language. They comment on language as an object of study, they wonder and raise questions about language use, they laugh at and play with language, and they build concepts about its functions and its forms. And if they are in a bilingual or multilingual community, they are able to do this in two or more languages.

Intuitive and Conscious Knowledge

Talking and thinking about language help students become conscious of the many aspects of language they know intuitively. The difference between conscious and intuitive knowledge in humans is important in considering language study. Intuitive knowledge includes the things we know but aren't consciously aware that we know. Conscious knowledge includes those things we know that we are also able to articulate. Very young children have intuitive knowledge about language as a result of being immersed in a particular language community since birth. When they self-correct or overgeneralize their personal language forms, children provide evidence of their intuitive knowledge. They might say, for example, "I runned . . . I mean . . . I ran all the way home." The use of *runned* provides insight into the child's intuitive knowledge about English—that past tense verb forms often involve an *ed* ending. Children often overgeneralize the past tense rule by shifting irregular forms to the more common regular pattern *(runned, sitted, taked)*. Their self-corrections demonstrate that they are intuitively aware of the irregularities of language rules as they become more experienced with the language use of the adult community.

At very young ages, children provide evidence of their intuitive knowledge about the grammar of their mother tongue(s). Child-language researchers conclude that children know a lot about the grammatical and phonological systems of their home language by the time they are five years old. It's clear from children's talk that they know what the objects and subjects of a sentence are and the appropriate order of nouns, verbs, and adjectives. A child intently reading a book orally without attending to the written language of the text has a very different intonation from that same child when he leaves a message on grandpa's answering machine, showing that he knows the different intonational patterns of oral reading and phone messages. Children show by their appropriate responses that what they have heard makes them sad or happy. Such young children aren't yet able to state overtly (conscious knowledge) what they are doing with their language, but their language use demonstrates their intuitive knowledge.

Because of their longer histories and experiences with language use, adults have a great deal more intuitive knowledge about language than young children do. Intuitive knowledge is for the most part not conscious. People often are not able to articulate what they know about language and why they do what they do when they speak, listen, read, and write. Most English language users, for example, are confident about which of the following sentences sound right and which don't, but few are able to state a grammatical rule that allows them to make that judgment:

He walked to store.
He walked to the store.
He walked to school.
He walked to the school.

Linguists have documented that humans know the rules of their language well and are able to communicate with others successfully. Not only do we use oral language appropriately, but we also know what style of language to select when, for example, we write letters to business establishments, as opposed to the language we write in letters to friends; likewise, we read advertisements differently from newspaper editorials. Linguists document intuitive language knowledge by studying the complex ways humans communicate through oral and written language. Children as well as adults provide such evidence based on their language experiences. Elementary and middle school children are also able to document language use and how it works. Through language study, learners raise their intuitive knowledge about language to a conscious level. Through discussions with teachers and other adults and by reading articles about language, learners become aware that they know a great deal about the languages they use every day and that this knowledge helps them develop understandings about the role of language in society.

Language Study in Elementary and Middle Schools

CHAPTER ONE

A Rationale for Language Study

The major purpose of this book is to consider a language study curriculum that provides students, especially in elementary and middle school, with authentic and enjoyable opportunities to talk, write, read, and think about their own language use and the use of language in their homes, families, and communities in order to raise language awareness to a conscious level. Through these experiences, students, along with their teachers, explore significant personal and social issues of language use and discover that language study is not only enlightening but interesting as well.

Language learning takes place as a result of language use and language study. Teaching about language in the context of its use provides rich opportunities for pupils to develop new language forms that serve new functions. Language learning in such contexts results in expanding, flexible use of language.

In presenting a language study curriculum, I suggest that the study of language grows out of the curiosity that learners show as their language develops and they encounter new language in many different contexts. Teachers are fascinated with the questions their students ask about the universe, the laws of physics, the way in which the body works, and how society is organized. Language is an integral part of this rich understanding of the world. Whole language teachers are aware that in the same way they and their students inquire into issues in the social and physical sciences, there are endless possibilities for involving their students in exploring language issues and concepts. In *Wally's Stories* (1981), Vivian Paley provides many examples of the discussions children as young as five have about language. In one episode, her kindergartners talk about the different languages spoken by the children in the class. They then shift the discussion to consider what would happen if everyone in the world spoke the same language (pp. 116–21).

The language study curriculum is embedded in a view of learning, teaching, and curriculum that perceives students as excited and serious about learning in a language community that can be trusted to raise significant questions about language, which is a major aspect of daily life. Language is considered an object of inquiry worth learning about, and learners are considered capable of constructing their own intuitive and conscious knowledge about language. The ways in which people use and learn language are valued and respected. This language study curriculum is built on a constructivist view of learning and is informed by a whole language philosophy (K. Goodman, 1986).

This language study curriculum stands in contrast to the long history in schools of teaching grammar, vocabulary, and the sounds of language as a series of rules disconnected from the use of language. This transmission model of language teaching treats knowledge as something to be memorized rather than as always open to exploration. It suggests that the learning of language rules is a prerequisite to the proper use of language. There are problems with this approach to teaching and learning language. First, the transmission tradition grows out of a prescriptive view of language instruction in which language is either right or wrong. When the student's language is different from the preferred high-status dialect (often called "standard"), the student's language is considered wrong, and it is the teacher's obligation to "correct" it by teaching the prescribed language rules explicitly and often out of context. This approach to language use doesn't value the range of dialects and multiple languages children learn from their experiences in their homes and communities before they come to school. It doesn't trust students' intuitive knowledge or ability to use different forms of language or shift language registers appropriately as they move from one social context to another. It doesn't trust the learning ability of language users to expand their language repertoires as they are immersed in new uses of language in school and as they expand their worlds.

A second problem with a prescriptive approach to language teaching is that people don't learn language only by learning *about* it. They develop their abilities to expand and change their language by *using* it. Halliday (1979), an Australian linguist, states that we learn language best by using it in real and meaningful social contexts. He believes that humans learn language as we use it daily; we learn through using the language of math, science, the arts, and so forth to build concepts and construct views of the world; and through these language events, we learn about language—its forms and conventions. In other words, we learn language while we use language to learn.

The prescriptive approach to teaching language is based on the belief that by direct and isolated teaching of skills, language itself improves—that if teachers teach grammar, phonics, and spelling through intense exercises outside the context of real language use, students will read and write better and be better users of language. Yet more than a century of research has provided little evidence that such direct teaching improves students' oral and written language (Hillocks, 1982).

Some teachers, parents, and researchers have mistakenly come to the conclusion that teachers who hold constructivist views of teaching and learning do not discuss the sounds, the structures, and the meanings of language with their students. There are even some novice whole language teachers who have developed the misconception that language concepts should not be the focus of classroom content. They do not recognize language concepts as something to be taught in school in the same way that concepts in arithmetic, the physical or social sciences, and the arts are part of instruction. A language study curriculum is a response to both misconceptions. It is a guide for teachers who want to help students become consciously aware of the ways in which they construct language knowledge and to provide opportunities for students to discuss their new and developing language schemas. It is a support for teachers who believe in holistic ways of teaching about language.

Knowledgeable and successful whole language teachers know a lot about language, and they continuously expand on that knowledge through their own language studies. They have a love affair with language: hearing it, reading it, singing it, writing it, playing with it, and exploring or studying it in order to understand

and make it work for their students. As teachers carefully observe and document students' development of spelling, grammar, and use of genres; edit students' writing; and document the quality of students' reading miscues, they continually inform their own knowledge about how language is used and learned. Whole language advocates do not reject the existence of phonics or grammar and vocabulary study in school settings. Rather, they *seriously* consider how students' intuitive knowledge of letters and sounds, the rules of grammar, and word meanings relate to students' proficiency as speakers, listeners, readers, and writers, and they help students become conscious about their own language knowledge.

Historical Overview of Language Study Curricula

For decades scholars in the field of English language arts have focused on using language for real and functional purposes. Believing in authentic language use as the basis for language learning, professional educators have explored ways to apply such knowledge in classrooms. This holistic application of embedding language within enriched curricula is central to educational programs such as language experience, individualized reading, shared book experience, whole language, language across the curriculum, the National Writing Project, process writing, reading as a thinking process, reader response, integrated curriculum, and the universe of discourse. All are grounded in holistic views of language, constructivist views of learning, and teaching as professional decision making. Materials for teachers contain a range of language study ideas, and some authors have developed materials and curricula focusing on language study in the context of using language. Over the years, these scholars have been influencing language arts curricula that are grounded in sound educational, linguistic, and psychological theory and research. The growth in the use of adolescent and children's literature and writing across the curriculum in elementary classrooms is a result of this work. Although most of the inquiry opportunities presented in these texts relate to grammar study, connections are made to the lives of students, who are encouraged to explore language and its purposes, interpretations, and points of view rather than to consider language prescriptively. I hope that *Valuing Language Study* adds new insight to this significant literature.

Beginning in the 1960s, James Moffett urged teachers to involve students in using language rather than analyzing it. His *Teaching the Universe of Discourse* (1968, 1983) provides a well-documented and theoretical rationale for the conceptualization of discourse as the unit of language to explore, in contrast to a focus on the grammatical nature of sentences. Moffett coauthored *Student-Centered Language Arts and Reading, K–12: A Handbook for Teachers* with Betty Wagner (1983, 1992), offering specific ideas for a language arts curriculum that highlights language as an "object" to talk and think about.

In 1963, Neil Postman coauthored *Discovering Your Language* (Postman, Morine, & Morine, 1963), and in 1966 he published *Exploring Your Language* (1966). These were unique textbooks for junior high or middle school English language arts classes. Notes to the teacher in *Discovering Your Language* establish its focus: "providing an opportunity for students to arrive by their own inquiries at sound generalizations about language." Bill Martin Jr., who influenced whole language practices and materials, published the Sounds of Language series (1966–1967) of readers about thirty-five years ago to help teachers understand the beauty and power of language and language learning and to share ways of getting children excited about the variety of forms that language takes. The teacher's edition of these books explores language and its forms. Through his miscue studies of a wide range of readers, Ken Goodman helped teachers see the control readers have of their language cuing systems. In his latest publications, *Phonics Phacts* (1993) and *On Reading* (1996a), he provides evidence of the knowledge about language that children bring to their reading. With other researchers and teachers, I have students talk about their own reading capabilities by examining their miscues (Y. Goodman & Marek, 1996).

Constance Weaver (1996) wrote *Teaching Grammar in Context*, updating her *Grammar for Teachers* (1979). Her new book provides teachers with information about grammar and linguistics, language acquisition, the writing process, and the teaching of writing, as well as information about learning theory and literacy development. Gutiérrez, Baquedano-López, and Turner (1997) discuss "Putting Language Back into Language Arts," arguing for the importance of teachers using their students' language, cultural knowledge, and sociocultural practices as resources for teaching and curriculum development.

In British schools since the mid–twentieth century, language study has had high visibility in language arts curricula as well as in teacher education. Teachers typically take a course called The Role of Language in Education, which not only provides them with opportunities to explore language learning, language development, language processes, and the sociocultural and political issues of language, but also focuses on language study in elementary and secondary schools with an emphasis on language in use. The language study curriculum I present in this book integrates ideas from my interactions with U.S. and British scholars about the potentials of language study. In addition to those mentioned earlier, these scholars include James Britton (1993[1970]), Harold Rosen (1998), Margaret Meek (1988), Catherine Wallace (1988), and Mike Raleigh, author and compiler of *The Languages Book* (1981), at the English Centre in London. Many of the ideas I present here are also influenced by the writings of New Zealand and Australian scholars such as Brian Cambourne (1988), Hazel Brown (Brown & Cambourne, 1990), Jan Turbill (1982), Margaret Mooney (1990), Marie Clay (1979), and Don Holdaway (1979), to mention just a few.

Principles for a Language Study Curriculum

We know that the young learn language all the time whether or not teachers are involved. On the other hand, teachers have significant opportunities to help students make explicit their intuitive knowledge about language, to reflect on what they know about language, and to see if what they know fits with what others know about language use and with how language scientists, or linguists, think language works. A language study curriculum allows teachers to organize opportunities and environments so that students expand on the language knowledge they

---

Principle 1: Language is a powerful tool with which to think, to communicate with others, and to explore the universe.

Principle 2: Language is best understood when it is examined in the context of human language events that occur in the real world.

Principle 3: It is legitimate to use appropriate linguistic terminology when talking about and studying language.

Principle 4: Language study needs to include the latest knowledge and questions that linguists raise about how language works and how it is learned.

FIGURE 1. *Principles for a language study curriculum.*

bring to school and develop sophisticated ways to talk and think about language. This language study curriculum builds on principles (see Figure 1) informed by whole language pedagogy (K. Goodman, 1986).

Principle 1: Language is a powerful tool with which to think, to communicate with others, and to explore the universe.

Through language study, students come to realize that as they talk and think about language in serious ways they are continuously learning about language. They become conscious that they know a lot about language intuitively and that they can talk about language with others, and they come to believe that they have power and control over language. Students realize that language is a tool used to collaborate with others as well as to explore the wonders of the world. John Dewey (1925) illustrates the role of tools in learning and their relation to language:

> The invention and use of tools have played a large part in consolidating meanings, because a tool is a thing used as a means to consequences, instead of being taken directly and physically. It is intrinsically relational, anticipatory, predictive. Without reference to the absent, or "transcendence," nothing is a tool. . . .
>   As to be a tool, or to be used as means for consequences, is to have and to endow with meaning, language, being the tool of tools, is the cherishing mother of all significance. (pp. 185–86)

In schools we sometimes ignore potentially powerful moments in which teaching about language could enhance students' conscious knowledge. When my oldest daughter, Debra, was in secondary school, one of her teachers edited her writing according to simplistic conventions: *Don't use short sentences! Don't start sentences with* and *or* but! Whenever she showed her teacher stories by John Steinbeck, Ernest Hemingway, or other well-known authors who included short sentences and sentences beginning with connectives, Debra was told that she had to follow the correct language rules: "When you become a published author, you can break the rules too, but in this class and until then you will follow the rules of correct English." She would have learned a great deal more about language and herself as a writer if her teacher had encouraged her to examine the works of Hemingway and Steinbeck closely to discover how and when these writers use short sentences and in what contexts they start sentences with *and, but,* or *or.* She would have learned that great authors use language structures flexibly depending on the meanings they are trying to convey.

Students discover that wondering about language, discussing it with peers and teachers, and asking questions such as "Why does language change the way it does from time to time and from place to place?"; "Why do adults get so upset about the way teenagers use language?"; or "Do people who are bilingual think in two languages?" allow them to use language with greater control. Such inquiry and the understandings that follow result in students revaluing themselves as capable language users and valuing the languages they use in and out of school (K. Goodman, 1996b).

The acceptance of linguistic diversity and variation is central to language study and acknowledged by those who teach it. Students know that their teachers and the school community respect their languages and their cultural backgrounds in all their forms. The resources of bilingual students (including the Deaf), students who are multilingual and multiliterate, students learning English as a second language, and students whose dialects are different from their teachers' are incorporated into the explorations of language and viewed as contributions to language growth and understandings about how language works in society (Ruíz, 1988). Many of these students already think about language in explicit ways.

At the same time, teachers help students understand the realities of language issues in society that establish the value of some language forms over others. Teachers help students face language issues honestly and organize forums to discuss cultural prejudices toward different forms of language. Students are encouraged, for example, to document how often they use tags such as *you know* or *OK* and then interview other students and adults with a range of backgrounds to find out how they respond when they hear such language use. The point is not to situate one language as intrinsically superior or more correct than others in its written, oral, or signing forms but to explore aspects of economic and political power in society.

Exploring language in this way with students openly acknowledges that language, including uses of literacy, is a tool that often renders students and even teachers vulnerable and powerless. When one language is designated an official language in a country where large groups of people speak other languages, the people whose languages are not considered official are disempowered. Students often don't understand the power issues behind decisions to target certain dialect forms as inappropriate for school or work settings, and they are forced to choose between their home language or the language of their peers and the language of school. Making students believe that reading or studying certain established literature is more prestigious than exploring literature that represents their own cultural and linguistic genres teaches students that their tastes are not valued and the languages of their home communities are not important. Such messages cause students to devalue themselves and their ability to use language. Language study into these power issues helps students examine the realities of language prestige and notions about hierarchical language and literary values and to decide for themselves how language attitudes will affect their jobs or academic futures. Language study critically examines the ways in which language is used to control and dominate their lives. Only when students believe that their language and language learning abilities are fully respected and accepted by teachers and the school community do they come to trust and take the risks necessary to study language in an open-ended and scholarly fashion.

Students come to realize that language rules are not inherently right or wrong but are instead social conventions evolving from people's use of and knowledge about language. These conventions vary depending on the speaker's linguistic community. The social conventions, or rules, of language can be documented through the scientific study of language: linguistics. Students discover that language rules are controversial and that linguists debate what some teachers and English language arts textbooks often proclaim is *the* correct form of language use. As they gain confidence, students consider, reflect, and define themselves as competent language users in control of their own language use rather than at the mercy of absolute rules about appropriate language use. Such students are not paralyzed into *not* using language. As they build positive attitudes and value themselves as capable language users, students are able to use their language more effectively to think about the world and to take risks as language users. They search for new language to express their new concepts. Initially, their conscious awareness may not result in high scores on standardized tests. But with growing confidence, their testing abilities develop as well.

Principle 2: Language is best understood when it is examined in the context of human language events that occur in the real world.

As students explore the use of oral and written texts embedded in real events, they come to understand how language is used to control, to dominate, to describe, to express feelings, to state beliefs, and to expand on personal thinking. Experiences such as field trips, science and math experiments, social studies explorations, current events discussions, and yearbook publications involve the use of a variety of materials such as tickets, advertisements, programs, notes, recording devices, letters, and other firsthand documents. These texts are embedded in social events involving all kinds of talk and problem solving.

I use the concept of "authenticity" to refer to this kind of real language in use (Edelsky & Smith, 1984; Wortman, 1990).

The development of a language study curriculum reflects the importance of using the wide range of personal and social functions that language serves in the real world to develop flexible and sophisticated use of language. Students are encouraged to explore and value diverse language uses in their world, including the language of their own youth culture such as jump rope rhymes, rap, or graffiti. Writing love notes or making lists of favorite stars is recognized as serving the same legitimate literacy functions as the writing of stories or reports. These are all authentic uses of language. Each genre has layers of complexity and the same potential for language learning.

When teachers treat students' language use respectfully and as worthy of serious study, students are likely to treat the language of adults with respect and interest as well. Students become aware that they are already competent oral language users; that they have been speaking, listening, reading, and writing to serve their purposes for many years; and that they are capable, therefore, of expanding their uses of both oral and written language to new uses they find challenging. The study of oral language use is valued the same as the study of written language use. In fact, it is acknowledged that written language rarely occurs without the accompaniment of oral language. Talk—discussion, conversation, debate, and critique—is viewed as a significant area of study.

Learning about language is never a prerequisite to using language. There are no readiness activities for learning how to talk and think about language. Rather, whenever students stop to think about language; wonder and ask questions about it; discuss, dialogue, and debate with others about it; and critique their language experiences, then language about language becomes necessary, and students discover language as a result of using it.

Principle 3: It is legitimate to use appropriate linguistic terminology when talking about and studying language.

Those of us who are whole language advocates are not opposed to the exploration of spelling, handwriting, grammar, phonics, language, or linguistics. Our argument is that such talk should take place as much as possible in authentic environments that provide opportunities to study the ways in which language is expanded and constrained and how appropriate language terminology relates to language use. In such contexts, students come to understand how the specific linguistic labels relate to the real world of language use. In the same way that it is necessary and appropriate to use scientific terminology when talking about the human body, it is appropriate to use linguistic terminology when talking about language. The study of terms such as *sentence, adjective, fiction, nonfiction,* and so forth outside the context of real language use does not help students develop understandings about such concepts. When students and teachers explore and describe language as linguists do, they come to understand the meanings and concepts behind the terms they need to use to talk about language. They become aware of the advantages of conventional language terminology. Some commercial programs confuse language learning by using terms such as *naming word* for *noun* and *action word* for *verb.* Terms such as *quotation marks, phonics,* or *grammar* are avoided, and teachers get involved in using cutesy language about language. I've heard, for example, quotation marks referred to as "sixty-sixes and ninety-nines."

In a language study curriculum, teachers use appropriate terms for linguistic concepts and relate them to the commonsense terms the kids use. When students are editing their own writing in conferences or groups, for example, they might talk about *big letters* or *naming words.* The students' commonsense terms are accepted. But when the teacher uses conventional terms such as *capital letters* and *proper nouns* in daily conversations, the students easily pick up the language of the teacher. Teachers might, for example, talk about the overuse of *adverbs* that get in the way of what the author wants to say; they express joy over carefully selected but rich use of *adjectives* in describing the setting of a story; they point out to students their knowledge of *phonics* as represented by appropriate *invented spellings;* or they admire students' ability to write good *alliteration.* Students come to understand that there is a conventional vocabulary with which to talk about language. In authentic settings, teachers and students use terms such as *grammar, dialect, composing, revising, comprehension, predicting strategies, fiction,* and *nonfiction* (and many others) when they are appropriate, and thus over time students develop the concepts these terms represent. It is much more important for students to understand the concepts related to particular terms and how they are used in written and oral language than it is to be able to state a rule about a linguistic term.

Dictionary definitions alone do not help readers and writers understand language terms. Dictionaries are helpful to confirm what a word means and to discover information about its origin and pronunciation when such information is important for the reader's or writer's purposes. By exploring the concepts that undergird the meanings of words, however, students come to realize that they understand the language use that surrounds them. I have been working with Zachary, a fourth grader, to help him understand the quality of the miscues he makes while he is reading. We discuss his reading while he listens to an audiotape of a story he has read. I use terms such as *miscue, substitutions, omissions, self-correction, comprehension, reading strategy,* and others. Because we are talking about his reading in a context in which he is comfortable, Zachary develops conceptualizations for these terms. In our conversations about his reading, he eventually uses the same terms appropriately and more frequently over time.

Principle 4: Language study needs to include the latest knowledge and questions that linguists raise about how language works and how it is learned.

Teachers continuously update their understandings of current scientific knowledge about language and language learning and avoid supporting myths, misinformation, and folk beliefs about language. Teachers become knowledgeable about the issues and concerns intrinsic to the teaching of elementary language arts as well as the teaching of English as a second language and bilingual education. Unfortunately, too many language arts textbooks contain many prescriptive, commonsense notions or folk beliefs about language that affect students in negative ways. These texts include comments on dialect variation: "People who talk *that* way won't get jobs," or "Such language is not correct." Or they promote scientifically unsound language rules such as "When two vowels go walking, the first does the talking." These rules are often oversimplifications of complex language issues; the rule about two vowels, for instance, doesn't apply even 50 percent of the time (Bailey, 1967; Clymer, 1963; Emans, 1967). Folk beliefs or commonsense myths about language provide students with rich opportunities to critique and raise questions. Language knowledge is expanded when teachers and students inquire together into the truthfulness of language prescriptions.

Through critical questioning, teachers and students come to understand that language rules are the result of scientific language study by *linguists, psycholinguists,* or *sociolinguists.* Such explorations are open to examination and critique by students. It is important for teachers and students to understand that *grammar* is a term used by linguists to describe how language is organized in order to study and explain it. Different linguists develop their own grammars to describe language based on their views of how language works. With teacher guidance, students learn that not all language issues have been resolved by language scholars, and there is a good deal of controversy about language issues within the public and academic communities. Teachers and students need to be familiar with the work of language scholars in order to support their own discussions about language and to become comfortable studying language with the openness that linguists bring to their discipline.

The work of language scholars is a resource that informs teachers and curriculum developers as well as students. Teachers concerned with language study can use the knowledge, debates, and issues in the various linguistic fields to organize a curriculum that engages students in teaching and learning experiences.

To support students' confidence in their language knowledge and use, teachers demonstrate confidence not only in their own language knowledge but also and especially in their ability to know where to find resources and plan research to answer their own questions as well as those of their students. It is not necessary to be conversant with the latest theoretical issues concerning generative grammar or systemic linguistics to begin language study. To help preservice and inservice teachers overcome a lack of confidence in talking about language, I help them discover that as language users they have a great deal of intuitive knowledge about language: they know how language works and whom it privileges, and they understand the power and control language has over people's lives. Once their basic competence is established, graduate students and teachers are more comfortable reading and researching in linguistics and other language study areas. Too often, language arts, English education, bilingual, English as a second language, and foreign language classes focus on prescriptive linguistics, which often results in making teachers as well as students insecure about their language knowledge. Such insecurity leads some teachers to become overly dependent on grammar textbooks for correct answers to linguistic dilemmas. As teachers take an inquiry stance in response to their own and their students' questions about language, both teachers and students benefit. They grow in their knowledge about language by learning together.

Teachers' knowledge about language also grows as they continue to take advanced graduate courses and programs, read professional literature, and attend conferences. Participating in professional organizations, being actively involved in teacher study and writing groups, and presenting results of classroom research to others are all avenues through which teachers can continue to develop knowledge about language. The National Council of Teachers of English (NCTE) (www.ncte.org) supports teacher study groups with teleconferences on topics such as spelling, reading and writing instruction, language evaluation, and classroom organization, among others. The International Reading Association (IRA) (www.reading.org), as well as NCTE, encourages teacher research through funded grant programs. Controversies about and inquiry into language are discussed in many nonfiction books, textbooks, and popular newspapers as well as professional journals. The list in Figure 2 is of journals (including addresses) that help teachers keep abreast of new knowledge, controversial issues, and ideas in the fields of linguistics, English language arts, and bilingual education.

I remember the impact on my teaching when I read *The Five Clocks* by Martin Joos (1962), written in the 1920s. The text was recommended in a linguistics for teachers course I took as part of my master's program. Joos helped me understand that all speakers change the way they speak whenever they change time or place. I read parts of the text to my seventh graders in order to share with them my new excitement about language. Much of

Bilingual Research Journal
www.nabe.org
1030 15th Street, NW
Suite 470
Washington, DC 20005
202-898-1829/202-789-2866 (fax)

Childhood Education
www.acei.org
17904 Georgia Avenue
Suite 215
Olney, MD 20832
301-570-2111/800-423-3563

Foxfire News
www.foxfire.org
P.O. Box 541
Mountain City, GA 30562-0541
706-746-5828/706-746-5829 (fax)

International Reading Association
  Journals
Journal of Adolescent & Adult
  Literacy
Reading Research Quarterly
The Reading Teacher
www.reading.org
800 Barksdale Road
P.O. Box 8139
Newark, DE 19714-8139
302-731-1600/302-731-1057 (fax)

Journal of Early Childhood Literacy
www.segepub.co.uk
Sage Publications Ltd.
6 Bonhill Street
London EC2A 4PU, UK
44-0-20-7374-0645

Language and Education
(Multilingual Matters)
www.multilingual-matters.com
Frankfurt Lodge, Clevedon Hall
Clevedon, England BS21 7HH
44-0-1275-876519/44-0-1275-
  871673 (fax)

Linguistics and Education
http://academic.brooklyn.cuny.edu/
education/jlemke/L-and-E.htm
100 Prospect Street
P.O. Box 811
Stamford, CT 06904-0081
203-323-9606/203-357-8446 (fax)

National Council of Teachers of
  English Journals:
Language Arts
Primary Voices K–6 (1992–2002)
Research in the Teaching of English
Talking Points
Voices from the Middle
www.ncte.org
1111 W. Kenyon Road
Urbana, IL 61801-1096
217-328-3870/877-369-6283
217-328-9645 (fax)

The New Advocate
1502 Providence Highway, Suite 12
Norwood, MA 02062
781-762-5577/781-762-2100 (fax)

Rethinking Schools: An Urban
  Educational Journal
www.rethinkingschools.org
1001 East Keefe Avenue
Milwaukee, WI 53212
414-964-7220

Teaching Tolerance
www.teachingtolerance.org
Southern Poverty Law Center
400 Washington Avenue
Montgomery, AL 36104
334-956-8374/334-956-8488 (fax)

TESOL Journal
www.tesol.org
700 South Washington St., Suite 200
Alexandria, VA 22314
703-836-0074/703-836-7864 (fax)

FIGURE 2. *Journals with language/linguistic information for teachers.*

my knowledge about grammar comes from the miscue analysis I do with readers and my analysis of children's writing. The more I understand the nature of miscues, the more insights I have about readers' intuitive knowledge of grammar. I now share this knowledge with readers and writers of all ages to help them become knowledgeable about the role of their errors in developing comprehension and compositions.

Linguistic Knowledge Informs Language Study

As I developed a language study curriculum, my work was informed by the knowledge of language scholars, the methods they use to explore language, and the kinds of questions they ask as they try to understand language and its uses. The study of language is always changing, new questions are being formulated, new knowledge is discovered and being considered, and the field is filled with debate and controversy. It is within this spirit of open-ended scientific inquiry into language issues that teachers and students become interested in and excited about exploring questions and ideas about language and expanding their knowledge about language use and its forms. As teachers express their excitement about language study, students develop interest and find satisfaction in the explorations as well. Teachers and students gain in-depth understanding of language as they consult language scholars and use these scholars' knowledge as resources in their own explorations.

Figure 3 identifies six areas of language study that inform the development of a language study curriculum. These six areas, rich with insights from linguistics, psycholinguistics, and sociolinguistics, provide supporting knowledge about *language use,* which includes the functions and purposes of language; *language processes,* which are concerned with how humans use language both individually and socially; *language variation,* which includes dialect, registers, and different languages; *language history and development,* which involves language change over time within individuals as well as in society; *language form,* or the conventions of language use; and the *power and politics of language,*

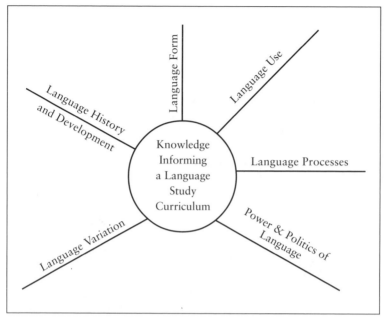

FIGURE 3. *Areas of language knowledge that inform a language study curriculum.*

which examines the ways in which language is used to control others and takes into consideration equity and social justice. In the following sections, I discuss each of these areas. The references at the end of the book also contain many sources on linguistics and related fields.

Language Use

Language use refers to why people use language in the ways they do and to the purposes or functions language serves. Because language use is strongly influenced by the context in which it occurs and the functions it serves, development of a language arts curriculum must acknowledge the diversity of sociocultural contexts and how language changes from one setting to another and from one person to another. Scholars interested in sociolinguistics raise questions about the interrelationships between language users and social structures as well as about the environment in which these interrelationships occur. The study of how women and girls use language in contrast to how men and boys use it has become a recent focus of many linguists in response to their attempt to understand female roles in society. Language scientists explore how the different functions of language influence language use; how power relationships among a group of speakers influence the ways in which each person speaks; how context and audience affect the ways in which people read and write; and how the sociocultural status of the user influences literacy use. The ways in which people know when to use language formally and informally or when to use oral or written language are also aspects of language use.

Language Processes

The exploration of language processes helps explain how language works as individuals and groups read, write, speak, and listen, and various disciplines make contributions to this exploration. Psycholinguistics helps explicate language processes because it studies the interrelationship between language and cognition—in other words, how language and thinking influence each other. Neurolinguistics seeks to explain the role of the brain and how it functions in the production, perception, and comprehension of both written and oral language.

Language Variation

Language or linguistic variation refers to dialects, registers, bilingualism, and multilingualism. Language variation issues strongly influence the attitudes of students, their families, and educational professionals (teachers, researchers, specialists, test developers, etc.) toward language and language users. Scholars interested in language variation examine issues such as which aspects of society influence language variation and why variation occurs. Sociolinguists as well as anthropologists address the relationship between language and culture because cultural variation affects language variation, and vice versa. A study of language variation also takes into consideration the idiosyncrasies of an individual's language or idiolect in relation to the social dialect of the community. It examines the differences between oral and written language and helps explain how written languages come into existence. In recent decades, scholars have become interested in written language variations in writing systems, genres, and multiliteracies.

Language History and Development

School curricula have always included aspects of language history, but too often such study involves dry facts about word origin rather than inquiry into the historical influences on language change. Rarely do traditional school language programs examine either historical linguistic changes or those taking place in the present. The study of how languages change over time and their relationships to one another includes how words come to be, how they are modified and changed, and how languages change in relation to population mobility and changes in personal and family language histories. How the forms of both written and oral language change over time is also an aspect of the history of language. Scholars often raise questions about how and why written language came to be, and why there are alphabetic and nonalphabetic writing systems. Studying how language changes because of major historical events such as the launching of Sputnik or the latest technological revolution is another important aspect of language history.

The influences on historical language change are similar to the influences on how individuals learn and develop one or more languages from birth. Developmental psycholinguistics considers not only how children come to learn their first language but also how language develops as a lifelong process. Scholars are also interested in how children become bilingual or multilingual and how biliteracy develops within individuals and society. This study of language includes the personal history of an individual's language development.

Language Form

The forms language takes in order for communication to occur are an important aspect of language study. In too many English language arts textbooks and programs, "correct" linguistic form is a major concern that is influenced by authors who take a prescriptive stance toward grammar and language use rather than a scientific or inquiry stance. When teachers and students study how different linguistic forms are used differently in different contexts, they have many opportunities to explore which rules are appropriate and most conventional in specific contexts and to explore the ways in which language use is flexible and creative.

As I explore aspects of the conventions of language forms, I refer to the subsystems of language, which derive from various fields of linguistics. Different schools of linguistics use different terms or organize the subsystems in different ways because of their theoretical orientations toward language study. The terms I use in this book for the subsystems include:

Phonology—the systems of the sounds of a language or languages.

Orthography—the ways in which language is organized in a written text. Initially, the term was used in relation to the spelling system of a language, but in recent years it has come to include systems of punctuation, capitalization, and paragraphing, as well as aspects of nonalphabetic print.

Graphophonics—the relationships between the sound systems of languages (phonology) and the written systems of languages (orthography). Such study is important in order to understand how oral and written language relate to each other and are reflected in other language systems such as phonics and spelling. The relation between intonation and punctuation is also an aspect of the graphophonic system.

Syntax or *grammar*—the study of the systematic ways in which sentences are organized and related to one another. Syntax reveals how words relate to one another within sentence or paragraph frames for meaning to occur and how words change meaning based on smaller meaningful units such as prefixes and suffixes. This latter aspect of syntax is often referred to as *morphology*.

Semantics—the study of vocabulary and terminology and how words and phrases relate to objects and ideas. Semanticists also study the ways in which words come to have the meanings they do historically and the influence of context on word meaning.

Pragmatics—the study of the ways in which language use changes depending on the context, taking into consideration time, place, and the social relationships between speakers, listeners, readers, and writers. Those who study pragmatics go beyond focusing solely on linguistic issues and are concerned with how language is influenced by society. Pragmatics relates to the ways in which people use language based on who and where they are and on the topics being addressed. Scholars interested in such language issues sometimes call themselves sociolinguists. If they are interested in how individuals process language, they consider themselves psycholinguists.

Power and Politics of Language

Many of the aspects of language introduced in the previous sections are also central to a study of the power and politics of language. Both socio- and psycholinguists are concerned with the power and politics of language. Often applied linguists become involved in this area of study as they focus on national language policies; legal constraints on language use; language in the political arena; constraints on language in advertising, classrooms, and courtrooms; and the ways in which language is used as a tool to manipulate the thoughts and rights of others. Applied or educational linguists are concerned with the language of teaching and testing and the impact of language policies on schooling.

An important part of considering issues of language power is asking questions such as who benefits from certain language policies or conventions and in what ways the lives of people are better or worse because of language teaching and decisions about language use. Sociocultural theorists concerned with critical language analysis raise important questions about equity and social justice in language curricula, such as the role of translation for non–English speakers in books as well as in classroom and conference contexts.

Although the work of scholars in psychology, anthropology, linguistics, sociology, and education is important to the development of a language study curriculum, knowledge from these fields must not be used to mandate a rigid program of memorization or a study of language trivia based on outmoded or even modern grammars. It is helpful to remember the disaster of Robert's English series (Roberts, Ross, & Boyd, 1970); this textbook series introduced generative transformational grammar (the latest theory of linguistics in the United States at the time) for primary through middle school students. Although the purpose of the series was to provide students and their teachers with a perspective on grammar that was new, there was no attempt to involve students in studying questions about language or in helping teachers understand the purpose of a shift from one school of linguistics to another. Transformational grammar was presented in the series as *the* truth. Although the series was touted as a program that would miraculously improve students' language use, this assertion was never supported by any kind of evidence.

Teaching/Learning Experiences

The language study curriculum presented in this book is developed by organizing an environment in which students are invited to inquire into language issues; wonder about the conventions of language use; consider why language works the way it does; demystify the absolutes about language that have often characterized the English language arts curriculum in schools; and discover that language study is fun, interesting, and educationally stimulating.

In planning a language study curriculum, I explore classroom episodes and opportunities that are authentic, holistic, and integral to English/ESL/foreign language courses and language arts programs for elementary or middle schools, including bilingual and biliteracy programs. I use different classroom experiences to organize the chapters that follow: critical-moment teaching, strategy lessons, and theme cycles (focus on language and linguistics, focus on language and literature, and focus on language as power). Figure 4 identifies the classroom experiences that frame a language study curriculum.

Critical-Moment Teaching

Almost all teachers have experienced spontaneous and incidental teaching moments when the students (or the teacher) discover significant language concepts, ask questions important to them, or get involved in a discussion of controversial language issues. Often these result in the "Ah ha!" responses of critical learning

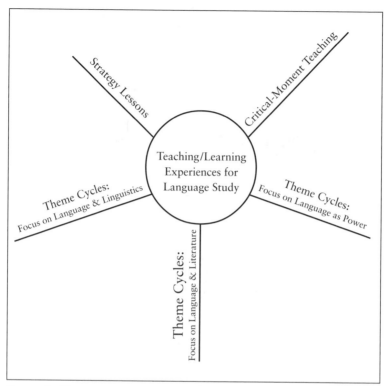

FIGURE 4. *Classroom experiences in a language study curriculum.*

moments or intuitive leaps, as Jerome Bruner (1966) calls them, that all learners experience. In Chapter 3, I discuss why these critical teaching moments are powerful for language learning in the classroom community. Since this kind of learning tends to occur spontaneously, it is not well documented in the professional literature and often isn't even considered legitimate teaching practice. I stress the importance of spontaneous critical-moment teaching, suggest opportunities teachers can take to follow up on such moments, and urge teachers to document these moments in order to share with others in the field.

Strategy Lessons

In response to students' questions about language or to issues that arise from critical-moment teaching, teachers often organize short, focused lessons to extend language learning or to get kids to think about language in new ways. Sometimes these strategy lessons are planned for a small group or the whole class in response to problems or questions that arise from the students' reading, writing, speaking, or listening. Strategy lessons are developed to raise students' intuitive language knowledge to a conscious level and to highlight aspects of language that are important to students' learning.

Theme Cycles: Focus on Language and Linguistics

When language issues are important to the lives of students and they decide to explore them in greater depth, teachers plan for language study that involves more research and reflection than a strategy lesson or a critical teaching moment can provide. Teachers sometime introduce theme cycles because they consider a specific curricular study to be particularly significant, such as a study of dialect differences in the community. But as often as possible, topics should emerge from the questions or problems students raise and are interested in exploring, such as whether the city should paint over graffiti on city property. These theme studies often involve students in fieldwork that is similar to the kinds of inquiry in which linguists or anthropologists are involved.

Theme Cycles: Focus on Language and Literature

Much children's and adolescent fiction and nonfiction focuses on language, its use, and its issues. Authors, not surprisingly, are fascinated by language, and their explorations of language as a major aspect of plot, theme, or conceptualization (idea) offer students many opportunities to explore language issues. Sometimes the focus on language is central to the story line, as in a biography of Frederick Douglass, who overcame many obstacles in order to become literate, and other times it is less direct, as when characters in stories written by authors such as Walter Dean Myers and Christopher Paul Curtis speak different dialects. Literature written for children and adolescents often explores the role of language in the lives of characters, which can precipitate rich theme cycle studies.

Theme Cycles: Focus on Language as Power

In a democratic society, the uses of oral and written language need to be demystified for students, who often see language as a subject to study in school but not as something that affects their lives daily in social, political, and economic ways. Critical language/ literacy study allows students to explore the power of language and helps students analyze how they are influenced and controlled by the language use of others and how their language influences and controls others. The consequences of such influence and control are thoughtfully considered and critically examined.

Language Study Curriculum

In this chapter, I show that the rationale for involving students in language study is rooted in scientific knowledge about language, has historical support from scholars and researchers, and is founded on understandings of language, teaching, learning, and curriculum development. I provide a rationale for and an overview of a language study curriculum for elementary and middle school students.

The following chapters explore the learning experiences identified in Figure 4: Critical-Moment Teaching (Chapter 3); Strategy Lessons (Chapter 4); and the theme cycle chapters, Language and Linguistics (Chapter 5); Language and Literature (Chapter 6); and Language as Power (Chapter 7). In Chapter 2, I present overall considerations for planning a language study curriculum.

It is not necessary to work through the chapters in the order they are presented. It is most appropriate to study language issues when they are raised by the students, considered relevant and significant by the teacher, or appropriately integrated into other areas of the curriculum. Teachers will find it helpful to be familiar with the different sections and to focus on them when they fit curricular needs. The classroom, the school, and the community are rich in opportunities for teachers and students to pursue language study. In the following chapters, the suggestions for learning and teaching experiences come from episodes and opportunities in my own teaching and from those I have read or heard about or observed in the classrooms of successful teachers.

CHAPTER TWO

Organizing for Language Study

In this chapter, I present teaching and learning concepts that I consider to be at the heart of organizing a language study curriculum. They include:

- establishing a learning cycle and acknowledging the importance of its recursive nature in encouraging in students a high level of interest

- raising language and language learning to a conscious level

- implementing language inquiry to involve kids actively in language study

- kidwatching or evaluation

Perceiving, Ideating, and Presenting

To enhance and excite students' language learning, I plan curriculum by keeping in mind the learning cycle processes of perceiving, ideating, and presenting (K. Goodman, Smith, Meredith, & Goodman, 1987; Langer, 1957). In the following discussion, I conceptualize each phase of the language cycle; each should become even clearer through the specific ideas presented in subsequent chapters.

The *perceiving* phase of the learning cycle engages the students so that they focus intently on what is to be learned. This phase is key to motivating the "wanting to learn" experience. Students explore and discuss language issues enthusiastically when the ideas come from their own questions and interests and connect to their lives. Preschooler Brian asks his teacher as he takes an order during restaurant play, "Is this the way you spell *crab*?" (Owocki, 1999). Through questions about what Brian is doing, the teacher draws out Brian's interest in exploring his own writing. Older students also get involved in perceiving when, for example, they work on their writing in a group setting. I remember a long discussion with Gabriel, a fourth grader, when he was writing about a football game he had attended the previous week. He started to write, "When I was coming home from the football game." He stopped after the word *home* and asked, "Is *coming* home from the football game the same as *going* home from the football game?" The other kids at the writing center who were tuned into Gabriel's question looked up, and we discussed what they thought was the better-sounding sentence. This led to an animated discussion about antonyms and synonyms. In both Brian's and Gabriel's cases, the teachers used the perceiving or attention-grabbing learning phase to extend the students' exploration of language issues.

Although whole language teachers integrate and build on their students' questions and interests as the basis for language study, they also sometimes plan for language study because they believe that students need to think about and understand specific language issues. A crucial part of a teacher's responsibility is to help students expand their knowledge beyond their own provincial experiences, but at the same time to organize the environment so that the students develop interest in and excitement about new ideas. In my teaching experience, for example, students rarely on their own raise questions about the role of prediction strategies during listening and reading. When students are asked what words or phrases they think will come next in a story, they sometimes are surprised that they are able to predict appropriately. I not only explored with students what knowledge they had that provided the opportunity to predict, but also shared with them how I predict when I read. In response, the kids often said, "Yeah, I never thought about it in that way." Teachers not only share their own inquiries but also sometimes decide that it is important to organize instructional episodes to prepare students for standardized tests or to focus on objectives or standards recommended or required by state or district guidelines or frameworks. They plan for such experiences by establishing connections with students' interests and questions.

Teachers initiate planned language study a few days before the beginning of the study. They draw students' attention to a particular aspect or issue of language by inviting students to consider the topic and organizing activities that will engage the students' perceptions: they plan field trips; invite speakers with relevant expertise to class; arrange a table or a section of the room for browsing with pertinent books, magazine articles, recordings, videos, and audiotapes; set aside a section of the wall or a bulletin board to be illustrated with photographs, charts, or time lines; and display students' "I wonder if . . ." questions and statements in prominent places in the classroom. Teachers help students become aware of the significance of the language issue in order to highlight interest and motivate and stimulate talk. As a result of this environmental "seeding," students begin to think about and reflect on the topic even before it becomes a focus of the study. The physical environment for language study should be rich in language artifacts, such as newspaper clippings and favorite sayings displayed prominently (Loughlin & Martin, 1987). I often describe such classrooms as having literacy hanging from the ceilings and dripping down the wall.

The second phase of the learning cycle sustains and extends students' reflections and thoughts on what they have seen, heard, or read. In the *ideating* phase, teachers organize opportunities for thinking and reflecting. Eve Merriam (1991) provides insight into ideating in *The Wise Woman and Her Secret*. The characters in this illustrated text are anxiously seeking the secret of the woman's wisdom. After a number of explorations, the wise woman tells Jenny, a curious child, that she has found the secret: "[T]he secret of wisdom is to be curious, . . . to see and touch and taste and smell and hear. To keep on wondering and wandering" (p. 26). I think of seeing, touching, tasting, and smelling as aspects of the perceiving phase of learning and the wondering and wandering as ideating aspects. Although the perceiving phase involves many social interactions, the ideating phase also involves opportunities for personal introspection and self-reflection. Whenever ideating is personal, students can respond to stimulating social interactions and share budding ideas with others. The teacher sets aside time within the school day for individual kids to have a quiet place to think and for small groups of kids to think about issues together. The classroom is organized, and members of the class are respectful of one another's opportunities:

- to reconsider developing ideas or concepts and to establish new ones

- to consider new questions in light of the results of previous explorations

- to hypothesize or make informed guesses

- *to wander*—to the school library/media center to expand on inquiry questions, to a space in an outdoor patio, to the loft or a thinking chair

- to *wonder*—to stare into space, to listen to music, to write personal reflections, to doodle or draw, and, yes, even to daydream

Geane Hanson (1991, pp. 22) has documented daydreaming as an ideating state during which learning matures.

The third element in this learning cycle is the opportunity for students to present their thinking to others. The *presenting* phase is akin to Emily Dickinson's (1944) poetic metaphor, "This is my letter to the world" (p. 2). Kids have all kinds of opportunities to tell the world about the mysteries of their topic (K. Goodman et al., 1987, p. 180). It is in the telling that ideas take shape and are given voice. Students discuss and debate, listen to one another, and talk with family members or friends outside of the classroom to get responses to their ideas. Language and thought are expanded as students write to pen or e-mail pals, participate in computer chat rooms, and express themselves through various artistic media in order to share their thoughts and receive responses that challenge their thinking. In this way, language learning always involves the personal and the social. As they talk about what they think and mean, students expand their language use, inventing or discovering language they need to express their ideas. They explore new language and new uses of familiar language.

As students name what they are thinking about, share it with others, and receive response, they broaden their thinking and use of language. Such activities provide evidence of Halliday's (1979) idea that as students use language to discuss new concepts and ideas, they learn about the world through language. Students find new ways of talking and writing. Sometimes they dialogue informally, intimately, and quietly with the teacher or one or two other students, other times they participate in excited conversations with peers, and still other times they plan more formal uses of language to report to a whole class or to put on plays or demonstrations for the entire school or their parents.

Although presentations occur orally through discussion, argument, debate, or retelling, students are encouraged to compose through multiple sign systems such as written language and drama (Langer, 1957). Students are actively engaged with nonalphabetic writing systems such as math equations, science formulas, music and dance notations, computer logos, webs, diagrams, designs, illustrations, models, sketches, or photographs. They discuss the ways in which the various sign systems relate to their language and extend the possibilities of their communication.

The three learning phases are recursive and interrelated. Perceiving, ideating, and presenting never occur in isolation. As two students present to the class historical information they have researched on the U.S. Civil War, for example, their perceptions and thoughtful ideations about civil war stimulate discussion about the civil wars taking place throughout the world at the present time. As students ideate or wonder about why civil wars occur, they present possible reasons and become aware of new perceptions gleaned from what others are thinking. Students make connections between what they know and what they still want to know. They pay greater attention to and become more critical of TV and newspaper coverage. As they read more sophisticated historical texts or novels, this accumulation and history of their language experiences stimulate their need to express or present new thoughts in new ways to others. Perhaps they remember books they have previously read such as *Across Five Aprils* (Hunt, 1969), *My Brother Sam Is Dead* (Collier & Collier, 1974), *True North* (Lasky, 1996), *Nightjohn* (Paulsen, 1993), or *Cecil's Story* (Lyon, 1991). They establish connections between the Civil War and the Revolutionary War that lead to new perceptions and expanded thinking about issues and concepts that relate to all wars.

Teachers play an important role in stimulating students' perceiving, ideating, and presenting. They raise provocative questions based on their own wonderings. They keep seeding the environment with resources and expertise, reading to students from firsthand resources or complex texts the students aren't yet able to read for themselves. They show their interest in the students' ideating by engaging seriously in authentic conversations that extend students' opportunities for presenting. They provide evidence that they value students' learning by discussing with students how they are learning and by engaging students in self-evaluation of their learning. Teachers seed the environment with a rich array of resources in order to highlight opportunities for perceiving and ideating; they also provide space, time, and freedom of movement for ideating and exploring so that students use classroom and community resources and have time to think, discuss, and organize for continuous learning and social interaction.

Time is an especially significant issue when organizing for the learning phases and is often a constraining factor in planning language study. Although critical-moment teaching and strategy lessons are usually completed in a short time, theme cycles work best when sufficient time is set aside for teachers and students to follow the paths they want to explore. Some intense studies take from three weeks to two months of an hour or more a day and end with a major production for parents or presentations to the entire school. Others work better spread throughout a semester or year, and presentations are in the form of reporting to the whole class or writing newsletters or journals. When language study is organized in this manner, the teacher sets up an area in which to display the ongoing study so that the class revisits it on a regular basis.

Revisiting is an important concept that supports the cyclical nature of the learning phases. Revisiting prompts the recursive thinking that is stimulated when ideas are left open at the end of a period of study and students are reminded that they will revisit the ideas later. To provide opportunities for revisiting, students place charts, webs, photographs, or writings in strategic places so that they return to them at appropriate times later and throughout the semester or the year. Revisiting allows students to view their own learning historically as they discover how they elaborate on their ideas, how they make connections between ideas, and how they come to tentative conclusions, rethink ideas, and reconceptualize.

Just as it is critical to provide time for a thoughtful study to develop, it is equally important to terminate a study when it has run out of steam. If students don't sustain enthusiasm or excitement, the teacher should eliminate any pressure on students to continue a study that isn't engaging. Evaluating why enthusiasm has waned can be done with the whole class and provides insight into what didn't work and the best ways to keep students engaged in their own learning. Sometimes only a part of the class will decide to stay involved while other students move on to other interests and new studies. Opportunities for small groups of students to be involved in parallel or related studies reflect the teacher's flexibility in organizing the class. Sometimes when only one or two students sustain interest in an idea, they become experts in a particular area and are encouraged to develop individual expert projects. A major aspect of the learning phases is the opportunity for talk about language to become a conscious experience in the classroom.

Raising Language to a Conscious Level

Students' language growth is enhanced as a result of classroom talk about language and their ability to use language in non-threatening environments (Barnes, 1995; Britton, 1993). The critical moments, strategy lessons, and theme cycles discussed in later chapters involve suggestions for open-ended discussions that enhance opportunities to perceive, ideate, and present in relation to language study. Conscious awareness of how and why language is used takes place whenever language becomes an object of study.

By becoming conscious that language issues can be talked and wondered about, interrogated, and debated, students come to know that understanding language and developing their abilities to solve perceived language problems puts them in control of their language use. As students explore language use in overt ways, they perceive concern about language not simply as a reason to produce single correct answers or high test scores, but as a way to follow up on their own inquiry. In transmission model teaching, students view teaching and learning as having an isomorphic relationship: What I am taught, I must learn. But when students are immersed in a supportive environment in which they ask their own questions about language and discover ways to answer those questions, they become reflective about the role of language in their lives and in the lives of others: they wonder and wander about language.

Through the discussions that take place during either short lessons or in-depth study, students become aware that they have intuitive knowledge about language. They come to know that they have been using language effectively since birth in many different ways in different contexts. They learn that some strategies of language use are successful for them and that others actually interfere with their learning and communication. As a result of their growing awareness, they become more effective users of language.

Some students, however, believe that their language is poor or inappropriate because they speak a dialect that is not considered acceptable in school or because they speak a language in their home that is not valued by teachers or the school community. In addition, some students talk out of turn, hog a conversation, pay too much attention to letter-sound correspondences rather than focusing on meaning, develop "blocks" that interfere with writing, or are timid about asking questions or taking part in discussions. Negative attitudes and responses to these kinds of language uses affect students' views about themselves as language learners as much as they influence the ways they use language. Teachers need to organize discussions in sensitive and supportive ways to explore negative attitudes and responses to language learners. Having students write language-learning biographies or keep language-learning journals or logs provides a means by which to discuss and explore such issues.

As students write and talk with others about how they feel about themselves as language users and how they use language, they discover their language strengths and develop the confidence that helps them revalue themselves and others as competent language users.

Language Terminology: Metalanguage

In Chapter 1, I indicate that one principle of a language study curriculum is the use of appropriate linguistic terminology when talking about and studying language. In order to be conversant with any subject, it is necessary to use the language that signals that particular subject. Discussions with students about appropriate language terminology always involve raising language to a conscious level. As people learn to cook, for example, and come to understand and use terms such as *colander, spatula, coddle,* and *braise,* they realize the importance of cooking terminology for the purposes of reading recipes or talking to other cooks about how to achieve the best results. The language about cooking develops as cooks read, write, listen to, and talk with others about cooking. The same thing happens in talk about language. When kids are involved in discussions about how to conduct a debate, how to improve their reading or spelling, or how stories are structured, to mention a few examples, they come to use terms such as *argumentation, expression, prediction, sentence, adjective, whispering, comprehension, making sense, talking nonsense, taboo words, phonics, plots,* and so forth. The concept of any term develops best when it is used within the context of authentic settings. Awareness of language is at the heart of vocabulary development. As students discuss the skillful ways in which their favorite authors use language, why students select the language they do for their own writing, and how they use language differently with friends and family, they come to use and understand language about language.

As students talk about language, they develop *metalanguage* and *metalinguistic awareness.* Because of the nature of language, different language scholars use different terms for similar or even the same linguistic meanings. Some terms are popular at particular times but soon go out of fashion. Varying terminology grows out of different histories, paradigms, and controversies in fields such as linguistics or anthropology. It is helpful for both teachers and students to be aware that discipline-specific terminology is legitimately used in different ways. Knowing that there is varying terminology for similar concepts helps students become flexible in their discussions about language.

Students' test-taking strategies improve when teachers are able to point out that the language terminology of standardized and other high-stakes tests is sometimes different from the terminology conventionally used in the classroom. Exploring varying terminology is an important part of language study and provides flexibility of language use. Keeping a chart on the wall where students and teacher list terms about language that they already know, hear, or read is a good starting point. The following chart was developed in a fifth-grade class. The teacher and students listed these items when they began to wonder about the meanings of these terms. They interviewed other people about the meanings and consulted language arts texts, grammar texts for teachers, and standardized test sample questions.

Different Language Terminology

Adjectives	Sometimes called descriptive words (Everyone says my sister is a *beautiful* baby.)
Verbs	Sometimes called action words (Turtle *jumped* all over the place.)
Articles	Sometimes called function words or determiners (They traveled on *a* fast train through *the* countryside.)
Schwa	Sometimes called an unaccented vowel (work*e*r, *a*bout)
Adverbs	Sometimes called "ly" words (He ran very quick*ly*.)

This chart was generated over time and added to throughout the year. When confusions or contradictions developed—such as when some students asked, "Why do so many people say, 'do it quick,' but some teachers say you have to say 'quickly'?"—the question became the focus of a strategy lesson. Such lessons sometimes develop into a full-fledged theme cycle study. In this case, the teacher told the class that adverbs were going to be on the fourth-grade test, so she first wanted to show them what they already knew about adverbs by developing the chart, and then they would continue to discuss and think about adverbs during the next few weeks. Without belaboring the issue, the teacher had the students focus on adverbs in their writing and reading during this time, and they continued to add to the class charts. She asked the class to listen to conversations and take notes of the adverbs they heard. Some of the students spoke Spanish, and she invited them to discuss with their parents how adverbs worked in their other language.

The more connections the teacher helps students make, the more likely their language concepts develop in meaningful ways and become a permanent part of their schema and knowledge base. In my graduate classes with many international students, we become aware of the variations among languages as students from different language communities compare how similar terms work in different ways in different languages. We don't need to become proficient in these languages. Rather, we become better language users when we understand the complexity of language and think about the language we use in new ways. We also have to find common terms with which to discuss the language issues. This often sends us scrambling to linguistic texts and to raise questions with linguistic scholars on campus. Such discussions are also possible in elementary and middle school classrooms, especially when some students speak different languages. Students love exploring language differences when the exploration takes place in a supportive environment in which wondering about language is valued.

Although young students often use their own invented terms or the overgeneralized terms they have learned during previous instruction or at home, it is helpful for teachers to use linguistically appropriate terms and to make explicit connections to the students' uses. In this way, students expand their storehouse of language terminology and don't come to believe that somehow what they know or how they say it is wrong. Students do not become proficient at talking about language when teachers use only language such as "action words" for verbs or "descriptive words" for adjectives. Such attempts at simplifying language add an unnecessary step to a student's learning. They have to understand the teacher's metaphoric uses and then relate them to conventional terminology. The most supportive strategy is to use appropriate terms with students from the beginning. Although metaphors such as *action* or *describing* are helpful when making connections to students' knowledge, as teachers use the conventional terminology in context over time, students develop appropriate concepts, and as a result, begin to use the terms conventionally.

Becoming a Language Scientist: Inquiry Study

I keep emphasizing that language is as amenable to study as subtraction, galaxies, the presidents of the United States, rap music, or any other topic. A language study curriculum allows students to explore ideas in innovative ways that make sense to the learner: the focus is on inquiry.

In my elementary and middle-grade classes, students kept lists of their questions and crossed them off as they discovered answers, adding new questions. Their questions often related to why their language was not considered acceptable by other people and why their words were considered taboo or offensive. My students became inquirers into language issues—they were interested in language study. Scientists' burning questions drive their investigations and lie at the heart of their inquiry. When students follow their own questions into an inquiry study with similar passion, they add dramatically to their learning about language. Even when the teacher knows that the students' explorations may not be fruitful, he or she encourages them to follow their own leads. When explorations lead to unclear or even wrong answers, students discover how to inquire more deeply. The uncertainty of inquiry is at the heart of Piaget's (1977) concept of disequilibrium. Just as scientists learn when their hypotheses don't work out, students experience the satisfaction that comes from learning from their false steps. During such times, teachers also discover that some of the ideas or knowledge about language they were previously sure about are actually considered controversial or questionable. Through inquiry, teachers also become learners about language. As teachers share their own reconsiderations with their students, they demonstrate for students the value of risk taking.

Students benefit from descriptions and discussions of how linguists go about doing research in their fields. They become aware that exploring their own language use or the language use of others is the method linguists use to research language. It is helpful to invite linguists or anthropologists to the classroom to share information such as what they like to study, what questions they ask, and how they go about researching in their fields.

Language researchers often start by considering what they know. Based on that knowledge, they ask questions designed to uncover things they do not know. Their questions grow out of wondering and being curious. *The Wise Woman and Her Secret* by Eve Merriam (1991), referred to earlier, is a wonderful book to read with students in order to explore the role of wonderment and exploration. Linguists discuss their questions with other language scientists and read what other scholars have to say. They interview the people they want to know about and collect transcripts of language samples from different people in different environments. Students, likewise, participate in such methods to discover how language works. They take field notes or use audio- or videotape recordings and then transcribe some of the tapings, depending on what they are trying to find out. They cut apart the transcripts or organize them in various ways to establish categories or themes. They become keen observers and investigators of language phenomena. A number of books help teachers consider ways to involve their students in such explorations (e.g., Heath, 1983; Taylor, 1998). As Judith Lindfors (1999) makes clear, inquiry isn't just about seeking information; it also involves seeking "to explore, to reflect, to wonder" (p. 23). Inquiry embodies rich opportunities for the ideating phase of learning.

After exploring how linguists work, the class should decide which questions they want to answer as a whole class or whether they want to pursue language issues individually or in small groups. They might decide to find out, for example, whether girls and boys use the same or different kinds of language to invite one another to parties. After interviewing and audiotaping one another and students in other classes, they report back to the class. In addition to discussing what they have discovered so far, they talk about ways to improve their interviews and then try out their questioning on another group of students. As students discuss their interviewing technique, teachers help them clarify ethical issues about privacy, interviewing, and reporting. *Harriet the Spy* by Louise Fitzhugh (1964) is a good read-aloud that allows fourth through eight graders to explore ethical issues. Harriet does a lot of note taking about classmates and friends and uses the notes in her writing, but she does it without the knowledge of the people she is inquiring about.

Depending on its purpose, language study can be planned for individuals, small groups, or whole classes, taking into consideration the recursive cycles of perceiving, ideating, and presenting. The students understand the purpose of their inquiry because their inquiry is based on their own questions. Edie, for example, a fourth-grade Native American student, discovered that each of the three encyclopedias she consulted cited a different number of moons for Jupiter. She needed to decide which encyclopedia had the best information for her purposes and whether she needed to consult different texts or ask more knowledgeable people. Not only did Edie find out information about the planets, but she also learned to be a critical reader. She led a discussion with her study group about the characteristics of the texts she was using and how she decided which was the most reliable.

Through inquiry study, both students and the teacher are encouraged to consider many different ways to go about answering their questions (Short & Harste, 1996; Lindfors, 1999). In transmission model classes, the language topics studied could be similar to those studied in inquiry classrooms, but the teaching and learning in the two contexts are very different. In transmission model classrooms, teachers often ask questions to which they already know the right answer and use textbooks as the main authority for specific knowledge. Knowledge is transmitted to the learner, who reports back this knowledge to the teacher in specific and "correct" ways. Let's say that in both types of classrooms the language topic is to use quotation marks appropriately in writing. In the transmission model classroom, the teacher tells the students the rules for placing quotation marks before and after the direct quote and where to place the comma. She writes an example on the board and shows the students where the marks go. She follows this with a worksheet containing a number of examples. The students mark where the quotation marks and commas go, and the teacher corrects and grades the results.

In inquiry-oriented classrooms, learners construct concepts or knowledge themselves through their questions, experimentation, and discoveries (Dewey, 1925; Duckworth, 1987). They are in charge of their own learning. More specifically, the students in an inquiry classroom explore quotation marks in response to their use in their own writing or when students notice them in their reading. The teacher asks the students what they know about where, when, and how quotation marks are used. The students keep records of their responses and then explore their writing and reading to see if quotation marks are used in different ways in different contexts. Teachers in inquiry-oriented classrooms ask the students questions to which they do not know the answers. Judith Lindfors (1999) reviews research on teachers' questioning and concludes that "[u]ntil recently, the one bit of advice that was rarely given was 'Ask real questions, questions you yourself wonder about,' . . . what I call acts of inquiry" (pp. 113–14). As teachers demonstrate their own sense of wonder by asking honest questions, they model for students ways in which to conduct their own inquiries. I have noticed recently that in Spanish, quotation marks are used differently than they are in English. In fact, sometimes dashes are used with no quotation marks. I wonder if such devices are sometimes used in English and how widespread this is in other languages.

Kidwatching: Record Keeping and Evaluation

The most informative evaluation is one that is an ongoing part of curricular experiences and involves learners, teachers, parents, and organized record keeping. There are many ways to develop record keeping for the evaluation of students' language growth. The presenting phase of the learning cycle, discussed earlier in this chapter, provides continuous evaluation of students' growth and progress. Authentic evidence for ongoing evaluation includes not only completed language study projects but also work in progress, small group discussions, data collected on video- and audiotapes, reports on the results of interviews, analysis of samples of reading and writing, and many other formal and informal presentations. Continuous evaluation involves teachers and students in reflecting on their products and progress in many different contexts. Many teachers and teacher educators use a range of forms and formats through which they provide authentic assessment of students' ongoing language study (K. Goodman, Bird, & Goodman, 1992; K. Goodman, Y. Goodman, & Hood, 1989; Kitagawa, 2000; Owocki & Goodman, 2002).

By establishing a kidwatching stance that includes careful interactions, observations, and analyses of students as they engage in ongoing, daily learning experiences (Y. Goodman, 1978; Wilde, 1996), teachers approach evaluation as a continuous process. Kidwatching includes the recording of anecdotal records or field notes as well as the collection and in-depth examination of samples of students' work. Kidwatching occurs during presentations of all kinds: reading and writing conferences, oral reading, retellings, and literature circles. Careful analysis of the range of documents that represent students' work not only provides teachers with information about students' growing capabilities, but also points to the aspects of language study that teachers most need to organize for individuals, small groups, or whole class instruction. Ongoing evaluation is one of the most important ways in which teachers inform their developing curriculum, and it updates parents and school administrators on the successes and needs of the classroom community.

Evaluation is most powerful when students are integrally involved in the process. Student-teacher conferences or three-way conferences (including parents) provide opportunities for self-evaluation and for all parties to assume responsibility for the student's future learning. Conferences help pinpoint opportunities for critical-moment teaching and strategy lessons (Chapters 3 and 4). In addition, the information gleaned from conferences allows teachers to respond to students' questions and help students formulate their wonderings into inquiry projects (Chapters 5 through 7).

In the writing study that colleagues and I did with Tohono O'odham Native American students, for example, we asked the third and fourth graders to examine five of the compositions they kept in their portfolios during the year (Y. Goodman & Wilde, 1992, p. 35). During conferences with the students, we asked them to place the writing in order, with their best piece of work on top. We then asked them to explain their ordering: why did they choose a particular piece as their best, their next best, and so on? After we collected information about their personal perspectives on their own writing, we asked them to put their papers in order according to what their teacher would like the best. In other words, which piece did they think was best and next best and so on from their teacher's perspective? Each child produced a different order when ordering their work according to their teacher's perspective. They also had different reasons for their choices. For the writing they chose as the best according to their own perspectives, they said they liked a particular piece best because it reflected an innovation they had worked on; it represented an important personal meaning; the actions had taken place in their lives; or the story line was interesting. Gordon, for example, liked one of his stories best "because of a little surprise twist in the plot" (p. 187). The reasons they gave for their teacher's supposed choices included that the pieces were the longest, most neatly written, and spelled correctly. Gordon said his teacher would like one story better than the other because "I spelled the letters right this time" and "in the other one the lines are crooked" (p. 187). These conferences helped the teachers gain insight into the students' misconceptions about what the teachers valued. Likewise, the students developed a greater understanding of the realities of the teachers' views about their writing because the teachers shared their expectations with the students.

Evaluation is not just for individual students. Group evaluations are good for examining class discussions, projects, and interactions. I always ended theme study or periods of integrated work with a whole class conference by asking, "So how did we do?"; "What did we do well?"; "How could we do this better?" Through group evaluations, class members developed better ways to interact, sustain interest, support one another's work, converse with one another more successfully, and live comfortably together in our classroom. Evaluation is an integral part of all language study discussions.

The language studies examined in the following chapters describe opportunities for a rich language study curriculum that is informed by the teaching and learning concepts presented in this chapter. Each chapter provides suggestions and examples that serve as a framework for teachers, but as I say often throughout this book, the most satisfying language studies develop as teachers plan their own lessons, projects, or theme studies through negotiation with their students.

II

LANGUAGE STUDY EXPERIENCES

CHAPTER THREE

Critical-Moment Teaching

During many fleeting moments of the school day, the focus of attention is on language as students and teachers perceive language issues, think or ideate about language, and present their ideas about language to others:

> "How can *tropical* be a storm and mean a warm place at the same time?" asks fifth grader Rudy, who lives in snow-covered Buffalo, as he reads a novel.

> "How come," asks nine-year-old Marisue, reading a poem about a baby deer, "that a word like this [pointing to the noun *does*] is the same as this one [pointing to the verb *does* later on the same page]? It's really confusing!"

> Gordon, a third grader composing an article about a sports event, asks, "Do *foot* and *ball* go together when you are writing about a football game?" Inventing the need for compound words, Gordon decides to leave a smaller space between *foot* and *ball* than the spaces he usually leaves between separate words.

Younger children also spontaneously attend to language:

> Five-year-old Monica asks her mother as they are driving home from school, "How come *mom* means *mom* and *the* means *the;* why can't *the* mean *mom* and *mom* mean *the?*"

Legitimizing Critical-Moment Teaching

Kids often ask questions that reveal their interest in language—how it works and why it looks and sounds the way it does. In schools such wonderings about language occur within a range of contexts: during a current events discussion about problems in the Middle East, as teacher and students struggle with unfamiliar names; during a science experiment on mixing chemicals, as students notice similar word beginnings or endings (*aluminum/calcium* or *nitrate/nitrite*); or during a game, as one or two children express their shock at the language another child uses as the competition heats up. Wonderment about language is not confined to scheduled times labeled "reading," "writing," or "language arts." It occurs during discussions that relate to social studies, math, or music as the teacher and students use language to raise questions and learn new concepts about language. It occurs between the teacher and one student, in small groups, or during a whole class discussion. I call such language events *critical teaching moments*.

Such moments are *critical* because the queries, although often spontaneous, are of intense interest to the learner. They are critical because they heighten the students' awareness of language as an object of study. They are critical because the students begin to wonder whether the ideas and concepts they are considering are true or fair or confusing. Such wonderings often occur when students become uncertain because of new knowledge or ideas. During such moments, learners are deeply engaged in considering alternative reasons for their developing concepts about language and its use; if the teacher responds appropriately, critical learning and thinking take place. Often these moments occur during students' disequilibrium, in the Piagetian sense: when students are trying to understand and work out knowledge that doesn't fit neatly into the schemas or constructs they have already developed (Duckworth, 1987), or when they ask provocative questions or express their wonderment out loud. If the teacher ignores students' questions or doesn't support their wonderment, the opportunity to take advantage of the critical moment is gone.

Such moments are critical *teaching* moments because the sensitive teacher takes the time to encourage the student's inquiring stance, to encourage the learner's interest in the topic, and to support risk-taking opportunities when a student expresses bewilderment or wonderment. These moments reveal what Vygotsky (1978) calls the *zone of proximal development* as the teacher's responses to the students' inquiries mediate and support students' new and more complex learning. In this zone, learners, with the help of teachers and the classroom community, discover a safe environment in which to reflect on new ideas, relate them to established knowledge, and take risks necessary for new learning to develop. Successful teachers are well aware of the power of critical moments. They know how to exploit them for their students' benefit and are careful to respond in a timely fashion, because such moments pass quickly.

Whenever I think about critical teaching moments, the lessons raised by Albert Cullum's *The Geranium on the Window Sill Just Died, but Teacher You Went Right On* (1971) comes to mind. Cullum reminds his readers of the gulf that separates young peoples' views of school from those of too many teachers. His verse reminds adults in school settings of the importance of listening to students and learning from them:

> The robins sang and sang and sang
> but teacher you went right on.
> The last bell sounded the end of the day,
> but teacher you went right on.
> The geranium on the window sill just died,
> but teacher you went right on. (p. 56)

Critical-moment teaching is predicated on teachers listening attentively to their students and tuning into their questions and concerns, their wonderings and fears, their tentative beliefs, and the issues they raise. As I indicate in Chapter 2, this kind of careful attending is integral to ongoing authentic assessment, and I use the term *kidwatching* to refer to such observation and respectful conversation with students (Y. Goodman, 1978, 1985; Wilde, 1996). As we listen and observe carefully, students show us what they know and what they want to learn. By following students' lead, teachers help students establish an environment in which important questions can be asked without fear of reprisal, and thus significant learning results.

Many aspects of teaching are similar to the aesthetic composition processes of artists, authors, and musicians. These pedagogical creative compositions are not magical. They can be observed, reflected on, recorded, transcribed, and analyzed so that others can understand their power (Taylor, 1993). I call such awareness of teaching practices *metapedagogy*—the conscious reflection on why teachers do what they do (Whitmore & Goodman, 1996). As critical teaching moments are documented and analyzed, they become legitimized. Consequently, teachers become alert to such moments and refine the ways in which they respond to them. Such documentation becomes a regular part of teachers' self-reflection and affects educational practice. It provides specific evidence that teachers use to articulate their practice. The growing focus on teacher research in teacher education programs is an acknowledgment of the importance of such documentation (Watson, Burke, & Harste, 1989; Whitmore & Goodman, 1996).

While some critical teaching moments are resolved quickly, others expand into strategy lessons (Chapter 4) or theme cycle studies (Chapters 5–7). In this chapter, I examine the nature of critical teaching moments as they occur during:

- ◆ spontaneous language interactions
- ◆ human and physical resource use
- ◆ conferences
- ◆ exploration of miscues
- ◆ building language traditions

These critical teaching moments are drawn from my own teaching or the stories I've gathered over the years from other teachers in classroom settings.

Spontaneous Language Interactions

Exploring language comments and questions with students helps them become conscious that conversations about language, which occur spontaneously, reveal their thinking and knowledge and are evidence that they are good language users interested in developing greater competence.

Unfortunately, the process of students asking questions has sometimes been trivialized so that even in graduate school, students occasionally preface important questions about language with: "I know this is a dumb question, but . . ." Yet such questions in most cases lead to insightful discussions. The questions that students ask are just as important as the questions that teachers ask. In transmission model settings, teachers underestimate the importance of students' questions and overemphasize teachers' questions, which more often than not are trivial. Insightful teachers establish a tradition in their classrooms that there are no stupid questions, and they organize the language environment so that all students are comfortable asking any question and revealing their tentative thinking.

I was struck by the power of kids' questions many years ago when I heard Courtney Cazden talk about a second grader who said to her one day, "Do you know, Ms. Cazden, *big* is a little word and *little* is a big word?" What a powerful spontaneous critical teaching moment for the teacher to respond, "Wow, what made you think that? You're doing good thinking to ask such a question. I wonder if there are other big words that mean *little* and other little words that mean *big*? How could we find out?" When we discuss this language story in graduate classes, we learn a lot about morphemic forms of language and historical influences on the English language (for example, *mini* and *maxi*) as we explore the teaching and learning possibilities in response to such a question asked by a seven-year-old.

Inappropriate Language Use

When I taught eighth grade, I walked around my classroom observing my students' writing. One day I came up to two students who were editing their compositions with each other and arguing over whether *ain't* was an appropriate word to use in one student's story. One student claimed that *ain't* should never be used in writing, while the author argued that since it was part of the dialogue of the character in the story, it was not only possible but necessary. I asked the two students to present their arguments to the class. After a short discussion (the presentation and class discussion took less than ten minutes), we decided to write the question on the board: *Can you use "ain't" in writing?* Our discussion continued over time as we examined books and magazines, listened to television and radio broadcasts, and asked parents, high school English teachers, and a local journalist to contribute their views on this question. We learned about the variety of and strong points of view that people from different walks of life have about such language use. What started out as a critical-moment teaching event (students sharing their argument with the class) expanded into a strategy lesson (see Chapter 4) that focused on interviews the students conducted and reported on to the class. The students got so engaged in their learning that we developed an in-depth language study theme cycle on vernacular language (see Chapter 5). Although these discussions took place in the 1950s, not too long ago there was an article in the local newspaper about "a war of words" between the Houghton Mifflin publishing company and the *American College Dictionary*, published by Random House, over the acceptability of *ain't* (Sibley, 1993). Language issues that my eighth graders argued about fifty years ago are still debatable today.

I can't imagine a teacher not hearing at least once during the school year something like, "Oooooh, teacher, he say a bad word." For some this issue may seem too much of a hot potato to deal with in school settings. In the communities where I taught, however, responding to what kids perceived to be "bad words" helped me diminish the problem of kids using such language to disrupt class. At the same time, it helped students explore the purpose and significance of bad words, slang expressions, and teenage language registers. In my classes, I could always count on students bringing to the class's attention issues concerning questionable language. I realized that when students used inappropriate language in class, especially early in the year, they did so not simply out of anger or as a put-down; rather, the function was to shock the teacher—to test my responses and show their peers how tough they were. They were always disarmed when I didn't respond with righteous indignation but instead engaged them in several minutes' exploration of the functions such language served for them. They were surprised by my reaction and soon realized that the language they used had no shock value for me and that I used such language opportunities to focus the class on conversations about language. They were also astonished to discover that there were academic books dealing with the subject of such language use and that there were linguists who studied such phenomena (Andersson & Trudgill, 1990).

When teachers reject such language usage out of hand, it is easy for students to develop negative attitudes about themselves as language users. If instead teachers take advantage of such critical teaching moments, they can have students inquire into the nature of why certain usages are considered inappropriate and whether there are contexts in which they are acceptable. As a result, students become aware that language issues are controversial and that they have a role in exploring the issues and building their own knowledge and points of view.

Another example of a spontaneous critical-moment response to inappropriate language is described by Maureen Morrisey (1989), a third-grade whole language bilingual teacher:

> Bianca and Jessica came running up to me to tell me that Mara, a monolingual Spanish speaker, had told them "shut up." I laugh at the memory of the expressions on their faces when my eyes lit up and I exclaimed, "That's great! These are Mara's first words in English." I explained my reaction to the two girls as we went to tell Mara some other ways to say "shut up" in English. She was receptive to our offers of new ways to express herself and she walked away armed with new English words to meet her need for quiet or to be left alone. (p. 87)

A number of learnings took place during this critical-moment teaching. Not only did Mara learn that language she thought she understood meant something different, but also both Bianca and Jessica became aware that children learning a second language sometimes say things that do not fit the context. The students explored the pragmatics of language use—what language is appropriate and inappropriate given specific language contexts. Maureen Morrisey's elaboration with these students during the few minutes they needed to explore their concerns added a dimension to their understanding of second language learning.

It takes only a few moments to inquire with students into why certain language is considered inappropriate, to find resources to discover what others think about this issue, and to discuss solutions that include the responsibility language users must take for what they say and how they use language.

Exploring Punctuation

After considerable study of the animals they love in their homes, the third graders in Jodi North's class agreed that they would like to put on a pet zoo. Following class discussion, the students went off to their tables to write a profile of their pets. After working for a few minutes, Bill came up to the teacher and said: "You know, Mrs. North, I need a sad mark to write about my pet. Remember my dog got run over on Halloween night in front of the school?"

Mrs. North responded thoughtfully, "Bill, I don't think there are any sad marks, but maybe you could make one up." Bill returned eagerly to his writing. When he showed her his work, she told him that she had a university teacher who would be very interested in his invention. A few days later I received the following letter (note the punctuation mark after the word *died* in Figure 5):

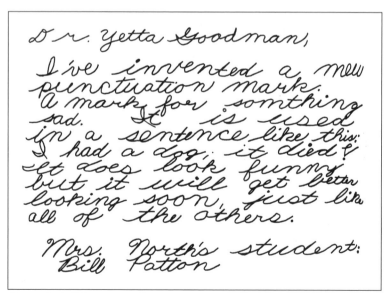

FIGURE 5: *Bill Patton's sadlamation point.*

While I was discussing with Julie Jensen, then editor of *Language Arts*, the possibility of publishing Bill's letter (Y. Goodman, 1979, p. 482), there was a flurry of activity in Mrs. North's classroom. The spontaneous language interaction she had with Bill, which took just a minute or two, led to interest on the part of all the third graders and experimentation in the uses and limitations of punctuation. Mrs. North took advantage of this critical moment to highlight the students' interest by involving them in Bill's invention of the sadlamation point (he named it), and the class thoughtfully began to consider the functions that punctuation serves in written language, thus moving them into a theme cycle study. The students and Mrs. North learned a great deal about punctuation as they extended their language study.

I may have learned the most from this experience because from that time on, I not only continued my research into students' invented spellings, but also began to systematically collect and study children's invented punctuation as well. Bill Patton clued me in to his inventive powers in the first sentence of his letter to me. I also noticed his use of the colon after his closing: "Mrs. North's student." Since then I have collected hundreds of young writers' punctuation inventions, become attuned to the fact that authors and poets experiment with punctuation, and have noted that the controversial nature of many punctuation conventions leads to interesting discussions among linguists and other language scholars. These are discoveries that teachers and students make as well as they explore the ways in which they segment written language and why they do so. Such explorations are often touched off during critical-moment teaching.

Human and Physical Resource Use

Resources available in the classroom, the school, and the community provide powerful contexts for critical-moment teaching, and discussions often help students become explicitly aware of the many possible ways to find answers to language questions in the social context of the entire community as well as in the school.

With a team of other researchers, I documented the learning that occurred when kids had the use of classroom resources during their daily writing time, and we discovered the ways in which critical-moment teaching influences students who are becoming independent language learners. We conducted this study with Tohono O'odham third and fourth graders in the Indian Oasis School District (Y. Goodman & Wilde, 1992). Wendy Kasten (1992), one of the researchers, categorized and analyzed the ways in which the students used both human and physical resources. As kids wrote, they interacted with teachers, other students, librarians, paraprofessionals, and other adults in the room and in the school. They used physical resources including dictionaries, trade books, chalk- and bulletin boards, calendars, book bags, posters, charts, and their own and other students' published writing.

We concluded that when resources are easily accessible to students, they learn to "live off the land," as Don Graves (1983) often says. In other words, they learn to be independent resource users who know they can consult many different materials and people to help them solve their problems and answer their questions. They become aware of ways to search for resources, especially when the teacher trusts them to be responsible and expects them to be mobile in the classroom and school in order to take maximum advantage of available resources. Students' flexible use of resources in the classroom establishes an environment in which a community of learners experiences a wide range of oral and written language. During critical teaching moments, it is possible to talk about ways to use resources most efficiently, how to use them flexibly, and which resources are most helpful depending on the students' purposes.

In Sr. Susan Caldwell's fourth-grade class, the students' resource use highlighted the importance of critical-moment teaching. Sr. Susan provided evidence of the critical role of the teacher and of the organization of the classroom environment in helping students use resources independently. The students had easy access to resources and used them whenever they were needed without asking permission. They went to the library corner in the room, used the charts on the walls, and discussed their problems with other students. Reference books, thesauruses, dictionaries, and atlases with a range of purposes, difficulties, sizes, shapes, and formats were set up on a rolling cart, and students were encouraged to move the cart to their table whenever they needed it. Sr. Susan made her students responsible for the care and organization of these materials, so they were familiar with all the resources. Although she was available to discuss resource use and to answer questions, Sr. Susan's goal was always to lead the students to work independently or with one another as much as possible.

Wendy Kasten (1992) documented a writing experience with Gordon, a student in Sr. Susan's class, when he was writing a story and began to search for the spelling of the word *surround*. Consulting a large Webster's unabridged dictionary, he turned to the *s*'s, starting at the very beginning of the section. He quickly became frustrated when he didn't find the word. Gordon talked about his difficulties with a group of other kids and decided to use a picture dictionary that included easy words; there he found the word *round*. When he returned to his seat, he wrote *sround* in his story. Later, when Sr. Susan came over to Gordon's table to observe the students at work, she asked Gordon to explain the strategies he had used to arrive at his spelling. The other kids at the table were rapt listeners. Gordon said that he knew that *surround* was a hard word, so he looked it up in the hard dictionary, but when he couldn't find it there, he decided that if he spelled *round* correctly, he could edit his spelling later. He knew that the word *round* would be in the easy dictionary (p. 100).

The group at Gordon's table considered different ways to use dictionaries and how they knew which words are in easy dictionaries and which are in hard ones. They explored the hard word/easy word issue and expanded their understanding of how to use dictionaries and which ones would be most helpful for specific purposes. A number of learnings emerged from this critical teaching moment. Wendy Kasten and I discovered that fourth graders have a sense of easy word and hard word categories and their placement in dictionaries (Y. Goodman & Wilde, 1992; Kasten, 1992). We concluded that having multiple kinds of dictionaries in a classroom was more beneficial to the students than having one set of the same dictionary for all the students. Sr. Susan learned about the strategies Gordon used in such situations, helped him become conscious of the knowledge he had, and, through discussion with other students, explored additional strategies for using various dictionaries and other resource books.

She helped him realize his syllabic knowledge, evident in his awareness that the word *round* was part of *surround,* and affirmed his
strategy of waiting to edit his spellings later. She also used
Gordon's experience to plan strategy lessons on suffixes and prefixes and to discuss the need to think about second and third
letters in a word when using a dictionary. Gordon, of course,
learned that he had knowledge about how words are patterned
and that he could use a number of acceptable strategies when he
was writing and needed information about spelling. Such dynamic
moments provide learning opportunities for all the participants
in the event and highlight the social nature of learning.

Mario, another Tohono O'odham fourth grader, was writing
about the Baboquivari Mountains, sacred to his people. He asked
aloud for the spelling at the writing table where he was working
with some classmates. Melanie ran to the window and looked
out at the parked school bus with Baboquivari Warriors (the name
of the high school football team) imprinted on its side. As she
returned to the table with the name written on a piece of paper,
Sr. Susan came over to the group, acknowledged the sophisticated use of resources, and engaged the students in a discussion
of the range of resources available for discovering conventional
spellings of unusual words. This spontaneous episode took less
than five minutes.

I observed a similar experience at a writing table with six
first graders in Vera Milz's classroom in Michigan. Timmy looked
at me and asked, "How do you spell *dinosaur?*" I responded
honestly that I wasn't sure of the entire spelling (I'm never sure
of the two vowels that immediately precede the final *r*). Jennifer
looked up from her writing and said, "Just a minute, Timmy,"
and she went over to the bookcase and selected a book. Ms. Milz
believes that primary-age children remember titles more easily
than they remember author names, so the students in her class
learn to shelve the thousands of books in their classroom library
alphabetizing by title. The kids not only come to know the alphabet, but also build knowledge about titles and ways to independently search for books. It was easy, therefore, for Jennifer to
take a book with *dinosaur* in the title off the shelf and bring it
back to the table for Timmy to use. Jennifer, Timmy, and the rest
of the group at the table talked for a few minutes about the kinds

of resources that are helpful when one wants conventional spellings and how it feels to be able to find such resources independently. These children use the terms *invented spelling* and *conventional spelling* with understanding because Ms. Milz uses the terms in their appropriate contexts.

Teachers such as Vera Milz and Susan Caldwell are aware of the rich resources available for both student and teacher use, and they organize their classrooms around these resources and discuss the independent use of classroom resources with their students. In addition, whenever the kids ask questions about how to find something, these teachers show the students how they themselves use specialized dictionaries and articles that are kept in a special file, or other materials that help the teachers support kids' learning. In such classrooms, students explore the range of resources that are available to support their spelling development, as well as the most efficient ways to use them.

After a few such critical teaching moments, the students and the teacher list these resources and the ways to use them and post these lists wherever the resources are kept so that the ideas can be revisited later when questions about resource use come up again. I have seen charts with titles such as "Going on a Spelling Safari" or "Where to Find Story Ideas." Both teacher and students periodically discuss and update the lists by adding helpful resources discovered as a result of the students' spontaneous questions. The teachers encourage the students not to list "Ask the teacher" or "Ask our aide," explaining the importance of students discovering additional expert human resources and not becoming overly dependent on the adults in the classroom. Librarians, the computer center teachers, and other specialist teachers are good resources for helping students become familiar with a range of new technologies. I recently took a graduate class that was working on a historical research project to the university library, and we were surprised by the new and expanding resources available on various networks that the resource librarian showed us how to access. Such research opportunities through or with new technologies are becoming more common in elementary and middle schools as well. It is important to help students find and critically use a range of resources that will allow them to explore their inquiries and discover the rich and voluminous materials available on the Internet. One search engine I use for a variety of topics, particularly to find lists of books for children and adolescents, is Google. Students learn to gather information from different sources, evaluate the status of experts, and decide why they think some materials are more informative or dependable than others. This kind of discriminating ability is especially important in response to sources on the Internet, with its explosion of information by authors whose expertise and points of view are not easily verified.

Students also need to develop criteria by which to evaluate the usefulness of specific materials. Different student committees in the class can volunteer to become familiar with the rich range of resources, to understand when and how to use them, and to share their knowledge with others. These committees help the teacher establish a collection of resource materials that extend the students' growing understandings. Students discover appropriate uses for dictionaries, thesauruses, and specialized word lists as well as becoming aware of the limitations of their use, and they learn how to recognize the latest information in dictionaries and thesauruses. These students become class experts who are available for other students whenever questions arise. Examining how bibliographies, telephone books, and Internet lists are compiled provides students with insight into questions about alphabetization, ways to establish categories, and the conventions of referencing. These explorations often lead to strategy lessons or theme cycles that culminate in students writing classroom resource books or producing lists of Web sites or bibliographies that focus on a range of language study issues.

As I work in classrooms with teachers and students, it is obvious that when the use of materials is constrained by mandates about what material is accessible and by limitations on when and how resources can be used, students lose precious opportunities to become responsible users and explorers of human and physical resources that enrich their language learning.

Funds of Knowledge

Everyone in the classroom should be aware of the funds of knowledge that other members in the class have. *Funds of knowledge* is a concept developed by Luis Moll and colleagues (Moll, Amanti, Neff, & Gonzalez, 1992; Moll & González, 1997) in studying the rich knowledge that members of working-class communities have as they support one another with their individual expertise. Members of a community, through their ongoing participation in the community, come to know which members are most helpful in specific instances: helping with medical problems, fixing cars, cooking special dishes, and so on.

Likewise, students in a collaborative classroom community become aware of their own and other students' expertise and come to appreciate that everyone in the classroom community has contributions to make. They come to understand that different members of their classroom, school, or home communities are important resources. Some students are best at spelling, others listen well to the writing of their peers, some class members are the illustrators and artists in the class, and others are capable planners and organizers. Highlighting and using the expertise of individual class members expands language use in many ways. Students, for example, are often involved in planning a field trip. During such opportunities, students discuss phone etiquette and strategies for following the long phone menus to find out when museums are open or how to get through to an appropriate party in order to talk to an actual person. Students learn polite ways to ask the school office staff whether they may use the phones to plan their trips. These experiences are good listening lessons and occur in a few minutes in response to a question. Critical-moment teaching often results in students becoming conscious of how they ask questions to discover how others can be of help, learning the language appropriate for inviting people to speak in the class, and finding the materials available for showing appreciation to others. Such opportunities relieve the teacher of many duties that kids are capable of handling themselves; the students in turn learn a lot about language.

Conferences

Individual or group conferences are rich in critical-moment teaching opportunities for language learning. As Donald Graves (1983) says, "When the child talks, we learn; when the child talks, the child learns; when the child talks, the teacher can help" (pp. 137–38). Although conferences are important settings for evaluation, they also include opportunities for getting to know a student well; providing students with the undivided attention of an interested and listening teacher; and helping students reflect on their own learning and future inquiries through self-evaluation. During conferences, issues arise spontaneously that lead to powerful critical-moment teaching, while others become the basis for planned strategy lessons or theme cycles. Teachers discover that conferences are integral to negotiating and expanding curriculum. Conference participants can include the teacher with an individual student, the teacher with a small group, or the teacher with the entire class. In some cases, as students become familiar with conference procedures a small group of students is capable of conferencing on their own and reporting back to the teacher.

In my university classes, I often plan whole class conferences during midterms. In my elementary and middle school classes, I held such conferences at a logical break such as the end of a day, a week, or a theme cycle. Such conferences are especially helpful when the learning experience in question has been either particularly constructive or ineffective. As a class, we evaluate and expand on the things that went well and make changes to improve those that didn't work. I begin such group conferences by asking:

- ◆ What went really well that we should continue?

- ◆ What could have gone better?

- ◆ What responsibilities should each of us take to make our time together more effective?

I do not focus on any individual who did or did not contribute well. Rather, our overall concern is to plan and work better as a group. During such times, spontaneous issues often arise about the kind of language we use as we talk to one another, how the power relationships in a small group affect the group dynamics, how we all need to listen better and be more patient during turn taking. Such talk leads to discussion of the pragmatics of discussion, which helps all the members of the class (including the teacher) consider how to relate to one another in positive ways. When students become aware of the value of conferencing and the teacher encourages discussions that are critical but positive, students learn to be supportive of one another. Not only do such conferences provide for critical teaching moments, but they also establish a sense of community in the classroom.

Conference Procedures

Holding conferences on a regular basis with large classes is initially overwhelming, especially to new teachers or teachers who have not conducted student conferences. Setting aside time for conferences means reorganizing class time. It is not possible to add to the school day without eliminating some aspects of the curriculum. Donald Graves (1983) as well as many other scholars concerned with the writing process discuss a variety of ways to organize conferences with students. They suggest questions the teacher can pose to help move students to think about language knowledge as they write:

- How can I help?
- What are you trying to say?
- What language are you using that you like?
- Have you described characters and scenes with enough detail for the reader to see what is happening?
- Does your dialogue sound the way people would speak to each other? (Atwell, 1998, p. 247)

Tommy Thomason's (1998) and Carl Anderson's (2000) recent books talk to teachers about their classroom experiences of conferencing with young authors. These authors include not only tips and myths about conferring with students but also check sheets, materials for teachers and students, and variations in procedures.

During reading conferences, I find the following questions useful:

- ◆ Are you understanding what you are reading?

- ◆ Are there words or phrases or sections of the text that you wondered about as you read? Show me what or where they are.

- ◆ Did the author use language that is especially interesting to you? Show me where that language appears.

Whenever it is appropriate, I follow up student responses with "Why do you think so?" This honest question on the teacher's part turns the questioning stance into a conversation that helps the student believe the teacher is not interested in correct answers only but is genuinely interested in the student's explorations, knowledge, and beliefs. Students' responses often give me insight into how to lead the students to consider ways to solve their own problems.

In order to schedule uninterrupted conference time, teachers plan carefully with the students the kinds of experiences they can engage in independently or in small groups while the teacher is involved in conferences. Students come to value class time spent on conferences and usually work quietly. The students who are not involved in the conference should be doing valuable work that interests them (Turbill, 1982). The students know they will have their turn with the teacher and anticipate the teacher's undivided attention for even a ten- or fifteen-minute period every few weeks. They are impressed with a teacher who demonstrates that students are important enough to spend time with, and they respond to such attention by taking their self-directed work in the classroom seriously.

As an upper-grade teacher, Debra Goodman often printed out weekly planning sheets for each of her students. She filled in the times on the plan when everyone was supposed to be together, such as class book reading, lunch, computer lab, and recess. In the conference time spaces, however, the students were responsible for filling in their own plans when they weren't the conferee.

Some teachers encourage the nonconferring students to participate in "written conversations" with other students during conference time so they do not interrupt the conferences with loud talking. In written conversations, students write notes to one another to simulate talk rather than talking aloud.

I observed the class of an Australian teacher who kept a small bulletin board next to her desk that her kids used to pin notes to while she was conferencing. Small pieces of blue, pink, and red paper lay in a box next to the board. The students wrote a request to visit with the teacher on a blue note if they wanted the teacher to respond to them within the next few days. They wrote on a pink note if they wanted the teacher to see them the next day. A red note designated an emergency, and the teacher would respond as soon as possible. This teacher had great discussions with her students that helped them decide how to categorize their notes. In addition, she helped her students develop greater independence and responsibility for their own learning.

All students need to participate in conferences, but all students do not need the same amount of conference time or the same number of conferences. The time and focus of the conference will change over time as well. Students who are more capable of organizing and taking initiative may need fewer or shorter conferences, whereas other students need more and longer conferences. In self-contained classes, some teachers set aside an hour or two at regular times during the week for conferences. With departmental classes, middle school teachers set aside approximately 50 minutes at a regular time out of a 250-minute week. A regularly scheduled time helps students become used to conference routines. Early in the school year, a conference sign-up sheet divided into 10- to 15-minute intervals is useful because students who are reluctant to conference with a teacher can observe how it works and how the other students who sign up are treated. Of course, the teacher explains to the class the purpose of the conference and the procedures. The teacher also keeps track of who has had a conference and usually makes sure that all students have had at least one before another round of conferences starts up.

Not all conferences need to be held during a prescheduled period. Alan Flurkey discovered what he likes to call "over the shoulder" conferences as a first-grade teacher. As he moved around the classroom to observe his students at work, he would stand next to a table and interact with two students during buddy reading, or he would look over the shoulder of a child writing in her journal but looking up at him for help. Such kidwatching provides opportunities to learn about the knowledge students have and the strategies they use, as well as a few moments for critical teaching (Y. Goodman, 1996a).

Language Study during Conferences

Conferences tend to spark conversations about language study that help students expand their language knowledge and give teachers ideas for strategy lessons or theme cycles that expand on language study issues.

Phyllis Whitin (personal communication, 2000) documents her discussion about language with Tony, a fourth grader, who was reading aloud during a reading conference:

> I noticed that when Tony came to the phrase "citywide monorail system," he repeated the word *citywide* and pronounced *monorail* slowly, saying "mon-o rail." I wondered if the word had made sense to him. Within a few paragraphs the word appeared again, and this time he read it smoothly and naturally. He did not repeat anything preceding the word this second time. When Tony finished reading, he told me about the story. I then asked him if he remembered changing his mind about any part as he read it. (We had discussed how readers revise their thinking in their heads as they read.) He did not mention any part with "monorail" but another place instead. Next I told him that I had noticed that he read *monorail* more slowly the first time, but he read it easily after that.
>
> He explained: "In first grade I'd stop and try to figure it [a word] out, or ask people. Then I found if you kept going you practiced the word. You teach yourself what it means." A little later in the conversation he differentiated between fiction and nonfiction reading strategies (he read a lot of nonfiction, especially books that explained how machines and scientific phenomena work). He explained that when he reads nonfiction, if he comes to something he doesn't understand, he often looks it up in the glossary.

Phyllis Whitin supported Tony's comments by sharing with him how she did the same kinds of things when she read. Then she broadened his thinking by asking him to write down some of the strategies he used that helped him the most when he read. They kept the list of strategies in his folder and during subsequent conferences considered how these strategies worked for him during his other reading experiences. With his teacher's encouragement, Tony also shared these strategies with some of the other students he was working with in a literature study, to see if they used similar or different strategies.

Nancie Atwell (1998) describes writing conferences that focus on the content and craft of writing:

> I listen, paraphrase, ask clarifying questions, nudge toward or suggest options if the writer needs them, and ask the writer to articulate what he or she plans to do next. My purpose is . . . to help writers discover the meanings they don't know yet, name problems, attempt solutions, and make plans. (p. 224)

It is important for students to reflect on their own language use and to be self-critical, but it is also important for the teacher to consider what the students already know and what they do when they use language, and at the same time to help students recognize what they already know about language. During conferences in which students' work is taken seriously, students come to value their own work. The teacher sends the message: "I think what you are learning about language is important. We are learning together what you know about language and what you still need to know."

Exploration of Miscues

How language works is revealed to teachers and students alike when we explore the "errors" we make as we speak or write and the confusions or misconceptions we have as a result of listening or reading. Such explorations are especially relevant when we are involved in learning a second language (Y. Freeman & Y. Goodman, 1993; D. Freeman & Y. Freeman, 2000) or interacting with others who speak a dialect different from our own (Shaughnessy, 1997). Miscues provide opportunities for critical-moment teaching as teachers and students discuss the role and purpose of miscues in language use and language learning (Bettelheim, 1982; Y. Goodman, 1996b).

Ken Goodman's (1965) study of reading miscues was initiated by his interest in what miscues tell teachers and researchers about how people read. He rejected the word *error* when he discovered that the unexpected responses readers make provide "a window on the reading process." Miscues illuminate the knowledge students have about language and the strategies they use in order to make sense:

> The reader is primarily concerned with making sense of everything. Sometimes that means keeping both the sense and the grammar but changing the wording; sometimes it means keeping the syntax but producing non-words. Most often in successful reading, the wording and grammar are the same as in the original text because readers control the process so well, not because they are accurately identifying words. Getting the words right is a by-product of making sense of the whole and not the other way around. (K. Goodman, 1996, p. 103)

I believe that all language miscues, whether in reading, writing, speaking, or listening, reflect our knowledge about language, language use, and subject matter, as well as our background. When a Chinese graduate student who has recently arrived in the United States asks my age, I could consider him rude. But when I understand that the student is showing his respect for me by asking such a question and I respond to him respectfully, then I show that I understand aspects of his culture. In my response, I share with him the information that it isn't common to ask such a question in a U.S. context, which helps him expand his knowledge of the new culture he is adapting to. Miscues, of course, do cause misconceptions and miscommunications, but they are based on knowledge; they are neither random nor unexplainable.

The more knowledgeable that teachers become about miscue analysis, the greater insight they develop into the linguistic and conceptual strengths students bring to language use (Y. Goodman & K. Goodman, 1994). Recently I have involved readers in examining their own miscues (Y. Goodman & Marek, 1996). Although in subsequent chapters I suggest strategy lessons and theme cycles that help students understand their own miscues, miscues often occur during oral reading, collaborative writing sessions, or oral presentations or discussions, paving the way for critical-moment teaching.

Student Miscues

During read-aloud time or when teachers are listening to kids read for evaluation purposes, teachable moments abound. Of course, not every miscue calls for a teachable moment—only those that present rich possibilities for interesting conversation. Following are a few examples that highlight miscues and critical-moment teaching.

Shoshana, an eleven-year-old with whom I have had many individual reading conferences, discussed what she does when she comes to something she doesn't know while she is reading: "Well, sometimes I sound it out, but that usually doesn't work. I usually pass it like a blank, like there was nothing there, and go on with the rest of the sentence until I can make it out, make sense of it, and then I know what it is." Shoshana then explained that she is a good reader "because I know a lot and I know how to help myself if I try."

> YETTA: And how would you do that?
>
> SHOSHANA: By just looking at the rest of the sentence. My mom says to use the context.
>
> YETTA: What does that mean, to use the context?
>
> SHOSHANA: To use the words around you . . . surrounding that . . . and try to make sense out of it and if it makes sense to you even though it's not the right word. It's like *funny*, and I say *silly.*

I responded to Shoshana by telling her that I value her thoughtful consideration of the reading process. I said that by focusing on what the language in her text means she is using strategies that proficient readers use. I let her know that her use of context showed me that she understood the story. We then discussed whether she might use her strategies differently depending on the importance of the word or phrase in the story. I encouraged her to continue discussing her reading with her mother and to share her insights with me as well.

During a reading conference with his teacher, second grader John was reading a story in which the word *oxygen* appeared a number of times. Each time he came to the word, he stopped and said to the teacher, "That's that word I don't know." The teacher encouraged John to keep on reading by saying, "You can omit it or try to substitute something in that place that would make sense in the story. I often do that when I read." She wanted John to discover that reading comprehension develops throughout the reading of a story and thus highlighted a strategy he could use when he was reading by himself. When he finished reading and was retelling the story to the teacher, John explained that the men in the story were not feeling well because something was wrong with the air. "*Oxygen!*" he called out, "that's the word I didn't know, *oxygen!*"

The teacher discussed with John how he was able to make personal discoveries about language and the reading process by trusting his own abilities, and she demonstrated that she valued his learning capabilities. She and John discussed the strategies he used to solve his own problem. He kept thinking about the word and developed meanings about the story by talking about it with the teacher. John came to believe that he was a more independent reader than he had thought.

As teachers and students explore the ways in which miscues reveal their knowledge and rarely reflect any serious language disorder, students come to understand the nature of error the way artists do. Illustrators of children's literature who talk to kids about their work often refer to the ways in which they incorporate their errors into their work to take advantage of the effects—in other words, the errors have creative consequences.

When I discuss with teachers ways of helping students without immediately correcting their miscues, they often say that the students correct each other's miscues immediately. I suggest that such responses are based on what students see teachers do. If teachers discuss the miscuing process with the class and explore the different strategies readers use during oral reading in addition to self-correction, students learn positive ways to help one another.

Teacher Miscues

Teachers' miscues also provide opportunities for critical-moment teaching. Don Howard, who has worked with a range of primary-age students, tells other teachers how he responds positively when students notice the miscues he makes when he reads aloud to them. Whenever his students draw attention to his miscues, he stops to wonder out loud about the possible reasons for making the miscue. Mr. Howard is convinced that his acceptance of the kids' responses to his miscues allows them to take greater risks as learners themselves and to be more comfortable when he helps them interrogate their own miscues. They begin to understand that miscues do not reflect something wrong but rather what they know about language and the strategies they use to make sense and communicate.

There are a number of ways for teachers to explore their miscues with their students (Y. Goodman, 1996a). When, for example, teachers are reading aloud to the class and substitute names for characters they are unfamiliar with or have trouble pronouncing, such as Rumpy for Rumplestiltskin or Ivan for Raskolnikoff, they should take advantage of a good critical teaching moment to stop and explain the strategies they are using. Or when they pronounce the names of authors (e.g., Chinua Achebe) or places (e.g., Warrambui) based on their own most informed guess using their English phonics rules for pronunciation purposes, they discuss these strategies with their students. This naming strategy—substituting a name that fits (maintaining characteristics of a character such as gender or ethnicity) or a place name that fits in terms of country of origin, and continuing to read in order to maintain the flow and interest of the story—is one that all proficient readers use to support their meaning construction (Y. Goodman, Watson, & Burke, 1996). Students need to know that teachers and other proficient readers make miscues similar to their own.

Although I am usually a good speller, I often find myself inventing spellings for some words as I write on the board. Once my principal called my attention to the fact that I had written *baloon* on the board. I shared that experience with my seventh and eighth graders and told them that since parents and administrators are not keen on teachers who display misspellings, the students could help me out by checking my spelling for me. I wanted them to call any of my misspellings to everyone's attention, and when they did, we discussed the kinds of invented spellings I made consistently, such as certain double consonants and double vowel patterns, and why I spell those particular words the way I do. Students learned about the stability of spelling rules and the importance of social conventions as we discussed my spelling. Then we would hold a short discussion about the social contexts in which it is usually important to use conventional spelling and when it is not so necessary. Through such discussions, I demonstrated for students ways to examine their own spellings.

In my university classes, I often discuss features of language as I'm writing on the board, reading to the class, or talking. I share my low-status dialect features, those differences in language use I have encountered and sometimes gotten in trouble over in different English-speaking countries. I share language that I am insecure about using in particular contexts because I'm not always confident that I understand their meanings. I often use as an example my history with the word *heuristic,* which I've learned to use more and more conventionally since I first read it almost forty years ago in Bruner's *Toward a Theory of Instruction* (1966). I share the fact that I looked up this word in the dictionary but then read it in another context where the meaning was different. Eventually over time I found myself using the term in oral conversations first and finally in writing. Even now, however, I check my spelling. I want students to know that concepts about word meanings develop over time and that certain words are easier to use in some contexts than in others. Realizing that teachers are not perfect spellers or writers of language, that they use strategies to solve language problems, and that they also struggle as language users helps students demystify the notion that language has some perfect and correct form that is inaccessible to most of them. Such discussions rarely take more than a few minutes and are often stimulated by a student's question or the teacher's exploration of his or her own miscues and insecurities as a reader, writer, speaker, or listener.

Building Language Traditions

Open discussions in classrooms about language lead to traditions that enrich classroom life. Examples of such traditions provide insight into language study traditions and critical-moment teaching.

We Do Not Tolerate Nonsense

Sr. Marianne Philips helped her fifth-grade students, during discussions about their reading, consider a principle that became a class slogan they then placed on posters around the classroom. The posters read: We do not tolerate nonsense. Sr. Marianne often taught children who were reading material they did not understand, and they seemed to believe that once they started reading, they needed to continue reading until they were finished. Whenever this happened, she took the time to explore with her class their options when they did not like or understand what they were reading. The children brainstormed a list of strategies they could use whenever what they read seemed to be nonsense:

1. If the material is interesting or important, keep reading. If things become clearer and make more sense, finish reading and then reread the problem section.

2. If the material is fiction and we want to read it, ask someone to buddy read it with us.

3. If the material is nonfiction and we want to know the information, ask someone knowledgeable about the subject to read it with us. Or ask someone knowledgeable to discuss the subject first and then try reading it.

4. If the material is necessary for a report or other schoolwork, ask the librarian for easier-to-read material that has the same information.

5. If none of the above works out, close the book and find something else to read.

Sr. Marianne wanted her students to know they had both the right to read and the power not to read. In other words, knowing when to terminate their reading is an important reading strategy (K. Goodman, 1996). The students came to understand that they needed to be honest with themselves about whether they comprehended the reading, and so they decided never to tolerate nonsense in what they were reading. This approach became a tradition in this classroom, and Sr. Marianne has introduced this language tradition in subsequent classes. She always waits for the issue to arise in class, when she can discuss it in response to a critical moment, and each class develops its own list. Occasionally she shows them a previous class list and asks the students if they agree or disagree with the statements; then they write their own.

In one class, however, this language tradition caused Sr. Marianne some consternation. One day when the students were taking the California Test of Basic Skills (CTBS), she was roaming the classroom to make sure the children were comfortable. She noticed that Ruben was sitting quietly with no test booklet in front of him. She quietly went up to him and asked, "May I be of some help?"

"No, sister," he replied. "I looked the test over and I decided it was nonsense, so I put it away." Sr. Marianne was respectful of Ruben's decision and didn't press him to take the test. "Fortunately," she said, "none of the other kids thought of that." Sr. Marianne told me that she often told that story to subsequent students and asked them what they would have done in the same situation if they had been either Ruben or her.

Asking open-ended questions during students' retellings or responses to literature helps students discover what they know and, even more important, to know "when and what [they] don't know." Eleanor Duckworth (1987) writes about the power of "not knowing":

> The virtues involved in not knowing are the ones that really count in the long run. What you do about what you don't know is, in the final analysis, what determines what you will ultimately know. . . . Accepting surprise, puzzlement, excitement, patience, caution, honest attempts, and wrong outcomes as legitimate and important elements of learning easily leads to their further development. . . .
> It would make a significant difference to the cause of intelli-

gent thought in general, and to the number of right answers that are ultimately known, if teachers were encouraged to focus on the virtues involved in not knowing. (pp. 68–69)

Helping students be comfortable with what they know and discover ways to respond to what they do not know are important aspects of learning, and can often be supported through critical-moment teaching.

As students reflect on their own responses, they have ample opportunity to critique the truth of what they are learning, explore the uniqueness of their language use, and legitimize their unique interpretations. They wonder about aspects that don't fit their prior knowledge and realize there are things they don't know. From this position, they discuss a range of language issues such as parts of speech, use of punctuation, genre variations, and pragmatic considerations for conventional language use. Helping students understand that it is legitimate not to know and discussing what to do in such cases is an important classroom tradition to establish.

My Powerful Language

Another example of a language tradition comes from my middle school teaching. We often started the day with a discussion of the current events students were most interested in from the newspaper, magazines, television, or radio. Sometimes the student presenting the current event would use language that other students weren't familiar with and questioned. I suggested that students write such words and phrases on the board and share with the class how they are used and what they mean. We then left the words and phrases on the board for a while, and other students would listen for them and add their definitions and the diverse contexts in which they were found. After we explored a number of specific words and phrases, I asked the class to decide whether they would like to keep a class language power book. Keeping such a book became a tradition in my class. We began to follow this procedure with any unfamiliar words and phrases the kids heard, read, or tried to use in their writing or speaking that intrigued or interested them. Usually we included the entire sentence, with the target word or phrase written in colored chalk. (Adolescents love to use colored chalk.)

One of my students began to keep her own personalized list in a notebook she labeled MY LANGUAGE POWER BOOK. I invited other students to do the same and incorporated this tradition in my other classes. An extension of this practice led to students writing their own dictionaries. We spent a few minutes once or twice a week discussing new language in their language power books. This was also a way to show my students that language is expanding and changing all the time. Some students asked questions about vocabulary meanings, dictionary organization, and other related topics, and these issues often expanded into strategy lessons or theme cycles.

Flora Ann Simon, a first-grade teacher, encourages her students to add new and interesting vocabulary to their individual dictionaries that are purchased by the district for each child as expendable materials. This helps students realize that dictionaries are always being added to and deleted from and that the process of using and producing dictionaries is dynamic rather than prescriptive.

Other language traditions that emerge from critical-moment teaching include class book clubs, choice activity times, author's chair, reading circles, weekly author teas, and organizing the class with students in leadership roles. Language traditions emerge from student interest and are sustained by student enthusiasm. I recently saw a middle school Teen Topics bulletin board that was developed and maintained by the seventh graders. They not only used charts and other graphics to depict the latest in video games, computer concerns, and their favorite rock music and sports figures, but they also collected a list of teen language they wondered about.

Many critical moments occur when the ongoing curriculum is not easily interrupted. I recently visited a fourth-grade class that reserved a section of the bulletin board for a chart labeled "Ideas To Come Back To." The teacher and her students used this chart to remember powerful ideas they wanted to think about and discuss at a later time. Such revisiting is important for recursive thinking and becomes a language tradition in the classroom.

Schoolwide Language Traditions

School administrators also establish schoolwide language traditions that lend themselves to critical-moment teaching. Some principals set up weekly lunches in order to read to a small group of students or to have student authors read to them (Harwayne, 2001). A schoolwide post office, a store run by students for selling school supplies, or a school newspaper, radio, or TV station are all examples of schoolwide language traditions. Robert Wortman, principal of a primary school, often asks students who are sent to him because of discipline problems to write their perceptions of what took place (Wortman & Matlin, 1995). It becomes obvious to everyone involved that each student has a different perspective on the same incident. Dr. Wortman discusses with the students why such differences of interpretation occur and the way language is involved in establishing and changing perspectives.

Documenting Critical-Moment Teaching

Every time a critical teaching moment involving language becomes the focus of discussion, students add to their schema about how language works and how to use language. Students become comfortable with tentative responses: the sense that questions are rarely simple to answer, that answers lead to new questions, and that learning is continuous and expansive. They learn that they are capable of revisiting ideas later and that they learn more in-depth over time. Unfortunately, we have not legitimized such critical moments to the degree we should have in professional education. These moments are not easy to document, and therefore even teachers who are aware of their significance don't always value them sufficiently. With the reporting of teacher research and collaborative university-school research to ever-wider audiences, however, the significance of these moments is becoming abundantly clear (Atwell, 1987, 1998; Bird, 1989; Ladson-Billings, 1994). It is important to discuss such moments in professional communities, to help describe them, and to legitimize their use as powerful teaching episodes. These moments emerge from a teacher's response to students' experiences as they eagerly solve problems and answer the questions they pose for themselves and others in the classroom.

We know that students' spontaneous questions and comments about language often result in language stories and literacy lessons. Such spontaneous interactions become learning opportunities for teachers and students alike. The teacher becomes a learner as the students' language stories provide lessons about students' learning that allow the teacher to plan for additional instructional experiences. Language stories, whether they provide lessons about teaching or insights into what students know about language, are "life vignettes that accent some important aspects of language and language learning and therefore help us understand how language works" (Harste, Woodward, & Burke, 1984, p. xv).

From such language stories all educators learn teaching lessons that legitimize the ways teachers respond to thought-provoking spontaneous moments that lead to significant student learning. Teachers and teacher education students should document such moments by keeping anecdotal records or field notes and transcribing video- or audiotapes of the language stories that provide evidence of students' knowledge and development. This documentation will help authenticate the results of teacher support of such development. These observations provide rich cases for teachers to reflect on for their own development.

The more the education profession finds ways to document and disseminate information about these critical moments and their impact and to situate them in the legitimate context of the overall curriculum, the more likely it is they will continue to be the focus of research about teaching; as a result, we may better understand and combat comments such as, "That's the art of teaching and we just can't explain how it happens," or "There are things about great teaching that just can't be learned. You have to be born a great teacher." Critical-moment teaching accentuates the curriculum and legitimizes the uniqueness of each professional in the classroom. There is no set curriculum or curriculum script when the teacher is responding to the authentic questions and concerns raised by their students in the classroom.

To help parents understand the power of spontaneous professional response to students in the classroom, and as a way of documenting for parents and administrators how involved students are in understanding and studying language, teachers often include vignettes of critical-moment teaching in newsletters sent to parents. Some teachers write articles for local newspapers or newsletters to document for the larger public the sophisticated ways in which teachers support students in their explorations of grammar, spelling, phonics, vocabulary, and many other aspects of language study.

But most of all, presenting on teachable moments individually or in collaboration with other teachers or with students at professional conferences and in professional books and journals contributes knowledge about innovative practices to the profession. I urge teachers to document significant critical teaching moments by creating language stories, cartoons, or diagrams for professional newsletters or journals. Such writing provides presenting opportunities for teachers as authors or speakers at the same time that it provides opportunities for perceiving and ideating for those teachers who are listening to or reading the work of their colleagues. These moments are the essence of teaching. As we expose them to others and explore and analyze the ways they work, we come to new scientific understandings of the art and science of teaching.

As I end this chapter, I want to emphasize again that the purpose of the chapter divisions in this book is to recognize the many ways in which language study is embedded in the ongoing language curriculum. The divisions do not suggest that the teaching/learning experiences and opportunities are separable or that any one necessarily occurs before the others. On the contrary, the ideas presented in each chapter are easily integrated into the others; they grow into and out of each other.

CHAPTER FOUR

Strategy Lessons

Humans, in their interactions with others, are always working at effective communication. In order to communicate effectively through oral or written language, humans consider the context, the participants in the context, and the topics being addressed (Halliday, 1975). In oral language settings, we anticipate what the other person is going to say. If we don't understand, we ask questions or make comments such as, "I don't understand. Say it in a different way." We tune into facial expressions and other gestures or body language to see if the person we are talking to understands and responds appropriately. Speakers (including teachers) scrutinize their audiences to determine who is paying attention and who is tuned out and then adjust their presentations to engage their listeners. As readers and listeners, we often continue to attend even when aspects of the written or oral text are not clear. We assume that the message will be clarified as we gather additional information from the author or speaker. These purposes for language use and how we accomplish them are, for the most part, intuitive (see Chapter 1). That is, we are rarely conscious of the plans or problem solving we engage in to make language comprehensible. These language and cognitive activities are *strategies* the brain utilizes to ensure that we accomplish our communication goals.

Before speaking or writing, we often take time to plan our compositions. When we write, we may wander around rehearsing before we settle down with a pen or at the computer to compose. We revise and edit some pieces many times. In informal contexts, however, such as taking phone messages, conducting friendly conversations or discussions about current issues, or reading a daily newspaper or an engaging novel, we are rarely conscious of how actively our brain is involved in a variety of strategies to make continuous sense of language.

In this chapter, I suggest ways to help students talk and think about how they use language effectively and at the same time discover what they know about the strategies they use. Strategy lessons help students become explicitly aware of the strategies they use intuitively. By exploring proficient language strategies, students can minimize their use of inefficient or dysfunctional strategies. Students also come to understand that at times language use results in miscommunication, especially when humans purposely use language to obfuscate the truth, control others, or hurt or discredit them. Planned strategy lessons involve students in critically analyzing such language use.

Planning for Strategy Lessons

A language study curriculum includes planned and focused experiences that engage students in conversations about the kinds of language strategies they use. I call these planned discussions *strategy lessons.* Over the years, colleagues and I have developed strategy lessons for reading and writing (Y. Goodman, Burke, & Sherman, 1980; Y. Goodman, Watson, & Burke, 1996). Many writing-process authors often use the term *minilesson* (Atwell, 1998; Calkins, 1994; Graves, 1983; Harwayne, 1992), which I consider synonymous with *strategy lesson.* I prefer *strategy lesson* because the term emphasizes that the major purpose of these instructional experiences is to help students become consciously aware of the ways in which they use their language strategies and discover what they know about language. Through inquiry into their own language strategies, students discover that they already possess language knowledge. As a result, they expand their knowledge and develop greater confidence in themselves as effective language learners and users. Strategy lessons are integral to a range of instructional lessons, including guided reading (Fountas & Pinnell, 1996, 2001), individual and small group conferencing, and writing center and oral language experiences. In a language study curriculum, however, strategy lessons also incorporate the principles and learning cycles discussed in Chapter 2 that focus on students' efforts to construct new knowledge about language as a result of their personal inquiries into the ways people use language.

Strategy lessons support students as they plan and predict, make inferences, interpret, self-reflect, self-correct, revise and edit, and learn to be selective in their language use. Teachers know their students well so that when planning strategy lessons they are able to take into consideration their students' experiential and language backgrounds, connecting new knowledge to what the students already know. Strategy lessons rarely last longer than twenty minutes (the "mini" in the minilesson). Some lessons serve their purpose after a single interaction. Other times, students explore their ideas through additional strategy lessons or a series of related strategy lessons throughout the year. Strategy lessons are often integrated into studies in other content areas. Some strategy lessons result from critical-moment teaching (see Chapter 3). When a strategy lesson results in discussion that is especially interesting, however, the teacher and students may expand their new discoveries into theme cycles (see Chapters 5–7) organized by the whole class or as an expert project for an individual or a small group.

The teacher's role in the strategy lesson is to ensure that *all* students feel safe expressing their beliefs, to help students listen with courtesy to the opinions of others even if they disagree, and, finally, to raise issues the students may not have considered as alternate points of view or as new roads to explore. In all lessons, conversations, and discussions, teachers voice their beliefs and knowledge in such a way that students are comfortable about challenging and questioning the teacher's point of view. In other words, teachers are authorities or experts but not authoritarian about imposing their views as the dominant or "correct" ones. Experts are open to new and challenging ideas, and teachers should be able demonstrators of such a stance toward learning and knowing. Earl Kelley (1955) states: "[W]e believe in freedom of the mind and freedom of speech for teachers, but it is difficult, even untenable, to defend freedom for teachers while denying freedom for learners" (p. 68). In this kind of intellectual climate, students come to understand that their teachers are knowledgeable about language because of their greater experience and study of language. But at the same time, they come to realize that all knowledge is open to challenge and debate. The way in which a teacher responds to students during discussions sends a strong message about whether students' views are valued and about who has power in the learning community being established in the classroom.

In addition to the strategy lessons discussed in this chapter, others can be found in sources listed in the references (also, visit www.ncte.org/notesplus or e-mail notesplus.ncte.org to check on *Classroom Notes Plus*, which is published annually by NCTE). The strategy lessons in this chapter are organized into the following sections:

- ◆ Understanding Language Use
- ◆ Using Oral Language
- ◆ Listening
- ◆ Using Written Language
- ◆ Language Inventions and Language Conventions

Understanding Language Use

Exploring the functions and purposes that language serves helps students become consciously aware of the range of language events that permeate their lives and of the ways in which they already use oral and written language. Functions refer to the ways in which language serves general societal use, while purposes are more specific and personal to the individual. When I want to know where Herzegovina is, for example, I might look up the information in an atlas. A general societal function of literacy is gathering informational knowledge. My specific purpose, however, relates to my intense interest in the part of the world where my parents and my Jewish heritage came from. I want to be informed about events in that part of the world. Interest is a driving force in establishing the purpose of language use (Anders & Guzzetti, 1996). When people are interested in an activity or experience, they are likely to know its purpose. Students, for example, need little help finding baseball scores when they want to know if their favorite team won, or selecting a CD of their favorite musical group. Because of their intense interest in engaging in the activity, their purpose is intrinsic. In life outside of school, we rarely engage in experiences that are without purpose. In school, however, when teachers control curriculum or strictly follow commercial programs, they often ask students to engage in tasks without first helping them understand why they are being asked to do a particular assignment—its purpose. When I visit some classrooms, I often sit next to students and ask them what they are doing. Some say "schoolwork," and when I follow up by asking why they are doing this particular schoolwork, they usually respond, "because the teacher told me to." It is easy to conclude from such responses that the kids do not understand the purpose of their activity. When students know the purpose of their work because the activity grew out of something they are curious about and find engaging, they reply specifically such as, "I'm reading to find if bears really sleep the whole time they hibernate. We're arguing about this in our class," or "I read every Gary Paulsen book I can get my hands on."

It is helpful to illuminate purpose and function in strategy lesson discussions with questions such as, "Why are we learning this?" or "Is this interesting? Why or why not?" Teachers need to be ready to support students who indicate that they are not interested in particular topics or experiences by having alternative options available. The whole purpose of such lessons is to emphasize that learning results most often when experiences interest the student. Through such discussions, teachers are able to connect their students' intrinsic interest in language learning to the ways they use language in and out of school.

Categorizing Language Functions

Eliana Winston plans strategy lessons with her fifth graders to highlight the literacy practices that students participate in daily and to explore the functions and purposes that reading and writing serve in their lives. In order to initiate the *perceiving* phase of the lesson, she asks her students to keep track of everything they read and write on two different days: one weekend day and one school day. The contrast between the literacy events that occur on the two different days helps the students identify the different kinds of literacy events that take place at different times and in different contexts. Before the students bring back their findings for the strategy lesson, they talk about the range of reading and writing that people do. They need to understand that reading the cereal box or the medicine vial or writing a telephone message or a note for their mom is a literacy event. The students present their lists to the class while one of the students or the teacher lists all the literacy events on the board. Ms. Winston then plans a series of follow-up strategy lessons. Working in groups of three or four, students share their lists with one another and categorize the items on their lists, considering the purpose each serves. Making the lists and categorizing the functions allows the students to *ideate* about literacy use even as the students *present* their literacy events to each other and discuss the reasons for their categories. The students' lists often include categories such as information, survival, fun, schoolwork, religion, and so forth. Ms. Winston places the list of literacy interactions, along with the categories, on the overhead and adds to them throughout the semester as her students' understanding of the functions of language use expands. By looking at such visible lists, the students become aware of the multiple ways in which language enriches their lives, and they are often surprised at the myriad of literacy events in which they engage.

Subsequent strategy lessons might examine a few of the literacy categories in depth, such as the kinds of literacy students engage in outside of school (environmental language functions); the kinds of language they use for work or school (occupational functions); the language used to gather and interpret information (informational functions); and the language used for fun and relaxation (recreational functions) (K. Goodman, Y. Goodman, & Hood, 1989).

Bob Wortman holds discussions about purpose and function with his kindergarten students, but his strategy lessons are most often embedded in ongoing curricular activities. When the students are writing menus for the restaurant they are organizing, for example, Dr. Wortman talks with them about why people write menus, and then they examine their menus to make sure they have all the items the customers might order. Or, when the students decide to put signs on their block constructions so that over night or over the weekend no one puts away the buildings they are constructing, the class discusses the kinds of language they need to use as authors so that the readers of their signs understand their messages. Based on the purposes of their signs, they decide whether they need to use different languages for the custodian and other kids in the room since these readers of their signs are not native speakers of English (Wortman, 1990). I find that most students, regardless of age, are interested and become engaged in understanding the functions and purposes of their own language use but that the sophistication of the lesson focus and discussion depends on the age and interest of the student. I plan similar assignments for graduate students.

Such lessons are easily adapted for oral language use and for examining the kinds of oral language that accompany written language. Exploring the ways in which people talk during their writing of shopping lists, for example, is very appealing. Young children are often part of this process in their households. Students need to learn that in many different contexts, such as at home, in the community, or at school, language processes and functions are not easily separated, and sometimes the same language event serves multiple functions.

If students show great interest in this topic, it is helpful to examine the lists of language functions described by ethnographers who study these functions. Students may compare their lists with those of researchers. Some researchers examine reading functions (K. Goodman, 1996a; Taylor, 1998; Taylor & Dorsey-Gaines, 1988); others categorize functions in writing (Staton, 1988; Peyton & Staton, 1993; Smith, 1985). Sulzby and Teale (1991), Heath (1983), and Halliday (1975) all write about oral language functions or domains of language use.

Variation of Written Forms and Their Functions

As students become aware of the different functions of language, they notice that the form language takes has a relationship to the function it serves. Shopping lists are written in a different way from notes to parents. Comics take forms different from the students' favorite storybooks. Strategy lessons therefore often explore the forms language takes in relation to different functions of language use. Pat Griesel, working with community college students, many of whom are learning English as a second or third language, brings into class a variety of printed material. She displays on a table the local phone book, a TV guide, candy and gum wrappers, advertisements from a popular pizza parlor, a bowling score sheet, a job book, medicine vials, a popular video in its jacket, tickets to a play, and notes written by students that were retrieved from the wastebasket (displayed with the permission of the students). Next to each item is a small pad of paper. A placard on the browsing table reads:

> When do you need to read this? Why would you read this?
>
> What purpose(s) could it serve for you? Who wrote this?
>
> Why was it written? What purpose(s) does it serve the writer/author?

In the perceiving phase of this strategy lesson, Dr. Griesel explains that the purpose is to explore the uses of each item, the functions each serves, and how the material is organized or formatted. She asks the students to examine each item, consider the questions listed on the placard, and write a short response on the pads of paper. She gives the students a few minutes at the beginning of class for a few days to examine the items, discuss with one another, and write their responses. She also invites the students to bring similar items to add to the display.

The strategy lesson discussion focuses on exploring the questions listed on the placard and analyzing the language critically. Sometimes Dr. Griesel shows overhead transparencies of some of the items so the whole class can examine them together. Other questions that often emerge from the discussion include:

> What does the author need to know about the reader to write/print the item?
>
> What does the reader need to know about the author to understand the purpose of the item?
>
> Why do different materials use different print sizes and formats?
>
> Why is some language ambiguous?

She often includes incomprehensible materials such as directions for assembling a toy or instructions from a computer manual. Small print that says, "Do not remove this label" or "Labor donated" leads to interesting discussions about economic and political issues. From such experiences, students develop their own literacy awareness and consider the complex purposes and functions that language serves in their daily lives. Dr. Griesel has shared these strategy lessons with elementary and middle school teachers who have used them successfully with their age groups by incorporating material more familiar to their students.

Once students become aware that language serves various functions that take different forms, they often ask questions about the forms and functions of language during other curricular studies. As part of strategy lessons, they examine graphs, maps, and mathematical statements or formula from their reading and writing, the purposes they serve, and the forms they take.

Comparing Oral and Written Language

There has been a tendency in language arts instruction to separate written and oral language. Planned strategy lessons examine the complex relations between the two. Although oral language often takes place in face-to-face contexts and readers and authors of written texts rarely meet, it is evident that oral language and written language often occur simultaneously and that they influence each other. It is therefore helpful to develop strategy lessons that help students perceive the similarities and differences between written and oral language as well as their relations to each other.

In order to initiate the perceiving phase of a strategy lesson that involved his sixth graders in comparing oral and written language, Ross Hammond collected and displayed written materials and photographs depicting people in various oral and written language contexts. The photographs and pictures cut out of magazines and newspapers showed people engaged in a range of written and oral genres: a minister reading from a text to parishioners holding hymnals; two people whispering; a parent reading to a child; a waiter taking an order from a group of people reading menus; an executive talking to a group of workers sitting around a table, with all kinds of technological equipment visible; teens buying videos in a music store. In addition, the display included a range of written materials such as personal letters, books, receipts, play scripts, cards, and posters of famous people. Mr. Hammond invited the students to browse and examine the items and discuss with one another the kind of language being used in each context and how the language was the same or different from context to context. He asked the students to consider the ways in which the language was helpful from the points of view of the producer (writer or speaker) and the receiver (reader or listener). He used terms such as *oral* and *written language, genre,* and *formal* and *informal language* to provide students with the language to talk about language differences. He encouraged the students to work in small groups to develop a chart to describe the material, the oral and written language used, and the form the language took. One student was responsible for filling in the chart while the other students agreed on the placement of the items. This activity provided opportunities for student talk as they were ideating and presenting their ideas about the forms, purposes, and functions of the language being used. In primary grades, this lesson might be done with the whole class, especially the first time the lesson is initiated.

One of Mr. Hammond's groups generated the following:

Oral Language	Features	Written Language	Features
Talking on the phone	Chatty, informal	Writing a phone message	Clear information, Need date, number
Talking with friends	Chatty, cool talk	Writing a letter	Beginning, date, signature, formal
Waiter's introduction to specials	Talks about food in interesting ways	Menu	Organized by types
Items needed	Words, phrases	Shopping List	In a long row
Mother to daughter	Depends on mood	Book	Formal, cover page

In this class, one of the groups concluded that written language is formal and oral language is informal. Some of the students didn't consider how often reading, writing, speaking, and listening occur simultaneously, so the teacher encouraged them to consider additional questions and activities:

> When you are talking on the phone, do you ever write anything?

> Let's watch political talk shows over the weekend and take notes about the kinds of talk we hear.

> Do talk show hosts read while they talk? What kinds of talk do people do when they are reading?

As a result of class explorations and questions, the students expanded their understanding of the diversity and complexity of oral and written language genres, became aware of the ways in which oral language and written language take place simultaneously, and considered how the forms of language are affected by their functions. They kept adapting the chart they developed over a period of months to incorporate their new learnings.

Using Oral Language

Too often in language arts programs, time is spent on reading and writing conventions, but oral language is taken for granted. By comparing oral and written language use, as suggested in the previous section, students become aware that oral language plays a pervasive and powerful role in communication. In this section, I highlight strategy lessons that involve students in self-reflection and evaluation of their oral language use, including a focus on listening.

Evaluating Oral Presentations

Strategy lessons that evaluate oral sharing, whether show-and-tell, current events, or science or social study reports, enrich these language experiences. Sometimes, when oral language sharing becomes institutionalized, it becomes formulaic, and everyone, including the teacher, loses sight of the rationale for oral presentations; the result is often a succession of boring classroom experiences. I've sat through show-and-tell presentations in which kids got up one after the other to tell about events that the teacher and other students paid very little attention to. In these cases, the form of the activity took precedence over the purposes for sharing and presenting. Professionals sometimes joke about show-and-tell as "bring and brag."

Oral sharing provides opportunities for students to express their ideas in small groups or to the whole class, share expert knowledge as well as personal information, take positions on significant issues, and listen to others with patience and interest. Taking center stage during a formal oral presentation helps students develop new language forms that do not occur in conversational settings. Students learn new ways to use language to lead others, respond to questions and comments from an audience, and develop ways of interrupting talk without being disruptive. Sharing experiences, ideas, and knowledge orally shifts the focus to the content of the message. But planned strategy lessons that precede or follow the sharing allow students to reflect and become consciously aware of how successful and articulate they already are in their language use and to explore ways to become even more effective.

I used whole class evaluations with middle-grade students as a strategy lesson after sharing, discussion, conversation, and debate by exploring questions such as:

◆ How did the talk the presenters gave help or hinder getting their message across?

◆ What was most helpful and successful?

◆ How did the audience help make the presentation effective?

Although we talked about the things the students found problematic such as complaints about one another and personal squabbles, our major concern was how to make the situation better for the next sharing. We listed concerns and possible solutions and developed charts variously labeled "Taking Turns in Discussion Groups" or "Learning to Listen to Each Other." Such charts are easily kept on overheads or in computer files for continuous revisiting and revising, which we did whenever we evaluated oral interactions.

Sue Martin, a second-grade teacher, documents in her teacher reflection journal the sharing in her classroom and its development through evaluation strategy lessons:

> Originally at the end of our morning meeting, I'd ask if anyone had anything they'd like to share—usually a couple did. As the year went on more and more kids each day wanted to share and we needed to develop systems to control the number sharing and to keep our sharing interesting. The kids decided that they'd sign up on a dated sharing sheet on the board so we'd have an organized order. I was so pleased with their involvement in the process because the level of sharing rose, as we talked about the best ways to share and how it could become more interesting and relevant to our learning. We started off the year talking about stuffed animals, gifts, and grandma's visit, etc., which was a great experience because it got the kids comfortable speaking in front of the class. But by the last quarter of school, kids were signing up in groups—presenting plays, experiments, reading books about artists before our trip to the Art Institute, etc. It was amazing how they took responsibility. We all looked forward to sharing time every morning. (personal communication, 1998)

In Anita Edersen's fourth-grade class, the students decided to transcribe selected portions of their oral presentations and duplicate the transcriptions so everyone had a copy. They discussed the following questions as they listened to the tapes and followed along in the transcripts:

- What topics are worth sharing?
- What kinds of questions are good to ask?
- How much time should we take when we share experiences?
- How do we keep each other on time?
- How do we show that we are listening respectfully and help the presenters make their talk more effective?
- What suggestions are helpful and don't hurt the speaker's feelings?

Evaluation strategy lessons are important throughout the year to help students understand their roles as listeners as well as presenters. Involving students in planned strategy lessons in order to discuss their roles as members of an audience before and after school visits to concerts or plays or when listening to and watching videos or movies helps them appreciate what it means to be responsible participants. Planning a lesson before the audience experience involves the students in generating a list of the characteristics of an appreciative and attentive audience. The evaluation strategy lesson that follows the presentation gives students time to revisit the list generated earlier and plan for successful subsequent audience events. Students also benefit from being prepared for their audience experience by knowing what will be involved and having background knowledge about the performers and the performances. When students are involved in the performances, as in introducing events or speakers, writing letters to invite performers, thanking them following the event, and considering the appropriate questions to ask performers, they are more likely to be a good audience.

Current Events and Language Lessons

In many primary grades, show-and-tell is a language tradition. The extension of oral sharing into upper-grade and middle school classrooms through activities such as News Time or Current News of the Day provides opportunities for older students to discuss important issues on a regular basis. I planned my middle school students' daily presentations of their newspaper and magazine reading as part of my social studies and science curricula. Encouraging students to become critical newshounds is a basic objective of a democratic society. Teachers I've talked to recently have had students select current events topics such as the role of the presidency in relation to Presidents Clinton and George W. Bush; secrets being leaked to China; the genome map; various wars and skirmishes in the world; bilingual education; and companies such as Coca Cola having exclusive sales contracts with universities and schools. To facilitate such discussions, the teachers planned a range of language lessons to involve students in learning about the origins and pronunciation of names of people and places, the worthiness of languages and dialects, vocabulary and concept development, and how language is used to persuade or purposely confuse.

As oral sharing or current events become a classroom tradition in which students are interested and engaged, they are eager to take the lead in planning the current events periods. They organize the sign-up sheet and decide on the amount of time to spend on each presentation, the most appropriate ways for presenters to maintain class interest, when and how to take notes, how to use notes during presentations, ways to involve the audience in discussion, and how to develop guidelines so that arguments are respectful. The students consider how and where to find interesting articles or news reports that focus on significant issues, and they become adept at finding current information in the print media, on radio and television, and on computer. *The New York Times* Learning Network (at www.nytdirect@ nytimes.com) provides stories and theme lessons to engage students in newspaper reading.

The presenter of the lesson leads the rest of the class through the perceiving phase of learning by sharing thought-provoking ideas or concepts. The student summarizes the news event, indicating why the event is important, and provides his or her interpretation. Class members respond with their opinions, comments, or questions. Students learn to listen carefully to one another, to respect diversity in opinion, and to discover ways of substantiating their own points of view. The teacher is alert to issues of language study and raises questions that expand on those raised by the students. As the school year progresses, the procedures for the presentations are evaluated and revised to accommodate students' growing sophistication.

Alternatives to oral presentations include having the leader pass out photocopies of a selected article that are then read silently by the class or aloud. After the presenter shares his or her interpretation, the rest of the students respond. Audio- or videotape selections of news provide other ways for students to lead discussions.

Formal and Informal Presentations

Oral language takes as many different forms as written language, and strategy lessons encourage students to use and talk about oral language in its many different forms. I use the term *genre* to refer to the categories of a particular text in terms of its style, form, and content (Gove, 1967, p. 947). Fiction and nonfiction are different forms of written language, but genre also categorizes the diversity of forms in oral language. The range of formality of language presentations depends on the genre. The most formal oral genres, such as a speech given by an expert to a large audience, a sermon presented by a religious leader, or vows spoken during a marriage ceremony, are constrained by the conventions of specific language forms. But informal language genres such as personal conversations or telephone talk also follow social convention.

Small group or whole class conversations provide many opportunities for informal oral presentations that lead to rich language study. These include, among others, the kinds of language that students use as they assume different leadership roles. I, for example, always organized my classes to encourage students to assume leadership positions such as president, secretary, book and supplies monitor, current events leader, or musical director. In different years, we organized different roles, depending on the students' suggestions and interests. In these capacities, students took responsibility for starting the class day, taking attendance, leading discussions, reporting to the office, giving directions, and establishing rules for our daily classroom life. In her upper-grade classrooms, Debra Goodman has the student secretary sit at the (teacher's) desk near the door to greet visitors to her fifth-grade class, respond to their queries, show them around the room, introduce them to class members, and explain projects the kids are working on.

The different kinds of language used in these settings are a potential topic for an oral language strategy lesson. The teacher initiates the discussion by asking what language is best for each of several different situations and why the language changes from setting to setting. Later the students, with the help of the teacher, tape-record their conversations and analyze transcripts of the tapes to explore how language forms change, considering factors such as clarity, politeness, and turn taking, among others. Some of the questions students have explored during such lessons include:

- What are the different kinds of talk we use with principals, parents, and classmates?

- How do we have a discussion without raising our hands?

- What kinds of turn taking are best to prevent people from interrupting and overlapping one another?

- How do we make sure that all students have opportunities to talk?

- How do we involve classmates who are usually too quiet?

- Are patterns of talk different for kids who talk most from those who talk least?

- Is it always necessary to have a discussion leader for discussions to continue smoothly?

Such questions and the discussions that follow often lead to theme cycle studies in which students research, for example, the role of gender and race differences in interruption patterns or turn-taking styles.

As students become adept at carrying on different classroom discussions, the teacher plans strategy lessons that focus on the formal ways organized groups ensure democratically led discussion, decision making, and debate. The teacher reads relevant sections about formal aspects of discussions from, for example, *Robert's Rules of Order* (Robert, 1977), or about official debating practices, and discusses with the students the reasons why such formality developed in particular contexts. Members of a high school or college debate team might be invited to talk to the class about the conventions of formal debates as a way of exploring differences between formal and informal debating. The class can examine their informal classroom procedures to see if they want to adopt the conventional rules used for voting or debating.

Such strategy lessons are relevant to and can be integrated into social studies discussions revolving around governmental procedures. In a democracy, disagreeing, offering counterevidence, helping one another consider the views of others, and building consensus are valuable experiences, which holds true for the classroom as well. Planned strategy lessons provide opportunities for students to explore the strategies that work best to persuade, build consensus, or agree to disagree. And to gain familiarity with language that shows respect for the ideas of others, students can study their own language use during literature study group interactions, current events discussions, and science and math experiments. As students discuss styles of argumentative language, they can shift the focus to differences between oral and written argumentation. Point-counterpoint arguments in newspapers and magazines provide texts that students can use to examine the characteristics of written argument. Students write their arguments in response to those they are reading. Newspapers have e-mail addresses and encourage students to write online, and they often publish students' letters to the editor.

Mrs. Kinzie, a fourth-grade New Hampshire teacher, finds that oral discussions lead to many writing opportunities for her students. She sets aside the first fifteen minutes of her class for students to share orally with one another in small groups. She then follows the oral sharing with quiet writing time because the oral presentations and small group discussions often stimulate topics that students are eager to write about (Watson, 1987, pp. 181–82).

Many areas of the curriculum benefit when the teacher plans strategy lessons to help students explore ways to report on the conclusions of their investigations. The best time for a reporting strategy lesson is at the end of a learning experience or at the point in a theme cycle when time is set aside to consider reporting information. Although the most common form of reporting is an oral or written presentation to an audience of peers and parents, strategy lessons can help students plan presentations that integrate various symbol systems such as sketches, music, constructions, and scientific notations. If the teacher doesn't encourage students to consider interesting and multiple ways of reporting, it is easy for reports to become boring and formulaic.

A strategy lesson on note taking encourages the development of interesting reports. The discussion of note-taking procedures should take place at relevant moments such as when students are observing science experiments, searching for specific information they want to remember, giving directions for playing games or building models, or preparing to listen to presentations given by class members or guest speakers. A note-taking strategy lesson focuses on ways to collect field notes, when to take notes, and how to be selective and collect information only on important ideas or concepts. Students then list the important principles or ideas they learned from their note taking and compare them to those listed by other students. The teacher also takes notes and shares her or his thinking as a demonstration for the students. If the students don't consider alternatives to "writing" notes, the teacher provides examples of a range of note-taking devices such as outlines, webs, and diagrams so that students become flexible in their note taking. When students are encouraged to selectively take notes on their reading, listening, and observation experiences in order to develop unique reports, they are less likely to copy uninterpreted sections of published resources. Note-taking strategy lessons include ways to elaborate on notes for presentations, how to rewrite and transcribe notes into progress reports, and how to keep folders of data, analysis, and original or rewritten notes.

The teacher and the students evaluate the success of their note taking in relation to the development of a formal and innovative report. By evaluating reporting experiences and revisiting previously established rules or procedures, students develop their reporting abilities. The decisions students make during such evaluation result in charts labeled, for example, "Things to Remember during Reporting," charts that change as the students become more sophisticated. Such lists should never be followed slavishly; rather, each class will discover what works best for them.

Listening

Teachers often document students' understanding by observing and noting the ways in which students respond to the language of others, interact with their teachers and peers, follow directions, and attend to stories or other presentations. Careful recording of such events provides teachers with rich resources for planning listening strategy lessons. Students themselves can be involved in such research. During listening strategy lessons, it is appropriate to highlight for students that whenever talk is involved, listening is taking place. As discussed earlier, students need to consider their responsibilities as listeners as well as their abilities as speakers. Audiences need to be respectful and make a personal contract to listen thoughtfully to the ideas of others, attempt to sense the feelings of the speakers, and respond and question respectfully.

As students are immersed in discussions about listening, teachers consider their own listening capabilities. *Kidlistening* is an essential part of kidwatching. Paying careful attention to what students mean is an important goal for teachers. A teacher who is a good listener demonstrates a powerful message for students and helps them become aware that listening to others establishes a caring social community.

Following Directions

Strategy lessons on following directions are most authentic just before or after students have an experience of giving directions. A short list of such experiences includes how to get to specific places in the school, how to play a specific game, how to organize and move around the space in the classroom, and how to participate in a science experiment. The activity varies based on the interest and age of the students, but the general topics about listening are similar. Kindergarten students, for example, might be involved in following a recipe given by a fellow student for making a peanut butter sandwich, while older students might work on their portfolios following a number of organizational proposals suggested during classroom discussion. The teacher (later this can be done by designated student observers) takes notes about the successful responses as well as any confusion that occurred as the students followed the directions. The strategy lesson discussion focuses on how the organization worked, whether the language used to give directions was clear, and whether the students who followed the directions were listening carefully or did not understand. The discussion includes evaluating the problems and deciding whether they are related to the presenter's language or to the listener's misunderstanding, or a combination of the two, and the group decides on ways to best resolve the problems. These are treated as problem-solving discussions, not as disciplinary actions. As students experience and then discuss their responses to following and giving directions, they develop greater expertise in both giving and following directions. Many so-called discipline problems in classrooms occur because directions given to students are not clear. Discussion following directions given by the teacher or classmates should focus on the importance of formulating clear directions. Such discussion about following directions should also address positive ways to question directions that are ambiguous, unclear, unsafe, or don't make sense.

Listening Games

Helping students become aware of their listening abilities is easily accomplished through listening games. Some kindergarten teachers conduct a game in which one child is blindfolded and the other children in the class or group are asked to talk about a specific event. The blindfolded child is then asked to guess who is talking and explain which voice features helped the child make a decision. Teachers often tell me they are surprised at how accurate many of the children's guesses are and how adept they are at discussing the characteristics they were listening for. This helps the teacher gain insight into the students' listening abilities and development.

The telephone or gossip game, familiar to many teachers and students, is another listening strategy that encourages discussions about careful listening. The students are seated in a circle around the room. One student whispers a message into the ear of the student next to him or her, and that student whispers into the ear of the next person in the circle. The message is whispered from person to person until all the children have been involved. The last listener says the message out loud, which allows the students to compare the final message with the original message. The goal of the strategy lesson is not only to enjoy the game and the funny distortions but also to prompt discussion about why the language changes through the listening process and the role that interpretation plays in communication. Playing this game is a good way to handle classroom gossip that has resulted in kids getting their feelings hurt. Students learn that language and ideas are interpreted based on the ways in which people listen.

Participating in musical chairs leads to discussions about whether music distracts from or supports different kinds of work. It gives teachers the opportunity to broaden children's musical tastes and to find out what kinds of music the students appreciate. The teacher then moves naturally from the musical game to a discussion of issues such as music pollution from loud speakers, the impact of loud videos and radio on listening and hearing, laws related to noise pollution, or the physics of sound. These can become theme cycle language studies (Lundsteen, 1979).

Perceiving the Sounds of Language

Poetry and singing that involve rhyme provide students with rich opportunities to play with and talk about the sounds of language. Children's phonemic awareness is evident as they predict and write rhyming patterns. Making up songs and poetry by building on the patterns they find in literature is an excellent way for students to explore (and for teachers to document) their knowledge of phonics, spelling patterns, syllable awareness, and other conventions of word formation. On charts or word walls, students categorize word families that relate to rhyming patterns.

A songwriting strategy lesson lets students make up the rhymes for a song by focusing on children's names; the class also discusses rhyming patterns. First the teacher teaches the song to the students. After the children learn a few stanzas, they pick up the pattern easily and add to the song (or poem). A good example is "Hey Lolly, Lolly," a traditional camp song:

Hey lolly, lolly, lolly, Hey lolly, lolly, low
Hey lolly, lolly, lolly, Hey lolly, lolly, low
I know a girl whose name is Rosie [or name of someone in the class]
Hey lolly, lolly, low
When we sit together, we're cosy
Hey lolly, lolly, low
[Repeat chorus]
I know a boy whose name is Kenny
Hey lolly, lolly, low
He is always bright as a penny
Hey lolly, lolly, low . . .

If the kids and the teacher are not familiar with the song, the verses can be treated as a poem. Poetry collections and songbooks include many selections that the students can easily build on as part of the strategy lesson. The children-authored poems or songs are placed on charts and hung around the room and published as a songbook or poetry collection to add to the class library. These become part of the reading materials in the class. Bill Martin Jr. (1966–1967) developed a reading series that invites exploration of the sounds of language. A rich classroom collection of songbooks and poetry anthologies keeps the class immersed in the sounds of language.

Read-Alouds

Teachers who read regularly to their students become master oral readers and should use their expertise to help their students become dramatic oral readers as well. Read-alouds are satisfying listening experiences and should be provided daily for students at every age level throughout the school years. In fact, one of the major purposes of oral reading is to help with dramatic presentations. A number of books written for parents and teachers include a range of suggestions for selecting good read-aloud books and for successful procedures that teachers and students can follow to learn how to read aloud effectively (Roney, 2001; Fox, 2001; Trelease, 1982; Larrick, 1982). Read-alouds are also wonderful for settling down students after lunch, recess, or times of stress.

Strategy lessons help students explore ways to read orally to others, especially younger students. As students read to others, they become aware of how others listen to them. Deaf students sign stories to younger deaf children, and bilingual students can read in their first language to younger children who speak the same language. During read-aloud strategy lessons, students list the characteristics of oral reading that they think engage them most in intense listening. One class listed items such as having a strong voice, changing your voice when you change characters, looking up as you read, and showing the pictures to all the kids slowly. Students use these characteristics as a checklist for their own read-aloud experiences, evaluating their oral reading as well as the listening behaviors of the audience. Students observe one another when they read aloud to a group or class and take notes as they listen to help evaluate one another's performances. They discuss ways to involve the audience when they read aloud. Developing reader's theater scripts, in which a favorite book is turned into a group oral reading production, or choral reading of books or poems is an extension of oral reading that also emphasizes listening skills.

Listening Centers

A classroom listening center provides a range of experiences for students to develop their own tapes as well as listen to commercial or teacher-made tapes, CDs, and records. Teachers use listening centers for read-alongs, sing-alongs, miscue analysis, poetry readings, transcripts of classroom discussions, and many other listening experiences. Marcia Omura, working in Hawaiian classrooms, told me about a first-grade classroom that uses a plastic shoe organizer in which to keep a cassette player for each child, along with a headset that each student brings from home, encased in a plastic bag.

Using Written Language

The best times for teachers to plan strategy lessons that highlight the process of literacy use are when students are engaged in authentic reading and writing experiences such as reading self-selected books, writing reports, or writing stories. Planned strategy lessons during which teachers and students talk and think about how and why people read and write provide opportunities for students to develop realistic notions about literacy use. Many students, even into graduate school, have perfectionist or unrealistic notions about reading and writing. They believe they are not competent readers or writers if they struggle with reading and writing, if they don't write neatly, if they don't spell or read accurately 100 percent of the time, if they write an occasional ungrammatical sentence, or if they can't remember everything they read and write about. Through reading and writing strategy lessons, students and teachers discover the realities about reading and writing and demystify the processes. As they build confidence in the reading and writing they are already capable of doing, they become willing to risk participating in more sophisticated reading and writing, and as a result become more competent readers and writers.

Writing and Reading Demonstrations

The concept of *demonstration* is a major aspect of strategy lessons, especially during the perceiving phase of learning about reading and writing. Frank Smith (1983) and Brian Cambourne (1988) discuss the role of demonstration and its significance for learning. Cambourne suggests that "classrooms should be places where learners are exposed to a multiplicity of relevant and functional demonstrations" (p. 47). He describes demonstrations as "actions and artifacts from which we can learn" (p. 47).

The teacher's writing demonstrations on an overhead projector involve students in perceiving the many facets of composing. As the teacher writes and thinks out loud, inviting students to wonder with her or him about the writing and to make suggestions, the students participate in the teacher's ideating phase of the learning cycle. Demonstrations include students as apprentices to the teacher's writing as students perceive a more expert writer engaging in her or his craft and have opportunities to wonder with the teacher about the solutions to the teacher-writer's composing problems. Nancie Atwell (1998) discusses writing demonstrations as

> taking off the top of my head. . . . Everything I wrote in front of my kids was true, it all mattered to me in my life, and none of it was an exercise done for their benefit. Because of that I'm convinced it benefitted them enormously. (p. 368)

Demonstration strategy lessons also help students observe revision in action, which I discuss in more detail in a later section. Teachers demonstrate for students that they do not always accept revision suggestions from others. Students realize that ultimately they themselves need to decide which changes they want and need to make to their writing rather than changing their writing in response to every suggestion. As the teacher demonstrates her or his composing process, including revision, the students are writing, revising, and editing with their peers in small groups in a similar way.

Other forms of demonstration are subtler and often emerge from critical teaching moments. If, for example, students see teachers keeping a journal for jotting down writing ideas and recording quotes and important sayings from their reading that they then share with the class, the students believe that such writing has authentic purposes. When teachers share with students snippets of stories or poems they are writing or reading, students realize the power of sharing their work with others. Planned strategy lessons provide time for students to share their work and to organize places in the room for sharing and posting favorite quotes, sayings, and ideas. Too often teachers give assignments without indicating that these are authentic activities in which the teacher also engages. Toby Curry, a middle school teacher in Detroit, never gives an assignment to students that she doesn't do herself first and then discuss with the students, including providing information about any problems she had. Her demonstrations allow her to make sure the assignments are doable but also prove to students that she values the work.

Reading Strategy Lessons

Reading strategies, like listening strategies, include initiating, selecting, predicting, inferring, and confirming activities, among others. Reading strategy lessons are planned to demonstrate to students that they actively use these strategies to make sense of reading and to impress on them the importance of these strategies to their comprehension. Readers initiate their engagement in reading when they decide to participate in a specific reading experience. They select significant print or orthographic features of the text they need and predict the language and concepts of a written text as they read based on prior knowledge and experience. They make inferences about their reading, constantly checking or confirming to make sure they understand the meanings being expressed in a particular context. And, yes, sometimes readers decide not to read something because it is too hard or too boring. A number of texts document reading strategy lessons, including *Reading Strategies: Focus on Comprehension* (Y. Goodman, Watson, & Burke, 1996) and books by Dornan, Rosen, and Wilson (1997), Harvey and Goudvis (2000), Tierney, Readance, and Dishner (1980), Tovani (2000), Weaver (1998), and Gilles et al. (1988).

A reading strategy lesson often begins with a class discussion that is fueled by questions such as, "What do you do when you are reading and you come to something you don't know?" The discussion reveals the reading strategies that students and the teacher employ when they come to unfamiliar or unpredictable words or phrases. Some readers say they skip the word or phrase and continue reading in order to develop its meaning in the contexts that follow. They don't worry about the pronunciation until they need to use the term orally. Other readers say they produce a substitution by using an initial letter of the word; others just use a synonym. The discussion helps students understand that there are a variety of strategies they can use to solve such reading problems and that it is legitimate and necessary for readers to substitute, skip, or continue reading with uncertainty as long as they continue to develop a meaningful understanding of the text. All readers must understand that every reader makes miscues (mistakes) when they read.

Dorothy Watson (1996) examines strategy lessons that lead to similar discussions and that involve readers in self-selection of their own miscues. These lessons follow a planned silent reading time in the classroom. The teacher asks the students to mark with a light pencil any problems they have during their reading, and tells them that she will stop them after they have read for about fifteen minutes so they can share their problems with the class. After they finish their reading, the students write the entire sentence in which the problem occurred on a sheet of paper or card that is then collected. The teacher, along with the students, categorizes the miscues. The various categories usually include substitution of names, punctuation issues, unfamiliar words, complex syntax, unknown concepts, and so forth. These categories become the focus of strategy lessons that the teacher plans using the students' examples (pp. 46–47).

The teacher might, for example, photocopy or write on the board all the examples of the reading of names. The students then discuss the strategies they use when they come to unfamiliar names, such as substitute familiar names for unfamiliar names, and explore the appropriateness of such strategies during reading. Students become aware that all proficient readers meet names and labels they cannot pronounce, and they list the variety of strategies readers use to handle such situations. Students revisit these discussions through very short strategy lessons whenever they read a novel that includes names that are difficult to pronounce, or they read social studies or science texts in which they encounter unfamiliar names of species or geographic regions (Y. Goodman, Watson, & Burke, 1996, pp. 61–74).

Writing Strategy Lessons

Writing strategy lessons also explore the composing processes that emerge from the teacher's writing demonstrations as well as from writing conferences that reveal common problems students face. Some strategy lessons focus on big ideas such as: "Where do I get story ideas?" or "How do I start a piece of writing?" Others focus on specific writing conventions such as: "How do I punctuate when I am writing dialogue?" Nancie Atwell (1987, 1998), Lucy Calkins (1994), Donald Graves (1983), and Shelley Harwayne (2001) discuss writing strategy lessons (which they refer to as minilessons) that focus on planning, composing, revising, and editing strategies. These and many other authors present ideas and references for selected instructional strategies designed to meet the writing needs of students.

Planned writing strategy lessons take place during individual writing conferences; before, during, or at the end of a writing workshop; with small groups; or with the whole class. Lucy Calkins (1994) suggests that students keep at the back of their writer's notebook a list of the possible writing strategies they use. Some teachers post the strategies students brainstorm on a classroom chart or in a computer file. Calkins cautions that problems may occur if teachers expect that "every student will use the content of a mini-lesson on the day of that mini-lesson" (p. 200). Rather, she asks teachers to consider that not all writers have reason to use a specific strategy at the time it is presented. She suggests that "children have tucked the idea into the back of their minds, and they may draw upon it when they need it" (p. 200).

As students write reports, lists, letters to different audiences, captions, dialogue journals, poetry, and many other genres, planned strategy lessons allow them to explore the different genres they use, how they write in different ways depending on the genre and its purposes, and ways to record the developing range of their writing abilities. Portalupi and Fletcher (2001) provide examples of lessons for the writing of nonfiction.

Revising and Editing

Planned strategy lessons help students learn when it is appropriate to edit their writing and when no editing is necessary. One fourth-grade teacher told me that she reserves a special area of the board for questions her kids ask about writing. One question she hears every semester is "What writing do we need to edit and what don't we need to edit?," so she has her students consider this question in a strategy lesson. Her latest class generated the following chart as a result of their discussion:

To Be Revised	Not to Be Revised
Letters for job applications	Phone messages
Science projects	Notes for our parents
Letters to the principal	Letters for friends
Cards for our grandparents	

Even when a piece is considered for final draft, students often need help focusing on revising content and ideas first and leaving editing for format and spelling until the end of the process. Planned strategy lessons about revision include having students and teacher brainstorm the kinds of questions they ask themselves as they write and reread: Does this piece say what I want it to say? Am I using appropriate language for my audience? Am I using the same words too many times? Would my piece be easier to understand if I reorganized it? The students keep the list of questions on a card in front of them as a reminder as they write. Additional suggestions for editing spelling and grammar appear later in this chapter and in Chapter 6.

When working on revisions, especially with primary grade students, it is important to consider that sometimes authors revise a story across several stories. Young students often write a similar story more than once. They seem to be revising across settings rather than reworking the same story. Revising and rewriting are often tedious for young students, and they are not interested in reworking the same piece. It is helpful for these students to realize that their sequels are ways of reworking their ideas. In fact, the idea that revisions can take place over time is a worthwhile strategy lesson topic. Composers often rewrite their compositions after they have been initially performed; plays and musicals are reorganized and rewritten after they have played off Broadway (and revivals are new versions of the original plays); poets and authors rework their pieces into sequels of stories or poems. The 2000 Caldecott Award winner, *Joseph Had a Little Overcoat* by Simms Taback (1999), is a reworking of a book the author wrote twenty years earlier (Taback, 1977). Sharing Taback's experience with students has a powerful impact on them. Strategy lessons on revision and editing continue throughout the school year and change to meet the students' growing writing sophistication. When teachers follow the same formulaic process of revision for all writing throughout the year, the purposes that revision and editing serve often get lost.

Another important lesson for young writers to learn is the strategy of rereading during the composing process. Students' lack of rereading is a consequence of having to finish assignments within a specified time period instead of having enough time to develop pride in their own compositions. Or the students figure that the only audience for the writing is the teacher, who is reading mainly for purposes of correction, so there is no reason to rework their own writing—after all, if the teacher is going to correct the writing anyway, why should they bother? Not rereading their own work suggests that students have not learned to value their compositions nor to understand the purposes of revision and editing. Strategy lessons that are organized to discuss the importance of rereading during writing for purposes of revision, to read their work aloud to another child or a small group, or to share their writing aloud to interested adults provide opportunities for students to hear their own work aloud, rethink their writing, and become aware of the importance of continuous rereading during composing. Teachers can demonstrate such strategies during demonstration strategy lessons.

Writing as Ideating

Writing in school most often focuses on writing for an audience, but it is also helpful to let students know that writing for oneself without an audience is a way to ideate or to wonder: to explore their own beliefs and thoughts. Encouraging students to keep a journal in which they can sketch or diagram, write down intriguing statements or ideas, and list writing ideas gives students a safe place to experiment with their ideas. Teachers demonstrate this kind of writing whenever they share their personal journals with their students and invite them to consider whether writing in a journal would work for them. Planning strategy lessons to explore how professional authors, illustrators, or journalists use personal journals is helpful for demonstrating the range of journals or computer files that authors use. Authors' Web sites often include information about what helps then in their writing. If writing a personal journal becomes a required assignment, however, it loses its significance.

Sharing and discussing personal writing journals, learning logs, or thinking journals invites students to discover how writing for themselves allows them to explore their own writing inventions, tentative ideas, real questions, and responses to new learnings. These journals help students think about their writing even as they help them explore the ways they do math problems, observe a science experiment, or respond to a video. Exploring their own thinking processes highlights students' awareness of their own learning capabilities. Teachers encourage students to personalize their journals or notebooks through tagging, artwork, sketches, or doodles. Although students may voluntarily share their journal responses with the teacher and other students, teachers should not evaluate these personal writings.

Language Inventions and Language Conventions

The history of language clearly documents the inevitable tensions between the invention of language functions and forms and conventional uses of language functions and forms. But these forces are not in competition with each other; each is essential to continuous language development in the individual and in society. Language invention is a necessary part of each person's development in much the same way that invention is part of the history and development of the world's languages and dialects. In the individual's need to communicate, infants produce sounds, words, and phrases that have never been uttered by anyone else (we relish the words of the babies in our families, such as *pasquetti* or *blinky*), and some remain in the language of the family, or *familialect*. As we read and listen to language, our understandings of meaning are unique, personal responses (inventions). As we discuss our personal responses with others, we often develop agreed-upon or shared meanings (conventions). We invent words and their meanings or take conventional words and change their meanings. We invent spellings, punctuation, and other aspects of written forms to make sense through our writing. Like much of language use, we do not think consciously about such invention since it happens continuously in the context of its use.

Groups also invent language in order to talk or write about concepts they are coming to understand and need to communicate to others. As people develop new shared beliefs, interests, and knowledge, they invent new language to express their ideas or discoveries. Such inventions often take place within the language use of particular groups, including age groups (e.g., adolescents); groups isolated or marginalized by society in terms of region, class, or race; or people within an occupational group such as computer programmers. Debates about the acceptability of such changes or inventions occur both in the popular press and in the field of linguistics. Some of the changes become universal and move into the language of the wider community (Smitherman, 1995). Some changes are incorporated into the dialects or registers of specific groups, others stay in the language only briefly, while still others are lost. If a goal of education is for students to become innovative authors and thoughtful readers, problem solvers, and critical thinkers, then their inventions need to be understood and valued.

Language invention is a major impetus for language change in both societies and individuals and a universal feature of language. It responds to the mobility of people and the need to express new ideas and to name new objects, and it reflects the ethnic, racial, and social status of groups within the language community. All aspects of language are in constant flux. The sounds of language, its phonology, change over years of use, sometimes even within the same dialect community. The sound of the letter *a* in the word *bag* and words with similar-sounding vowels, for example, has changed in my lifetime, and my daughters say it differently than I do.

As one example of grammatical change, it was common to say *someone's else book* at the beginning of the twentieth century, while now almost everyone says *someone else's book*. Currently people argue about the uses of *ain't;* the use of *me* or *I* as the subject of a clause (Me and Ken are going to the movies), and the object of the preposition (He completed his work for his mother and I). Words such as *cool, tough,* and *bad,* for example, change meaning and are interpreted differently from generation to generation. Many language changes become conventional in oral language forms but are not considered acceptable in written language until decades later. Graffiti artists produce their own written characters to avoid certain orthographic combinations that represent a rival gang, and many academics develop an abbreviation system to fit their need for specialized note taking. Adolescents are great influences on language change as they invent and adapt language to establish their own place in the sun. The term *hip-hop* has become so popular that commercial music and clothing companies use it, moving the invented form into conventional use.

Language conventions are also necessary because they enable people to communicate with each other and understand each other's meanings through a common form of language. Conventions allow groups of people—societies and cultures—to share ideas and beliefs through consensual forms of oral and written language. Sometimes teachers or language purists claim that conventional language forms are the only acceptable forms for school use, and they pass on the myth that "incorrect" language (read nonconventional) is a mark of "the lower classes," ignorance, and the decline of language use.

I suggest that teachers plan strategy lessons that focus on the legitimacy of language invention and explore the power that is generated as speakers and writers use language with flexibility and creativity. Strategy lessons on conventional language use examine the controversies about what is considered "correct" language use and help students use language flexibly, teaching them to gauge the appropriate use of language in a specific context. Strategy lessons on inventive and conventional language use help students value their own language while highlighting what they already know about language conventions. Such exploration often extends into theme cycle study because students find such topics interesting (see Chapters 5–7).

Language Inventions

Strategy lessons that explore language invention involve students in documenting the language they use and that some adults react to negatively. The teacher stimulates the search for new inventions by encouraging students to think about and report back to the class new influences on their language from popular music videos, books such as the Goosebumps series (R. L. Stine) or the Harry Potter series (J. K. Rowling), games such as Pokémon or Masters of the Universe, the latest clothing fashions, instant messaging, and advertisements. Teachers who pay attention to the movies, radio and TV stations, video advertising, and other aspects of youth culture are able to extend the discussions with relevant questions.

The teacher might, for example, engage the students in exploring the inventions taking place in their instant messaging interactions. Many students spend many hours after school instant messaging, and they are often more knowledgeable about this genre than their parents and teachers. A *USA Today* article reported on kids' use of instant messaging and the abbreviations they have invented, such as j/k (just kidding), brb (be right back), OMG (Oh My God), and POS (parent over shoulder) (Thomas,

2001). Such articles stimulate discussions, including a consideration of how such adolescent inventions eventually become part of adult language use. Students are encouraged to collect these abbreviations and other instant messaging terms, including how they are used in the context of the message, when and why the terms were invented, and what they mean. The teacher can also suggest unfamiliar terms that she or he has noticed. After students develop their list of terms or their Dictionary of Kid Language, they interview parents, grandparents, and others and then share their findings on adults' reactions to the language they have documented. They ask members of older generations to recall language they used as teenagers that is no longer in use or has changed over time. The teacher should introduce the concept of *metaphor* at this time since metaphor plays a major role in language invention. Students explore the reasons for adolescents' development of their own language forms and the different responses to such language based on their interviews with older generations.

Social inventions of language are easy to find in newspapers and specialty magazines and lend themselves to planned strategy lessons. Activities related to scientific discoveries in fields such as astronomy and computer technology often lead to language invention, as do the areas of games, sports, and fashion. Terms such as *English Only* (related to bilingual issues) and *high-stakes testing* (representing concern for accountability in schools) are suggestions the teacher might add to the students' explorations of language inventions.

Concepts and Labels

Planned strategy lessons help students consider their own development of new concepts and the labels for these concepts in relation to invention and convention and the tension between the two. Conceptual knowledge builds over time as new terminology becomes part of students' language use. When students ask the teacher the meaning of words or phrases, the teacher should plan strategy lessons to explore the relation between concepts and labels. In traditional language arts or English classes, such study is called vocabulary development, which in too many cases simply means looking up dictionary definitions. Nothing is more boring than listing definitions and creating sentences for words that have no relation to what the student is exploring. In a language study curriculum, the focus is on conceptualizing or exploring understandings of particular words and phrases within the context of their use. As dictionaries clearly reveal, the same word has many meanings that are only disambiguated when they are used in oral or written language. Understanding the meanings of language (the concepts) should be the most important aspect of vocabulary study.

Planned strategy lessons that explore vocabulary should focus most on concept development because students need to understand that definitions are statements that relate to the meanings or conceptualizations of a word. Therefore, it is helpful to brainstorm with the students what they already understand about the words or phrases they are interested in focusing on in the context of their use. In this way, students come to understand that concepts develop over time and that meaning development is tentative and enriched over time as they meet such labels in additional and new contexts. Strategy lessons grow out of students' inquiry into what a particular word or phrase means, or from the teacher raising inquiry-oriented questions during reading, content area study, and oral discussions.

Strategy lessons also examine the resources that help students broaden their developing concepts, such as dictionaries, thesauruses, and other reference materials. Students come to understand that dictionary definitions have limitations and that other materials can help in their explorations as well. With my middle-grade students, I often demonstrated resource use during a critical teaching moment when a student asked about a word meaning or when I was reading aloud and came to something I wasn't sure of. We first discussed what we thought the word meant and then wrote the word on the board along with the various meanings suggested by class members. We read a number of sentences before and after the words under consideration to see if there were clues in the text that would help our understanding. I asked the students which reference materials would best help us confirm the meanings we had brainstormed, and I encouraged them to consider the appropriate uses as well as limitations of dictionaries.

We talked about which definition was the one we were looking for, how to look up hard-to-spell words, and what strategies to use when a word is not in the dictionary. We then considered the appropriate dictionary definition by relating the multiple meanings cited there to meaning embedded in the reading material. In their book on vocabulary study, Blachowicz and Fisher (1996, 2001) provide many strategy lessons that explore how to learn vocabulary from context and integrate vocabulary into reading and literature studies.

As students examine concepts and labels, they discover that people often develop misconceptions about the sounds or meanings of words and phrases. These misconceptions often lead people to use words inappropriately, which is a part of human language development. I often share with my classes an article by Celestine Sibley (1993) titled "Sometimes the Wrong Word Can Be Absolutely Right." Sibley explores the use of malapropisms (named for Mrs. Malaprop in Sheridan's play *The Rivals*) in which people use forms of language they are unfamiliar with in unusual, inappropriate, but almost appropriate-sounding ways. Here's a recent example from an excused absence note written by a parent: Mary could not come to school because she was bothered by very close veins.

Adolescents are wonderful inventors of malapropisms as they use newly discovered language forms to express new experiences. Teachers and kids can collect and discuss malapropisms found in the media as well as in their own oral language and writing. Such discussions expand vocabulary and concept development as students explore spellings, pronunciations, and misconceptions. Amsel Greene (1969), a secondary English teacher, published high school students' written malapropisms in a book titled *Pullet Surprises*. The title came from a student's paper in which he had written, "In 1957 Eugene O'Neill won a Pullet Surprise." Ms. Greene explored the knowledge behind the malapropisms and categorized them. Students could write a similar book with titles such as "The Menagery Line around the Equator" or "One Nation Invisible" based on the malapropisms they collect.

With this kind of strategy lesson, it's important to have fun with the misconceptions and treat them as a normal part of language development and change. Students need to understand that such language miscues are not a mark of ignorance but of their own risk-taking attempts to express ideas in new ways. Asking students to write down the songs they sing often, the preamble to the Declaration of Independence, or the Pledge of Allegiance is another way to gather malapropisms. As students categorize their mispronunciations and misunderstandings, they explore the ways in which concepts and labels develop. Cartoons such as *Peanuts* and *Family Circus* and books such as Art Linkletter's (1957) *Kids Say the Darndest Things!* are rich with examples of how children's language misconceptions prove them to be sophisticated language experimenters.

Language Conventions

Through strategy lesson discussions, students learn that sometimes in school they come to believe that they do not know how to spell, how to use proper grammar, or how to write in appropriate formats, or that they do not have large enough vocabularies. Once an open-ended inquiry approach to language study is established, all discussions about language support the stance that many language issues are controversial, that different scholars have different points of view about language, and that since everyone uses language, everyone has a right to an opinion about language use. Such discussions help students examine their attitudes about themselves as language learners. As they learn about conventions, students come to understand that they learn conventional forms best by using language in many settings and for different purposes and by having opportunities in school to discuss issues of language use. Teachers plan related lessons by collecting and sharing newspaper and magazine articles or cartoons that focus on language controversies. I've recently read newspaper articles about the influence on English of Yiddish, about state legislation against noise from CDs and boom boxes, and about how advertisers violate grammatical rules. William Safire writes the syndicated column "On Language" that appears regularly in the *New York Times*. When students follow controversies about language in such columns and in letters to the editor, they often end up writing to the newspapers with their own opinions. Such discussions raise the students' interest and help them learn that conventional language use is more than knowing "correct" language forms.

Planned strategy lessons on conventional language use often emerge from the editing process during student writing. One fourth-grade teacher planned a series of strategy lessons to discuss the conventions of punctuation that emerged from a student's composition. Gordon, a Tohono O'odham Indian student, wrote a coming-of-age folktale about a boy who went hunting because he needed to bring food home to feed his family. In his story, Gordon used dialogue appropriately, but his rule for punctuating dialogue was to always place opening quotation marks after the word *said* and ending quotation marks at the end of the sentence after the period ending the dialogue. This worked well for him when he was writing a straightforward quote such as:

His father said, "Little Nife, come with me."

But he also placed quotation marks in indirect quotation structures such as:

His father said, "that he can carry the deer with him."

Gordon also placed them in a construction in which the quotation marks needed to be around the phrases "Little Nife" and "don't worry":

Little Nife said, "his father don't worry."

During an individual conference with Gordon, after telling him how powerful she thought the story was and discussing the characters' motivations, the teacher explored with Gordon his use of dialogue. She made it clear that she was always sure how to read the dialogue because of his punctuation. She then asked him if she could share his composition with the whole class since others who were also exploring the use of dialogue would benefit from the discussion. Gordon, comfortable with his teacher and classmates, gave permission to use his paper with the whole class. The teacher made an overhead transparency of Gordon's original draft, and Gordon read the story to the class while the teacher noted how he read the dialogue and the indirect quotations. The teacher then asked Gordon to go back and reread the sentences with the quotations in them. Gordon used conventional intonation in reading the dialogue. The teacher and the students pointed to the conventional knowledge that supported Gordon's oral reading and his use of commas and periods in the written text. Then the teacher helped the class discuss the conventional ways in which direct dialogue is punctuated, including quotation marks, commas, and periods. With Gordon taking the lead, the class eventually decided that quotation marks relate to the language spoken by characters and not simply to the word *said*. The teacher involved the class in a discussion about how to recognize indirect quotes, and she established reasons why indirect quotes are not punctuated.

The teacher planned some follow-up strategy lessons. She duplicated a list of additional examples of dialogue from other student authors (with their permission) and had the class work in small groups on these in the same way they had on Gordon's writing; they then reported to the whole class on their results. On another day, she asked students to collect dialogue sections of their writing from their portfolios and to share examples in small groups to discuss whether they were punctuated conventionally. The class then discussed these examples in light of their previous discussions. The teacher encouraged the class to collect examples of punctuation from their reading materials, examining in particular how terms such as *said, asked,* and other related dialogue markers were used and punctuated.

For younger children, teachers use Big Books that are filled with dialogue as a way to examine conventional use of quotation marks in context and to list their characteristics. The teacher asks the students how they know which character is talking or what the author does to provide clues for the reader about who is talking. The students then check their own writing to see if they are using punctuation in conventional ways. After her students were using quotation marks conventionally in their own writing and were able to talk about the conventions they used, one teacher planned a strategy lesson in which she had the students examine *My Grandson Lew* by Charlotte Zolotow (1974), which does not use quotation marks to punctuate dialogue. She discussed with the students why authors and publishers experiment with invented punctuation and encouraged them to look for such inventions in their reading. The class also decided they would write to the author and publisher to ask why they hadn't followed conventional punctuation in this book. In a follow-up strategy lesson, these students read two or three pages in the book they were reading at the time and collected different authors' uses of punctuation with dialogue. They brought their lists back to the whole class for discussion. Students who participate in such strategy lessons on a regular basis pay close attention to the orthography of their books, reading like authors concerned with the craft of writing. Throughout the lessons, the teacher and students use appropriate terminology to name the punctuation they encounter, and thus the appropriate terms become part of their conventional use of language.

Cloze Procedure or Selected Slotting

The adaptation of cloze procedures to planned collaborative strategy lessons provides opportunities for students to become aware of their knowledge about grammatical and semantic language conventions. A strategy lesson that Brian Cambourne and I developed together is called *cooperative cloze* (Y. Goodman, Watson, & Burke, 1996, pp. 157–60). We reprint a short one- or two-page story or article, omitting every seventh or so word. The students work in groups of three and collaboratively decide on what word or phrase best fits the omission slot. As the students fill in the blanks, the teacher roams around the room taking notes on the language the students are using. This way the teacher discovers the degree to which the students are already using appropriate grammatical terminology. With older students, teachers eventually appoint a student to be the note-taking observer. During class discussions, the teacher refers to the appropriate terminology used by the students or uses the appropriate terminology to demonstrate new vocabulary in context for the students: "I heard Farley say that a 'thing' needs to go there, but Bryan said, 'You mean a noun?' Both of those terms are appropriate and refer to the names of objects, but *noun* is the term that is usually used in such contexts."

For younger children, teachers can use Big Books as a selected slotting activity. The slots the teacher selects are covered
with a sticky note, and initially the teacher works with the class
as a whole. After a few demonstrations, the students are capable
of working in small groups and reporting their results back to
the whole class. The sticky notes are used to cover up the same
word throughout a story, to highlight spelling patterns that are
common problems such as *their* and *there,* or to explore grammatical functions such as adjectives or past tense forms, contrac-
tions, or word endings such as *ing.* The teacher asks the students
to predict a word or phrase for the covered linguistic slots. This
experience, along with discussion, helps students realize they are
capable of predicting appropriately because of their language
knowledge.

Spelling Conventions

Students' conventional spelling develops best through a wide range
and large amount of reading and writing and through discussions related to when and why they need conventional spelling to
communicate with others. As students and the teacher discuss
spelling development, the relation between convention and invention becomes clear (K. Goodman, 1993).

Teacher-researchers often keep examples from their students'
writing portfolios in order to document their students' spelling
and punctuation development over time. Such record keeping
not only provides important evaluation data but also is especially helpful when students are encouraged to keep personal lists
of their invented spelling patterns as well as lists of conventional
spellings they have learned.

Debra Goodman has her middle-grade students keep a spelling check on selected writings at specific times during the year
(usually before report card time). The students calculate the percentage of words spelled conventionally in their writing. She also
dictates one piece of writing to the students around the same
time, and the students note the percentage of conventional spellings in dictation. Dr. Goodman uses these percentages to evaluate students' development in two different writing contexts (1991,

p. 254). Students not only are capable of recording their quantitative spelling data but, by keeping lists of their invented spellings and categorizing and discussing the rules they use for specific spelling features, they also are able to inquire into their own invented spelling patterns. Often students generate the same kinds of inventions, and these patterns can be used to develop individual or small group strategy lessons. In order to help my students, I kept a list of my own spelling inventions and discussed with the students the issues I face in developing conventional patterns:

Y. Goodman's Challenging Spellings

se/ce endings	double letters	*tion/sion*	*eed/ede*
license	accommodate	extension	proceed
pretense	balloon	pretension	concede
absence	occasional	position	precede
abstinence	councillor	convention	recede
obstinance	counselor		
reminisce			

I told the students that I overgeneralize using the feature that is most common in my writing. I tend, for example, to use the *ce* ending and am not always sure when *se* is appropriate. As a result, I check those words. By discussing my spelling challenges, I am able to demonstrate for my students the strategies I use, and they are able to discuss their own categories of spelling challenges in a similar way. Such documentation shows conclusively to parents and administrators that spelling is a carefully planned part of the curriculum and that invented spellings are the nature of spelling growth over time.

An example of individual and small group strategy lessons that involve students in documenting their own spelling patterns and considering why they use the inventions they do took place in a third-grade bilingual classroom. Eduardo, a Spanish-speaking student writing in English for the first time, wrote words such as *fur (food), liro (little),* and *erem (ate them).* Shana, bilingual in Spanish and English from birth, wrote most of the time in English. When she wrote a menu in Spanish, she wrote *lemonatha (lemonada/lemonade)* and *salatha (salada/salad)*. The teacher in this class understood the students' knowledge of the graphophonic features of English and Spanish that influenced these invented spelling patterns. She was able to discuss with Eduardo that the *r* in Spanish in medial positions represents the same sound that is represented in English by *d, tt,* or *t.* Eduardo documented these patterns in his own writing and listed similar spellings in his English and Spanish reading to check the consistency of the pattern. The teacher showed Shana that the *th* she used is an English spelling pattern representing a similar sound in Spanish spelled with a *d* in words such as *lemonada* and *salada.* Shana kept her own personal list of *th/d* patterns in her reading and writing.

Through such documentation and individual strategy lessons, students come to understand that when they invent spellings they are using their knowledge of phonics, their understanding of spelling patterns related to grammatical, morphological, and meaning features, and their understandings about how words look, and that often they overgeneralize what they know. They are encouraged to talk about their personal understandings of spelling with other students and the teacher and to look for the use of their challenging patterns in their own reading and writing, which helps them expand their developing knowledge about spelling conventions.

The teacher plans a whole class discussion of conventional spelling patterns regularly a few times a week for a short period when specific issues arise during a critical teaching moment or individual conference in order to focus on one or two related issues that are general problems for many students in the class. Unique problems are best approached in individual strategy lessons. Textbooks on spelling or lists of spelling demons are sometimes useful for teachers early in their careers (or because they are mandated by school districts to use them), but I was always aware that the more I was able to individualize students' study of their own spelling issues, the more comfortable students were in using and exploring spellings that were difficult for them. Even when I was required to give weekly spelling tests, I documented student growth by having them select their own spelling words from the list of invented spellings they kept in their folders, new words they were learning in content areas as well as in language studies, and words they found interesting to explore and wanted to know. I had partners give their self-selected spelling words to each other, or individual students would tape-record their own spelling words with sentences they had generated and take the test from their own recordings.

Reading to students the words of authors who write about their own spelling concerns helps place spelling in its proper perspective. Such presentations are good for parents' meetings as well. Many authors discuss the role of spelling and other aspects of conventions in thoughtful ways that help listeners think more realistically about language conventions (Dahl, 1984; Fritz, 1992; Thomas, 1997). Students carefully observe the writing in books, magazines, advertisements, and environmental print and list unusual spellings that then become the focus of a strategy lesson.

Spelling Inquiry by Kelly Chandler and a teacher-researcher group (Chandler & Group, 1999) in Maine provides a range of ideas for inquiry lessons on spelling as well as demonstrating how teachers are able to study the spelling development of their students, explore innovative spelling curriculum together, and learn about the spelling system of English.

Although sometimes the teacher plans a strategy lesson in which the relation between letters and sounds and the ways in which particular spellings relate to particular patterns are presented in isolation, the words used and the patterns examined come from the actual writing of the students and their reactions to spelling as they read. The planned lesson involves the students in expressing why they think particular spellings occur the way they do, and the teacher helps the students discover the historical and linguistic influences on spelling.

Young children need to develop the stability principle of spelling. Some young children don't recognize that the same word looks the same across contexts. Standardized or stable spellings didn't occur in the English language until the mid-1800s, many centuries after people started writing in English, so it is understandable that individuals don't develop this concept early. Encouraging students to reread their own writing to check on the various ways they spell the same word helps them become aware that spelling is stable across contexts. Many professional books

for teachers, in addition to those listed earlier, provide understandings about English spelling and include suggestions for
planned strategy lessons (Glazer, 1998; Hughes & Searle, 1997;
Read, 1971, 1974, 1986; Wilde, 1992).

Discussions about the relation between invention and convention are not meant to lead students to a devil-may-care attitude about their language use. Rather, the purpose is to help kids
understand the nature of language development and to explore
their strengths, their flexibility, and their ability to recognize the
contexts in which language conventions are appropriate. In this
way, teachers level with kids about the degree to which they need
to be concerned about conventions and at the same time help
students learn to value themselves as capable and inventive language users.

III

THEME CYCLES FOR A LANGUAGE STUDY CURRICULUM

Introduction to Part III

The chapters in Part III include exemplars of theme cycles that engage students in the learning experiences of perceiving the importance of language study in their own lives, ideating or wondering about the ways in which language affects their lives, and presenting their thinking and learning about language to others. The theme cycles are intended as demonstrations that teachers can adapt to their own settings, not as lesson plans to be followed as scripts (Smith, 1983). In addition, each of the chapters that follow focuses on a particular content of language study and includes relevant information about the importance of the section, including bibliographic references for teachers and students.

Getting Ideas for Theme Cycles

The ideas for many of the theme cycles come from students' interests and questions that occurred during my own teaching and from other teachers who engage their students in theme cycles. Oftentimes a theme cycle concludes with new questions or problems the students want to explore further, thus precipitating a new theme cycle. Authors who write extensively about theme cycles also include suggestions for language study. They conceptualize theme cycles in varying ways and sometimes use different terminology, but their underlying philosophy is similar.

Altwerger and Flores (1994) define theme cycles as "a dynamic, ever changing framework for thinking about life in our classrooms. . . . [L]earners (both teachers and students) are at the center of learning, asking critical questions, engaging in meaningful problem-posing and problem-solving, and creating and recreating knowledge" (p. 2). Manning, Manning, and Long (1994) describe their concept of "theme immersion" as "an in-depth study of a topic, issue or question." Students and teachers plan together in order to "determine the important issues for discussion, and decide how to communicate their learning" (p. 1).

Short and Harste (1996) envision curriculum as inquiry through "the authoring cycle." The result is "a community of learners in the process of collaboratively constructing knowledge as they continually seek understandings of personal and social significance from new perspectives . . . for purposes of creating a more just, a more equitable, a more thoughtful world" (p. 42). The authoring cycle includes making connections by building on prior learning; finding questions for inquiry by observing, conversing, and selecting; gaining new perspectives; and taking action (pp. 51–60).

The "Foxfire" concept involves language study about the students' local community and was developed by Eliot Wigginton (1972) while he was working with students in rural Georgia. He helped them value the richness of their own community—their Appalachian heritage and language. The results of their inquiries have become popular published histories, and the approach has caught on elsewhere. *The Salt Book* (Wood, 1977), compiled by elementary students, applied the Foxfire concept to the rugged North Atlantic coast. The editor introduces the published book by noting: "Its young authors have turned to their own people in their own communities to learn about living" (p. ix). Foxfire continues as an organization for teacher-researchers. Information about Foxfire is available at The Foxfire Fund, Inc., P.O. Box 541, Mountain City, Georgia 30562-0541; e-mail foxfire@ foxfire.org or check online at www.foxfire.org.

Some authors publish ideas about theme cycles for bilingual, ESL, and EFL students (Y. Freeman & D. Freeman, 1997; Kucer, Silva, & Delgado-Larocco, 1995). A number of teachers new to theme cycle planning make use of www.Big6.com to support students in gathering library and technology resources. The next three chapters focus on different aspects of theme cycles. Chapter 5 discusses language and linguistics, Chapter 6 shows the relationship between language study and literature, while Chapter 7 is concerned with the power of language use.

Focus on Language and Linguistics

Chapter 5 focuses on the areas of language study introduced in Chapter 1 in which the major focus is to talk and think about language itself. These theme cycles often emerge from strategy lessons or critical-moment teaching that piques student interest. In Chapter 3, for example, I describe a lesson in which students editing each other's paper disagree about the efficacy of using the word *ain't*. Such controversies lead easily into an extended theme study about vernacular language. Language is sometimes the primary focus of a theme cycle, and in other cases it is integral to other subject matter inquiries. Language is the central focus, for example, when the students wonder why kids in the class whose names sound the same use different spellings, and they decide to study the origins of names and naming practices. Or the students get involved in researching naming practices as part of a social studies theme cycle on kinship or in a geography study that involves mapping the local community.

Focus on Language and Literature

Often, theme cycles are initiated by a book the teacher reads to the class. *Chrysanthemum* by Kevin Henkes (1991), for example, is great for initiating a naming study (see Chapter 7). In Chapter 6, I suggest theme cycles that can be initiated and enriched by adolescent and children's literature. Responses to literature are integral to theme cycles as students develop their interests and raise their questions in small literature study groups or during whole class discussions.

Short and Harste (1996) use the terms *shared book sets* and *text sets* to describe different organizations for literature study. A shared book set involves the use of multiple copies of the same book, which a group of students reads at the same time; the students then discuss their responses and follow up on their questions and concerns. Since teachers need multiple copies for shared book groups, they often have approximately eight sets of different books for the five or six literature book groups that are ultimately selected by the students. The teacher or a student who knows the book gives a book talk to provide the students with enough information to facilitate their choices.

Text sets comprise different books and reading materials related to a central theme such as the role of literacy among slaves in the United States or children struggling in school with learning to read or write. The term *multitext* is often used for text sets in social studies or science, referring to the use of a variety of references in relation to the study of a major generalization or concept. Depending on the focus of the inquiry, some students choose to work with shared book sets while others use text sets.

Some teachers plan one or two literature study groups at a time so they are able to participate with each group, especially when literature study is new to the class. Other teachers involve all the students in study groups at the same time, especially as students become more expert at organizing and participating in literature study.

One of the most important aspects of literature study groups is the opportunity for students to explore ideas and respond to their reading in an environment that legitimizes student-generated inquiry and varied responses. The difference between literature study in whole language classrooms and literature study in a transmission model class is that with a whole language philosophy, teachers characterize their literature discussions as a grand conversation (Peterson & Eeds, 1990), similar to the kind of talk that occurs in a book club for adults. The result is a community of learners in which the teacher and students, through in-depth discussion about literature, increase their comprehension of a text and extend their inquiry. In this community, the teachers' questions are open-ended, while students are encouraged to interrogate one another and the text from their own understandings (Bird, 1991).

Focus on Language as Power

In Chapter 7, I present ideas teachers can use to involve students in thinking about language critically, especially in relation to issues of equity and social justice. Concepts developed through critical analysis of language issues, however, should be integral to all aspects of a language study curriculum. Carole Edelsky (1994) clarifies the importance of a critical stance:

> Re-theorizing language education to make it serve education *for* democracy means highlighting the relationship of language and power. It means trying to understand the connections between the language-power issue and the idea of . . . literacies as social practices, the idea of reading as transaction, and . . . keeping the language-power issue central. It means . . . spelling out how systems of domination are part of reading and writing, part of classroom interaction, part of texts of all kinds—and doing that as our constant and primary . . . enterprise. (p. 255)

Within a language study curriculum, being critical means becoming consciously aware of and understanding the ways in which language use affects power relationships in society and who benefits from such interrelations. Being critical means recognizing and responding to language that marginalizes others, keeps people in their "place" academically or economically, or is used for hurtful purposes. Being critical means searching for knowledge and evidence to reject, support, or expand one's personal view while at the same time trying to understand the ideas, beliefs, and attitudes of others. Being critical means examining knowledge about language to democratize and enhance equity. The role of teachers taking a critical stance is to provide opportunity for discussion and inquiry into a range of diverse understandings. Sometimes the teacher presents alternative perspectives to help students question their own provincial beliefs and ethnocentric notions about language.

The heart of theme studies is the concept of active engagement by students in inquiry processes. Regardless of the different terminology and focuses of the scholars who write about theme studies, the following concepts are commonly agreed-upon principles:

Student Generated and Relevant: The topics of the themes are relevant to students' lives and emerge from their interests. After brainstorming and discussion, the students state their significant issues as major generalizations or questions such as, "In what ways is the language we use at home and at school the same or different?" or, "Why are there so many different languages in the world?" In order to solve the problems they pose, students choose many different ways to make connections to their own schema. Both teachers and students are involved in negotiating the curriculum and are significant to the planning process.

Authenticity: The study, the materials, the questions, and the problem solving relate to real-world experiences and are authentic within the context of their use. Students have a variety of resources available so that they are able to make connections and verify their learning. If for specific purposes such as test preparation language features such as spelling and grammar patterns are examined out of context, teachers and students make connections between the study topics and the real reading and writing experiences that are relevant to students' lives. The class engages in discussions about language credibility by understanding the value of firsthand materials such as personal letters, face-to-face interviews, and literacy artifacts that are used by real people in real-life settings. They examine school or academic language to understand how it extends learning. They realize that language changes to fit the needs of specific contexts.

Content and Integration: The knowledge, concepts, and generalizations of a subject matter domain of knowledge are the content of that subject matter. The concepts and generalizations related to a topic emerge as students raise their own questions and express their wonderings. Conceptual development and language development are recursive as they interrelate and impact each other. As a result, the focus on language is fundamental to every theme cycle in every subject matter. The more students understand the content they are exploring, the more they expand the language they use to talk about and investigate their developing knowledge and emerging concepts. The more they are able to talk about their learnings, the more they consider and expand the understandings of their concepts. Content areas are related to one another or integrated whenever appropriate, and they are informed by the physical and social sciences, the arts, and literature, although care must be taken not to integrate in artificial ways.

Democracy and Action: Throughout their inquiry, as students come to important conclusions they problem solve by presenting their ideas to others in a myriad of ways. As questions emerge from their daily lives, students are involved in learning to learn and come to understand their own ways of knowing. Students actively engage in collaboration and negotiation as part of a caring community, carefully listening to each other; respecting the rights of minority opinion; recognizing the richness of the diversity of culture, language, and dialect; and working toward a common good. The students expand on their inquiry by actively engaging in field trips to courtrooms, museums of tolerance, environmental sites, and many others to find ways to improve their lives or the lives of others. Darling-Hammond (1998) clearly states the importance of action-oriented education for democracy: "For democracy to survive and flourish, those who have been silenced need to find their voices. Those who have been marginalized need to seek, create, and find a myriad of possible places for themselves in society" (p. 91). Tyson and Kenreich (2001) discuss how to introduce students to social action through children's literacy by using text sets.

Planning and Reporting

Theresa Plaggett initiates her planning of language study theme cycles for her fourth graders at the beginning of the year by brainstorming with her students questions such as, "What do we want to know about language this year?" or "What questions do you have when you think about how you use language?" During the brainstorming, it becomes obvious that not all of her students are clear about what she means by studying language. So she keeps the discussion going over a two-week period, encouraging them to talk with each other and their family members about language issues they want to explore. Each time the class gathers to brainstorm potential study topics, they add to their list of questions as the kids gradually come to understand the possibilities for language study. Questions from one of Ms. Plaggett's classes included:

Why do we have to use handwriting and why can't we print all the time?

Why do people have more than one name?

Why do we have to edit our writing?

How come our grandparents speak two languages and we speak only one?

How come my parents go ballistic when I say things like . . . *like* or *dis* . . .?

Why is *word* spelled *word* and not *werd* like *herd* or *wird* like *bird*?

I want to know when to use hyphens, dots, and parentheses.

Once the students begin to focus on language issues, Ms. Plaggett waits a few days to allow time for ideating, asking students to brainstorm in small groups of three or four and to develop their own list of language questions or ideas, focusing on those they believe are most important or interesting. The students report back to the whole class the lists they have generated, and then a new group is formed with one student from each of the previous groups. Students combine and categorize the lists according to general concepts such as adult responses to kids' language, naming practices, slang, what words mean, and so on, and post the lists in the classroom. The students examine the topics for a few days and discuss which would be most exciting or interesting to study. The students vote or come to consensus on which topics they want to explore as a whole class. Ms. Plaggett reserves the right to order the sequence of the studies in order to control the time she needs to plan and gather resources, and to decide which topics fit best into the ongoing curriculum and other school activities throughout the year. Often new theme studies emerge from previous ones or from a current issue, and they are added throughout the year. Teachers of very young children often act as scribes as the children generate their ideas, and the teachers write the lists and help students see relations between questions in order to combine and categorize topics.

When I taught middle school, once we negotiated the topic I placed two columns on the board or on a chart headed "What do I know?" (about the topic) on one side and "What questions do I have?" (about the topic) on the second column (Y. Goodman, Watson, & Burke, 1996). As students generated their questions, a student wrote the statements or questions in the appropriate column. Next to the questions they raised we wrote the name of the student or students along with the date. We agreed that no one could reject a "What do I know?" statement in the first column, but students could challenge a statement by listing a question in the second column in response to a knowledge statement. This postponed disagreements till after further research. The students then took responsibility for organizing into small groups to pursue particular questions, leading the small groups, facilitating any related class discussions, and reporting back to the whole class. As the theme cycle continued and the students learned new things, they would cross out statements or questions and add new ones in different colors with the date. In this way, we were continuously evaluating changes in our thinking as we revisited our earlier thinking. As the students wondered about statements and challenged one another, they posed new problems related to their discoveries, and their deliberations often became the focus of new and sustained inquiry. Students' expanded conceptual schemas involved the use of new and familiar language as they presented their ideas to others. Donna Ogle (1986) is often referenced for a similar planning organization called K-W-L, in which students make three columns headed K—What we know; W—What we want to find out; and L—What we learned and still need to know.

Debra Goodman involves her middle-grade students in planning their theme cycle study by using the recursive learning phases of perceiving, ideating, and presenting:

Perceiving: Topic Selection/Planning
Topic negotiated: What do we want to learn about?
Prior knowledge shared: What do we know already?
Questions generated: What do we want to know?

Experience, materials: How can we find out?
People, space, and time organized: How can we best learn to-
gether?
Engagements and invitations: How do we best get involved?

Ideating: Learning Experiences/Literacy Uses
Authentic experiences: How do real scientists find out things?
Integrated curriculum: How does language/literacy help us learn?
Interactions: What experiences allow us to explore with each
other?

Presentations/Evaluations
Sharing and presenting: What did we learn?
Evaluating together: How did we do and what do we do about
it?

Perceiving

The teacher organizes for a range of possibilities. Materials are
displayed in various learning centers on bookcases, easels, tables,
or ledges so that they are inviting and accessible. The displays
include collections of books, magazines, newspapers, charts, articles, letters, lists of Web sites, films, recordings, photographs,
and other artifacts related to the theme topic. Teachers post related poems, songs, and favorite passages from their reading on
banners or posters around the room and invite the students to
add to the collection as the theme cycle gets under way. Often the
teacher or a student reads aloud one of the relevant books or
newspaper articles to initiate a theme cycle and to raise its significance to a conscious level.

Ideating

Space and time are organized to provide many opportunities for
talk with peers and interaction with a wide variety of adults. To
legitimize ideating opportunities, learning centers are organized
as places for quiet talking, thinking, and dreaming: a classroom
library with comfortable furniture, including dolls and fuzzy toys
for younger children; an art and publishing center with art and
writing materials; a listening center with CD players and head-
sets; a class museum to facilitate labeling and displaying artifacts

(Jorgensen, 1993). Materials are readily available, and students have time to jot notes; diagram; sketch and illustrate; compose music, stories, and reports; and listen to recordings individually or in small groups. Students discuss the richness of these different symbol systems for their learning and, based on similar questions or problems, the class organizes into interest groups to provide each class member the opportunity to have an environment in which to wonder about the topic selected for in-depth study.

Students consider ways to conduct their research during this part of their planning. If, for example, students decide they need to interview others, they discuss successful ways to proceed and explore possible pitfalls. They discuss the ethics of getting permission from people and how to let informants know the purposes and limitations of their research. They become involved in interviewing academic experts; discussing topics brought up in class with family and community members; gathering additional data about features of language they need more information about; searching the Web and libraries, learning how to gather a range of human and physical resources; and taking trips to verify ideas, answer their questions, and continue their learning.

Presenting and Evaluation

Making decisions about reporting and evaluating is integral to the planning process. Although students' discoveries and understandings are reported and shared informally throughout a theme study, there are times when the project culminates in a formal oral or written report. In Chapter 4, I discuss strategy lessons that focus on informal and formal ways to share in class and ways to evaluate these presentations. Such lessons can take place early in the theme cycle or whenever they are most appropriate. Evaluations are integral to final project presentations and research conclusions.

Students present formal written reports when there are important reasons for doing so. Time is set aside so students have opportunities to revise, edit, and share their results with others. Their theme cycle group is often part of their writing group for these purposes. Teachers encourage collaborative reports written by a small group of students who refine their thinking as they discuss their discoveries together. Teachers who work with very young children ask them to gather the notes they've taken about a topic, and the children write the report together with the teacher as the scribe.

As students report on what they have learned, they revisit their inquiry procedures and share their excitement and new understandings. They often rewrite earlier questions and statements. Class members have the opportunity to respond, and students push one another's thinking into disequilibrium or tensions that result in new concepts and language. Reports are printed, shared with parents, placed in the library, and shared with other classes.

Not all reports, however, need to be written. Some theme cycle presentations work best when students share informally throughout the inquiry or present orally using written field notes. Other theme cycle inquiries are presented in the form of charts, models, or diagrams organized as poster sessions and displayed for a few weeks in the classroom, library, or school corridors. Other classes and community members can be invited to visit and participate in these demonstrations. Taking photographs during theme cycle study is another powerful way to record and present the learning that has taken place. As the students revisit the photographs in an album or on a poster board and discuss their activities, they reflect on their own development and expand their understandings.

Evaluation is obviously a part of all these experiences. Students not only evaluate their writing and other forms of presentations with one another and their teacher, but they also discuss when it is most appropriate to present their findings orally or in writing and whether the style should be formal or informal.

CHAPTER FIVE

Focus on Language and Linguistics

The theme cycles discussed in this chapter focus on aspects of learning about language, building on ideas and knowledge from linguists and other language scholars. The sections in the chapter include:

- ◆ Language Use
- ◆ Language Processes
- ◆ Language Variation
- ◆ Language History and Development
- ◆ Language Form

Because of the cyclical nature of language and thinking, there is often overlap among topics. In addition, teachers enrich students' learning experiences when they integrate language study into other aspects of the curriculum.

Language Use

A multiage fifth- and sixth-grade class in Australia is studying systems of the human body. The school is located in an immigrant community with families from Greece, Yugoslavia, Italy, and India. The teachers are aware that the students often are embarrassed about using their personal terms, often not in English, about body parts or elimination processes. And they often use the language of their English-speaking peers but not always in appropriate ways. Even the English-only speakers are not always sure about the appropriate language to use in school related to body parts and functions. In response to some students' arguments about such language use, the teachers plan a language study theme cycle to accompany the study of the various systems of the human body.

First the students trace each other's bodies onto large sheets of butcher paper. The drawings are then hung from the ceilings and on the walls, and the teachers encourage the students to label the body parts on the drawing of their own body and to compare with one another the terms they use. The students invariably use the terms common in their language community or commonsense English terms such as *bum* and *titty.*

The browsing area includes all kinds of scientific books, charts, and models about the human body as well as dictionaries and thesauruses, including ones in languages other than English that some of the students can read and write. Throughout the theme cycle study, the students search Web sites, invite speakers to their class, including parents who work in health professions, and plan fields trips to museums and science laboratories.

Although the focus of the study is on understanding how their bodily systems work and on related health issues that concern preadolescents, language is also a major focus. The students discover the similarities among family terms about the body and how these terms are used in different languages. They discover that some scientific terms have closer historical ties to their first languages than they do to English. Many scientific terms have their origins in Greek and Latin, while the English terms are often four-letter words derived from the Anglo Saxon. Students discuss the relative status of Latin and Greek compared to Anglo Saxon and wonder whether the historical status of a language has influence on whether some words are considered slang, even taboo, while others are acceptable in scientific settings.

By listing the settings in which different terms occur, students discover that the scientific terms are more appropriate for academic settings, such as writing or reading reports, and decide that some terms are acceptable in all contexts, others are acceptable with their friends, and still others are appropriate mostly in academic situations. Throughout the study, the students add to their body portraits the scientific terms they are learning, alongside their vernacular language.

Language use theme cycles help students become consciously aware of their language strengths. In *The Languages Book*, written for students and rich in language study ideas, Raleigh (1981) helps students discover their language expertise:

> Everyone has managed the amazing job of learning at least one language—and, when you think about it, you use even one language in so many different ways that even one is a lot. So you're the expert; make sure you tell the others what you know about language and the way it works. (p. ii)

In this section on language use, I suggest theme cycles that involve students in examining their own language use and the language of others to build understandings about vernacular or everyday language use, about literacy digs and the study of signs, and about students' use of language in group interactions.

Vernacular Language

The perceiving phase of a theme cycle on vernacular language often emerges from discussions, arguments, or controversies about specific language use that occur during critical-moment teaching or strategy lessons. Or the teacher reads a current newspaper editorial that bemoans the ways in which young people use language these days. The specific controversial items (an example might be "that sucks") are listed on the board, and the students interview each other, older and younger students in the school, and the adults in their homes and communities to find out whether people should use such language and what they think the phrase means.

With the students, the teacher anticipates what materials the class will need in order to collect data, such as clipboards, notepaper, and pencils, and they discuss ways to take notes, establish rapport, and introduce the study to their informants. The class discusses abbreviations to use in their field notes and the language to use in interviews so as not to influence their informants' responses. Elena Tapia (1999) recommends that students consider the kinds of words to avoid, such as *acceptable, correct, proper,* and *right,* during their interviews: "These words and their opposites simply evoke comments on good and bad grammar, preventing the candidate and the respondent from talking about social and educational issues which might relate to the usage" (p. 300).

The students take notes or tape-record their interviews and examine the responses in order to list examples of the language that people use. They discover the pejorative terms people use for language they consider inappropriate, such as *slang, profanity, blasphemy,* or *dirty words,* and discuss the attitudes and moral issues that such responses represent. Once the students have a list of terms, they organize into small groups, and each group selects a few of the terms to document further and records definitions and examples from a range of sources. My computer lists *colloquial, argot, cant, idiom, lingo, jargon, patois, pidgin,* and *dialect* among many others as synonyms for *vernacular.* Students explore whether they think the terms are negative, positive, scientific, or emotional. They come to realize that some terms such as *dialect* and *pidgin* have both scientific and commonsense meanings, while terms such as *bad words* or *lingo* are part of common usage but not considered meaningful terms in linguistic circles.

The small groups share their work with the whole class, and the students then categorize the terms, including their definitions. Students compare the terms and the categories, noting which groups of people such as friends, parents, teachers, linguists, and so on consider the language to be appropriate. Or students examine how language is labeled inappropriate or appropriate by people of different occupations, ages, or racial backgrounds. They then discuss why there are such strong differences of opinion.

During the interviews, the students ask their informants for additional examples of language they consider to be inappropriate or appropriate. Students add to their categories and keep notes on the settings in which different people believe that specific language is appropriate or not, such as school, home, the community, television, or videos. The class invites linguists or others knowledgeable about language to respond to their discoveries and to discuss their views about vernacular language use.

Many of the terms that emerge from such explorations are derogatory toward different ethnic, racial, linguistic, or alternative lifestyle groups. The teacher and students need to analyze critically such terms in relation to how the terms are used to maintain power relationships in society. I stimulate such discussions by asking students to consider whether people are more concerned about taboo terms that relate to sexual acts or cursing or about words that stereotype and demean groups of people, and why.

Explorations of vernacular language use prompt students to consider their own use of language in school contexts and the reasons for such use—for instance, to gain attention or to control others. Understandings that emerge from in-depth studies about taboo language include what function it serves, who benefits from its use, who is harmed by its use, when and where it is used, and why some language is taboo to some folks and not to others (Andersson & Trudgill, 1990; Thomas & Tchudi, 1999).

Many examples the students find fit into grammatical categories. These examples might develop into a theme cycle separate from one that focuses on taboo or "bad" words. A third-grade classroom listed the following examples of inappropriate sentences, which came up in interviews with their parents:

Me and Joan are going to the football game tonight.

I did good.

I don't do nothing right.

Terry, she, is really a good skater.

That was very fun.

You ain't doing it right.

We've gotta go.

Upper elementary and middle school teachers have successfully adapted to their classes an activity that Elena Tapia (1999, p. 297) uses with her teachers to study what the public believes are nonstandard uses of language and what they think about it. She asks her students to first complete sentences such as the following themselves:

It [drives me crazy, annoys me, irritates me, etc.] when people say [*ain't*].
When I hear them say this, it makes me think they [are ignorant].

(The brackets show what the answers might be, but students get the sentences with blanks provided.) After discussing their own responses to the sentences, the students interview members of the public to gather their responses. As the students categorize the responses, they explore grammatical categories such as pronouns, irregular verbs, negative concord, and subject-verb agreement (p. 299). Once they begin to notice the various language features and to categorize them, the students then conduct additional interviews and examine different books about language and linguistics in order to verify their categories and conclusions. The results of their studies can be published as individual or group dictionaries, thesauruses, or rulebooks that define terms, the controversies related to their use, and the contexts in which they are or are not considered appropriate.

A number of major language concepts emerge from theme cycles on vernacular language use: (1) language is neither good nor bad, neither correct nor incorrect; rather, what is considered appropriate language is dependent on the context in which it is used; (2) some language is acceptable with peers but not with members of older generations; (3) language acceptability often varies from one cultural group to another; (4) meaning is specific to the context in which language is used; and (5) some vocabulary terms have the same pronunciation but different meanings depending on the context, the content of the discussion, and the people participating. The word *problem,* which means different things in the context of the home and in the fields of math, science, and literature, is a good example.

Another important concept is that when people use language that others consider inappropriate, issues of power and control are involved. When, for instance, the most educated or wealthiest members of society label the language of certain groups as inappropriate or inferior, they are attempting to control those groups, sometimes oppressing them into voicelessness. Some people make negative statements about the language of teenagers or certain working-class groups because of their negative attitude toward those specific groups, not simply because of teenagers' or working-class individuals' language use.

Literacy Digs

In her seventh-grade classroom, Roberta Truitt asks her students to empty their purses, backpacks, and pockets and to set aside the articles they find with writing on them. They then organize these items into categories and list the articles according to the different functions they serve. Lynn Ward asks his second-grade students to fill a shoebox with things they write and read at home and bring them to school to demonstrate their personal uses of literacy. In these ways, the teachers initiate a theme cycle in which students explore the ways in which literacy impacts their daily lives. The teachers also participate in the activity and together with the students explore questions such as:

> What purpose does the print serve for the reader? The author of the print?
>
> Is the writing more important for the reader or for the writer?
>
> Why is the material written the way it is?

To extend their in-depth study of literacy uses, the students document the literacy events of parents and members of their community and interview them using questions similar to those they used to examine their own uses of literacy. They take field notes and photographs to document the many ways people use literacy. They develop charts to categorize who reads and writes in which contexts and what they read and write, and they compare the literacy uses and purposes of others to the categories and lists of their own uses. The students observe and document literacy events in restaurants, supermarkets, and hotels and on television, airplanes, and buses. The focus is on the contexts in which literacy takes place, the people in the contexts, and the ways in which they use literacy. Students report their results to the class and revisit previous charts and categories in order to make new discoveries and develop new questions.

The teachers in these classrooms are adapting Denny Taylor's (1993) concept of *literacy dig*, which refers to the ways researchers gather data about when, how, and why people read and write.

Students come to realize that literacy use is pervasive and that reading and writing are not limited to classrooms or only for academic purposes. They realize that different people have different notions about literacy, and they develop their own conceptualizations about the role that literacy plays in their lives.

Signs

As the perceiving phase of a theme cycle on the use of signs in the environment, kindergarten teacher Carmen Gonzales plans a sign safari through the school and another safari through the neighborhood. On their clipboards, the children take notes, draw the signs, and make lists of the print they see, indicating where print is placed, and they discuss with one another the functions the print serves and its meanings. Ms. Gonzales takes photographs of the safari so the children are able to revisit and discuss the experience later. (Teachers are sometimes able to get cameras for classroom use from the various camera companies such as Kodak. Some Web sites for camera companies include suggestions for ways students can explore the science and art of photography, which expands language study into other content areas.)

A day or two after the print safari, the students share their notes and discuss the role of the print, diagrams, color, font, and images on the signs. They consider the advantages and disadvantages of the print compared with the nonalphabetic symbols. The students interview family members and friends who travel to different states and countries for information on the ways signs are used in other places. When students take trips with their families, they are encouraged to keep a notebook or take photographs of new signs they discover. After the students have viewed the photographs of their safari and discussed additional aspects of signs in the environment, they culminate their theme study by writing an individual or class book titled "Signs I/We Can Read." They write a second volume at the end of the year to demonstrate their reading and writing growth.

Ilsa Curran, working with third graders, says that she plans the perceiving phase of a signs-in-the-environment theme cycle by sharing a favorite sign book such as Tana Hoban's *I Walk and Read* (1984). The students notice which signs are most common and which are unusual and raise questions that lead to discussions of the functions that signs serve, such as safety and traffic control, information and directions, and labeling and identification. Students chart the categories with specific examples from the book and add others as they read other materials. They keep notes about the signs they see on their way to and from school and bring their data to class to verify their categories and make appropriate additions or changes and add to the chart over time. Some of Ms. Curran's students become interested in the procedures that photographers or illustrators follow to organize and display their art in published books and use what they learn to design their own books. One year her students discovered that a street sign on a major road in the community was written as Wilmout Rd. instead of Wilmont. They wondered how such a misspelling could occur and why no one seemed to have noticed it over the long period it had been up. The students invited someone from the city government to their class to talk about the sign. Not only was the sign eventually changed, but also the students learned a lot about the complexity of sign placement in the city traffic control department.

Many middle school teachers adapt the print safari theme cycle that Pat Rigg (1992) uses with ESL students. Dr. Rigg initiates this theme with her students early in the year in order to build community and help students develop a sense of their reading proficiency. She sets up a browsing table that includes books featuring environmental print on streets, malls, shopping centers, billboards, and vehicles, as well as magazine pictures, photos, slides, replicas of signs available at teacher supply stores, and charts of signs originally belonging to a driving school or the license bureau. The students add related materials as the theme cycle develops. The class examines the environmental print in the room and records the signs they see. They discuss the purposes and functions of the signs and then leave the room in small groups or pairs to collect data on signs found around the school and the neighborhood, expanding their circle of environmental print during each data-collection period. As they pass stores, buildings, and food or money machines, they draw or take photographs of the environmental print they encounter.

When the students return to class, they compare notes and categorize their examples. Students not native to the United States learn a great deal about U.S. culture as they explore the meanings of environmental print and the functions it serves. Dr. Rigg encourages the students to transcribe their notes by writing examples on 3" x 5" cards. In this way, the examples are more readable and it is easy for small groups of students to place or move the cards into categories according to their functions and where they are found. The students present the results of their inquiry by developing rock music videos, slide shows, or posters to demonstrate the print they encounter and its control and influence on their lives.

In research about signs in the environment, students inevitably raise questions about graffiti and tagging. The controversies that surround the use of graffiti are of high interest to middle school students and lead to lively discussions about the rights of adolescents to express their own identities and the rights of private and public property owners.

Students also discover that signs are used for discriminatory purposes. In their reading, they encounter references to signs such as For Whites Only; No One Under 18 May Enter; No Irish Need Apply; Women and Children's Room. In a sixth-grade classroom, one student brought to class a photograph of a sign from a local bagel shop that read, We Reserve the Right to Refuse Service to Anyone. A group of students decided to interview the owners of the establishment; they also asked customers what they thought about the sign. The students discussed the sign from the point of view and purpose of the author of the sign (business owner) and considered what message such a sign sent to its readers (customers). They explored how the sign was written, where it was placed, and the ways in which environmental print is used to exclude specific groups.

Although most books about signs are written and illustrated for young children, middle-grade and middle school students also learn a lot from these books. An effective selection of books by photographers and illustrators that focus on signs and other environmental print and that are great for read-alouds, browsing tables, and text sets includes:

Tomie dePaola, *The Knight and the Dragon* (1980)

Candace Fleming, *The Hatmaker's Sign: A Story by Benjamin Franklin* (2000)

Ron and Nancy Goor, *Signs* (1983)

Tana Hoban, *I Read Signs* (1983)

Tana Hoban, *I Read Symbols* (1999)

Tana Hoban, *I Walk and Read* (1984)

George Ella Lyon, *A Sign* (1998)

Tiphaine Samoyault, (1997) *Give Me a Sign! What Pictograms Tell Us without Words*

The major concepts that emerge from in-depth study of the use of environmental print include the understanding that the ability to read environmental print is one of the strongest roots of the development of literacy (Y. Goodman, 1980). Throughout the world, children come to understand a great deal about their writing systems as they are immersed in print. In addition, students learn that written language serves a range of purposes and functions in their daily lives. Students appreciate knowing that they were already readers of their environment long before they came to school and that they know a lot about literacy in their world.

Language in Group Interactions

Tracy Smiles, a middle school teacher, enjoys discussing language with her students so much that Megan, one of her eighth graders, said to her one day in a teasing tone, "Ms. Smiles, you're just obsessed with language." In order to heighten her students' awareness of how they use language, Ms. Smiles researches the kinds of language her students use in her classes as they talk to each other. She tape-records her students' language in different settings and then has them listen to the tapes and discuss among themselves the functions their language serves. Initially, her students are surprised by their language, and then they become interested in learning more about why they use language the way they do. As they categorize the language they use, they discover that their talk is laden with teasing, insults, gossip, talk about other classes at school, and playful uses of language even while they are discussing their literature book or exploring experiments in science or problems in math. They begin to wonder why they banter, use sarcasm, and make negative and positive comments about one another.

The students discover that some in their group are silent participants and that *just listening* is safe. As they raise questions about their language use, they tape their talk in different contexts, take notes, and add to their conclusions. They discover that the less talkative students are actively listening, laughing at jokes, and writing down their own revelations. Students note how their different kinds of talk fulfill their adolescent desire to belong to and interact with their peer group. They come to understand that their talk builds self-confidence, social skills, self-understanding, and a sense of humor. They begin to suggest to each other ways in which the more silent participants can get more involved in talk and the ways in which the most talkative participants can become better listeners. They become aware that their bantering might hurt someone in the group and consider when bantering is recognized as teasing or as a form of endearment. With this newfound awareness, students conclude that they want to be sensitive about the feelings of their classmates and that language use is an important way of showing feelings and concern for one another.

The students also use language play and, with Ms. Smiles, they begin to document their inventions such as, in one particular class, *chick-n-frick, shock-a-baac,* and names for fruits such as *papalope* and *mangorange.* At first these students didn't understand why they made up words, but eventually they realized that when they used such language with one another they often laughed hysterically, which made them feel like buddies. The students became aware of the social nature of language, realizing that language play builds camaraderie or group solidarity but also can make some students feel like outsiders (see *Frindle* by Andrew Clements [1998]).

Ms. Smiles's focus on language was of great interest to her students, and a number of them followed up the class inquiry with individual expert theme cycles. Amy, for example, decided to study notes that students write to each other during and between classes. In her final report she wrote:

> That's what this [students' notes] is all about, the ungraded, misspelled work that has no length requirement. This is about the secretive, behind the scenes writing. This is where I tell you what the kids really want to write about, how much they really pay attention to mechanics and what the real due dates are.

Amy wrote notes to her friends and asked them to write back to her. She then analyzed the different kinds of language use and discussed her findings with her teacher and her friends. She discovered that when students write notes they engage with many different topics and use different styles and lengths in their writing. Amy wrote about privacy issues and in-group abbreviations such as "w/b" (watch your back) and "what's ↑ [up]" and showed how her peers write about the same event with differing perceptions of the incident. She concluded her study: "I still would like to know why kids write notes, especially when they complain about writing a paper in school two minutes later, but that's for another study."

Drew, another of Ms. Smiles's students, studied his own personal language use. He kept a list of the vocabulary he used that was not in common usage, defined the terms, and asked his friends if they understood what he was saying and what he meant. He then created an illustrated book of his day showing where and how he used different terms. One page of his book, for example, starts with:

> Drew enters the P.E. locker room and says *Yosk* to people he knows. He exchanges funny stories about things that have happened. [*Yosk* is defined in his glossary as "my way of saying hi."]

Taylor and a group of her friends explored a number of topics as they planned their theme cycle, such as, Why do alternate spellings and shorthand appear in our reading and writing? and Why do we talk in certain ways with certain people?

As the students began to discuss how to collect data, Ms. Smiles introduced the topic of ethical ways to gather information, focusing especially on the issue of privacy. Taylor shows an understanding of the issue in her final report:

> To start my research I collected actual data from my peers. I did this by logging a long and meaningful conversation I had with my friends on AOL. To keep the conversation real, I first started the logging and waited until the end to ask for permission to use that conversation for this research project. My policy was that if they didn't want me to use it, I would destroy it and later collect new data. Fortunately, my friends gave me permission and I was able to use the data.

Another kind of research into language interaction involves students in collecting language samples of different people in different contexts where lots of people talk to one another, such as the supermarket, park, movie, hotel or mall lobby, or bus station. Students pick a spot and observe for a fifteen-minute period. Or they observe people in places where language use is usually quiet, such as the church, library, or classroom. Students take field notes and record gestures, body language, and use of reading and writing while the informants are talking. The students need to be prepared to answer questions about their use of tape recorders and to consider whether they need permission from their informants and how to obtain it. One helpful strategy is for the class to compose a letter signed by the teacher for students to carry indicating that they are involved in a school-based language research study.

From these various settings, the students examine the kinds of language people use when they make requests, persuade, inquire, insult, or argue. A number of authors such as Barnes (1995) and Lindfors (1999) have studied students' talk in classrooms. Teachers who plan to involve their students in researching their language interactions find these works helpful.

Teachers need to keep in mind a few cautions during theme cycle studies. First, it is important not to run any research into the ground. If students lose interest, the teacher should consider terminating the study before boredom sets in. If a few students are still anxious to continue their research, individual or small group expert projects provide opportunities for them to do so. Second, teachers need to help the students be selective about the amount of data they collect, analyze, and report. Their transcripts should not be too long, especially for group discussion or writing activities. It takes a long time for a class to discuss even two pages of transcription.

Language Processes

Theme cycles related to the study of language processes help students become consciously aware of how their brains use and learn oral and written language. Since students' attitudes about their language abilities are integral to the ways in which they use language, theme cycles involve students in talking and thinking about how they read, write, and use oral language while considering what they are already capable of doing. When we help students became aware of what they do well in their use of language, they are more willing to take risks and explore unfamiliar areas of language use. In this section, I suggest theme cycles that focus on self-reflection, especially as it relates to writing and reading.

Self-Reflection

As a teacher of sixth to eighth graders, I often started my language theme studies early in the year by asking students to gather in small groups and list the kinds of talk, reading, and writing they do that is successful for them. At times, depending on the needs of the group, we would focus on one language process at a time. We then discussed the results of the students' lists with the whole class. This perceiving phase of a self-reflection theme cycle provided my students with a way to discover their own language strengths and to realize that their abilities and concerns about language use are legitimate areas of inquiry. At the same time, I learned what my students believed about their own language use and gained insight into their concerns and insecurities.

At this point, I shared with the students my language-learning goals, which included that they develop flexibility in speaking and writing by building on what they already know and can do well. I asked them to keep a list of their own goals in a language-learning log, which they shared with me and with their peers. For privacy purposes, the students had control over which parts of their journal they shared. The students and I revisited our goals and log entries prior to grading periods to note their growth and plan additional inquiries. Students' goals included items such as write better in cursive; talk less; do better on tests; not be afraid to talk in front of the class; get along better with my sister; find more authors I love to read.

I encouraged students to jot down their personal reactions to the ways they engage in reading, writing, and oral language experiences. In their writing journals, the students documented the kinds of help that got them started, what interrupted their flow of writing, and what slowed them down or caused them to stop. They also kept track of what they liked to write about and special quotations from their reading they wanted to remember or to share with others. Their journals included diagrams, doodles, and artwork that represented their responses to their learning. Students shared their journals in small study groups that met regularly to consider the successful strategies students used, what to do when their strategies were not successful, how to improve in areas in which they were not confident, and in general to continue to wonder about the process.

When my daughter was a student at the University of Michigan, Dan Fader, a nationally known writing professor, organized her writing class so that members worked together in pairs. Not only did they read and respond to each other's journals, but they also read each other's work, helped with revising and editing, and reflected on and evaluated their processes and products together. Ever since, I have used such collaborations in all my classes. When students take responsibility for one another in these ways, their learning expands, their quality of work improves, and their self-reflection process is enriched.

Self-reflection journals also become the repository for ideas for theme studies. Arguments or controversies that crop up in small groups are brought to the whole class for discussion, and students' questions become the focus of new inquiry studies. In my classes, students discussed issues such as whether people read books more than once, whether readers were permitted to stop reading a book they didn't like, when people used cursive or print in their writing, or when to handwrite or use a computer. Opportunities for ideating about their language processes helped the students realize that through discussion and talk with peers and teachers they were able to discover more effective strategies for solving their problems with reading, writing, or speaking. As a result of such explorations, students revisited their language-learning goals and set new ones.

Some teachers initiate students' self-reflection on their language processes by using interviews that prompt students to think about what they do as they read, write, or use oral language. A group of teachers who used a reading interview with their students adapted the questions to writing (Y. Goodman, Watson, & Burke, 1987, p. 219–20). The questions are easily adaptable to different areas of the curriculum such as spelling or editing.

Writing Interview

1. When you are writing and stop to think, what do you think about?

2. Name a good writer that you know. Why is _____ a good writer?

3. If you knew someone was having trouble as a writer, what would you do to help that person?

4. How did you learn to write?

5. Are you a good writer? Why or why not?

6. What would you like to do better as a writer?

These questions lead to a discussion in which students reflect on themselves as writers (in this case) and on the diverse ways in which others think about the writing process. In exploring the process, students are often surprised to discover that the practices they consider to be evidence of their status as poor writers are similar to the practices of peers, teachers, and even professional authors. They discover, for example, that good readers or writers do not look up in the dictionary every word they don't understand or don't know how to spell, and they explore the different strategies they use in such situations.

The Reading Process

Debra Goodman (1999) uses a learning-to-ride-a-bike metaphor to stimulate students' thinking about how they learn and to initiate the perceiving phase of examining their own reading processes. She asks them to remember how they learned to ride a bike, and then they compare those processes with learning to read. The students in her class conclude that in order to learn to ride a bike, a number of conditions must exist: (1) you have to want to ride, (2) you learn best by riding a lot or practicing, and (3) you fall down a lot but you have to get right back on and keep riding. As they consider the metaphor over time, students realize that in order to learn to ride they first need to have a bike. It's hard to learn without appropriate equipment. Students note that riding up a hill or around a curve is more difficult than riding on a straight street, and you need to learn to do each activity in its appropriate context.

With Dr. Goodman, the students then explore the ways in which learning to ride a bike is similar to learning to read: (1) they need to want to read, (2) they must have a range of materials and read a lot, and (3) when they make mistakes, they need to keep reading. She then extends the discussion by encouraging the students to compare the reading process to being a detective discovering clues in order to solve a case—the process is a continuous search for meaning. She invites her students to join the Reading Detective Club, through which they become aware of what they know about language as they read, what they do to search for meaning as they read, and the roles that miscues play in constructing meaning. The students become conscious of how they discover meaning and grammatical clues as they read and when it is most advantageous to use graphophonic clues. They explore questions such as: When you read and come to something you don't know, what do you do? What strategies do other readers use? What do the best readers you know do? Debra Goodman's development of this search for clues in reading resulted in the publication *The Reading Detective Club: Solving the Mysteries of Reading* (1999).

I call such self-reflection on the reading process *retrospective miscue analysis* (RMA) (Y. Goodman, 1999). Teachers working with students of a wide age and ability range involve them in examining their own miscues and the strategies they use to solve the problems they face while they are reading. These strategies are kept for the entire class on a strategies-for-reading chart or individually in students' reading journals. As students share their insights in class or in small groups about the ways they use strategies and language cuing systems, they consider which strategies are most efficient and how strategies change or are influenced by different genres, the complexity of the language, and the reader's familiarity with the concepts. In one fourth-grade class, the students made a bookmark that listed the reading strategies they used: keep on going; only correct when it doesn't make sense; make predictions based on what already happened in the story; if you don't understand a word, keep looking for it later; and use illustrations and diagrams.

Language Variation

A theme cycle about language variation is the focus of the Australian film *Language at Twelve* (Manefield, 1976). A teacher and her sixth graders are discussing why different people speak English in different ways. They organize in groups to plan interviews with people who speak very differently. They decide on a disc jockey, the chief executive officer of a major department store, a car salesman, and a union organizer (all of the interviewees are male). The class then discusses how to set up the appointments and plan for transportation. They brainstorm the questions they will ask and the procedures they will follow and gather the material they need. They are especially interested in finding out how the interviewees use language differently, if they are aware of how their language differs from others', and what they believe about the differences. The students tape-record the interviews, take field notes, and transcribe the most important conversations in order to report back to the class.

The students discover that a person's socioeconomic status helps determine how that person views language variation. The CEO of the department store believes there is only one proper way to speak and that he always speaks the same way, even when he talks to his dog. The other men are more aware of their language shifts. The disc jockey speaks Australian English during his interview with the students but explains that in order to be popular, on the air he has to use American English, speak fast, and use high and emphatic tones. The union organizer tells the students that he has to be conscious of shifts in his language. In order to communicate with "my mates [his fellow union members], I need to talk the way they do. I need to make myself very clear and they understand that language best." The salesman explains how he speaks differently to the older couples who come to buy a comfortable car than he does to a young man looking for something "sporty."

Because the students still have questions, they decide to listen to the language they tape-recorded more closely to discover other changes in their informants' language. Then they decide to use what they discover to interview these individuals again and to set up similar interviews with people from other walks of life, especially women.

Through their many experiences with different people's language, most students are already aware of language variation. At very young ages, children notice that people speak different languages and dialects and that they speak differently in different contexts and when they are in different moods. Students also become aware that language differences are represented in written forms as well. Variations in writing are influenced by the function and purpose writing serves, the audience, the subject matter, and the context. Some people read languages they do not speak and some speak and understand languages in which they are not literate. In this section, I suggest theme cycles that allow students to examine language, dialect, and register differences in oral and written language.

Language Diversity

I often initiate a language diversity theme cycle by writing on the board or on an overhead transparency, "What would happen if people didn't have language?" The discussion that follows heightens students' perceptions about the functions of language and language diversity. Vivian Paley's *Wally's Stories* (1981) skillfully documents her kindergarten students' sophisticated responses during a discussion considering whether they would create only one language or many languages if they were in charge of the world. Akemi concludes: "If everyone speak Japan, everyone have to live there. My country too small for the big America" (p. 120).

After an initial discussion, and in response to language diversity questions, I invite students to document their language variations and the flexibility with which they shift language by charting the different ways they use their language(s) as they speak, read, listen, and write. Although I provide a basic introduction to terms on the chart by responding to students' questions, I assure them that as they gather the information and discuss the results in class, we will continue to explore the terms and concepts in class.

In their language profiles (Figure 6), students note people, kinds of texts, their own abilities, and when and where they use reading, writing, speaking, and listening in their primary language. They do the same for any additional languages they use even if they use a second language only minimally. The teacher also shares her profile with the students.

After considering their personal language profiles, the students interview a range of people and develop their language profiles. If no students, family members, or community members speak a language other than English, the teacher helps the students find e-mail or pen pals who speak other languages. As students explore the various languages spoken in their communities, they discover lists of languages and language families and related terms. Students know that language is often constrained by national boundaries, but they are sometimes surprised to discover that some nations comprise many language groups and that the same language is spoken in different nations. They learn that a language belongs to a family of languages, although English, which is considered a Germanic language, is so different from German that German and English speakers cannot understand each other. Through their research, they are able to categorize the languages spoken in their communities and discover additional information about how many languages there are in the world and who speaks them. Many Web sites concerned with specific languages provide a wealth of information helpful to students' inquiries. The April 2000 issue of *Kids Discover* focuses

		My Language Profile		

Name _____ Age_____

Language(s) I speak, listen, read, write
(Write comments or examples where appropriate)

Language	Speak	Listen	Read	Write
L1	Where do I speak? When and where? With whom? How well?	Where do I listen? When and where? With whom? How well?	What types do I read? When and where? With whom? How well?	What do I write? When and where? With and for whom? How well?
L2				

FIGURE 6. *My language profile form.*

on a language theme and includes a language family tree ("Your Family," 2000).

Exploring the myths, folktales, and Bible stories about the origins of language is another way to initiate a theme cycle on language diversity. The Web site http://logos.uoregon.edu/ polyphonia/babel.html includes the story of the Tower of Babel in Genesis 11:1–7, as well as a range of stories from around the world that are comparable to the Tower of Babel story, which states:

And the Lord said, "Behold, they are one people, and they all have one language; and this is only the beginning of what they will do; and nothing that they propose to do will now be impossible for them. Come, let us go down, and there confuse their language, that they may not understand one another's speech."

Students plan and conduct interviews with both religious and secular leaders to get their interpretations of this story and then read and present the various interpretations, including their own, to the class. At this Web site, the term *myth* is used instead of *story,* terminology that raises issues for students and teachers to explore through a question such as, "Why are biblical narratives called *stories* and narratives that come from other belief systems such as Native American or Asian cultures called *myths?*" The result of this inquiry generally includes appreciation for the large number of languages in the world and positive attitudes toward world languages and the people who speak them.

Language diversity theme cycles often extend to an exploration of symbol systems that are considered "special languages" or other communication systems: e.g., drumming languages of Africa, computer languages, animal communications, picture languages, body language, etc. The students explore these "languages" as systems and their roles in communication, and compare characteristic similarities and differences of special languages and the languages they know such as English, Spanish, Hmong, or Russian.

Register and Dialect Variations

In a multilingual, multicultural school in Israel, a group of teachers, including the drama and music teachers, and their fifth-grade students planned to explore the different versions of English spoken in the world, at the same time that they were learning English as a second (or third or fourth) language. As a result, they examined both dialect and register differences. Throughout the year, they read and performed musical productions of *Westside Story, Romeo and Juliet,* and *Fiddler on the Roof* in English. The students wondered about the different ways that English is used by different people in so many different walks of life. They explored the English spoken in these musicals by the different characters, including the various dialects and registers, and researched the influences on English of people from different socioeconomic backgrounds, national origins, and historical periods. In each case, the role of convention in specific historical contexts was a major focus of discussion. In order to perform these works, the group also explored ways to use dialects that showed respect for the people they were portraying and minimized the possibility of inaccuracies and ridicule. Needless to say, the performances were enthusiastically received by the rest of the school, their families, and community members.

In addition to a language profile, students can develop dialect and register profiles to help them document language variation in their daily lives (see Figures 7 and 8). In the dialect profile, students record the phrases, words, or actions that represent their dialect. Students at first may not be aware that they speak a dialect, but as different members of the class, including the teacher, share what they know about their dialect, students are able to fill in specific features. Students sometimes use the term *accent* as synonymous with *dialect,* and the teacher encourages the students to search for the differences between these terms and how they are used. As students come to understand that every language has many dialects and that dialect differences are influenced by a range of factors based on race, class, region, gender, and the age of the language user, they add the categories that best fit their situation, along with specific examples, to their profile. They discover that dialects, like languages, are fairly stable for groups of individuals throughout their lifetime, although in the same way that people develop the ability to speak more than one language, they also are able to speak more than one dialect of their language as they move from one place to another or change their educational or economic class. When they move between one dialect community and another, they are able to shift their language accordingly. In Chapters 6 and 7, I suggest additional theme cycle studies that focus on dialect.

In the register profile, students include language samples and gestures they use in different settings. With the teacher, they add categories in order to explore register variation such as when

My Dialect Profile				
Name _____ Age_____				
Dialect(s) I speak, listen, read, and write (include examples)				
Language	Geographic Origin	National Origin	Race	Generation
Oral Language				
Written Language				

FIGURE 7. *A sample dialect profile form.*

My Register Profile				
Name _____ Age_____				
Register(s) I speak, listen, read, and write (include examples)				
Language Examples	Family (specify specific members)	Friends (specify male or female)	In Class (specify specific activity)	After-school Activities (be specific)
Oral				
Written				

FIGURE 8. *A sample register profile form.*

they report to the class, argue, talk on the phone, tell stories, or greet friends or family members. Questions such as the following help them focus on register differences: Do the girls and the boys in your class use words, sentences, voice, body language, conversational topics, and turn taking in conversations in the same or different ways? Is your language the same or different when you tell your best friend a secret than when you speak to people you know less well? How and why?

For written language, students consider language differences in their own reading and writing of, for example, folktales, scientific articles and reports, medicine vials, personal diaries, phone messages, and instant messages. Although people tend to call written language variations *genres,* they are similar to register differences, and examples of genre language variations can be listed on the register profile. As the students discover the different ways they speak or write in different situations, they add language examples and categories to their profiles.

The term *register* indicates the ways in which we change oral language from one context to another and with different people depending on what is happening. We speak differently in each of our social roles, such as teacher, wife, mother, and child. Students focus on register differences by listing their social roles in school and at home, such as student, friend, child, grandchild, sibling, pitcher on the softball team, or hall monitor, and then documenting the different kinds of talk and written language they use in each role.

Students add appropriate examples to their various profiles over time based on their social roles and the accompanying language they document. They then develop dialect and register profiles for other people by interviewing parents, members of different occupations, people with language backgrounds from different regions, and people from different ethnic or socioeconomic groups. They examine the ways in which vocabulary, grammar, and the sounds of language change depending on the context and when such shifts are or are not considered conventional. Students discuss the degree to which they are aware of their own language changes while they are talking or writing.

Comparing the ways in which prominent people use language in storytelling, poetry reading, and speeches to different audiences heightens awareness and is an additional way for students to explore the role of dialects and registers. Recordings of Donald Davis, Luci Tapahonso, Martin Luther King Jr., and Langston Hughes provide good examples. Each of these individual's Web sites makes reference to audio readings.

Language Attitudes

A major purpose for a theme cycle on language variation is to develop students' conscious awareness of their attitudes toward their own language(s) and dialect(s) and the language variations of others and to build positive attitudes about language difference. In a democratic society, if we are truly committed to equality and social justice it is necessary to help all students value one another's languages and dialects and to appreciate the ability of all language users to make appropriate language shifts (code-switching) depending on the context. Students who speak a high-status form of a language or dialect (generally because they belong to the privileged classes) need to understand the socioeconomic issues that influence language status and to recognize the right of all students to engage in the language forms of their social groups. Students who speak a dialect that is not considered high status (generally because they are poor or a minority) must learn to value the language(s) they speak and their ability to shift language use when appropriate. Students develop greater confidence in their language use as they become aware of the many decisions they make daily to shift dialect and registers appropriately. Because language variation is a marker of social and intellectual status, it is important to sustain such discussions over time; language variation should be a major focus of a language study curriculum at all age levels. As a result, students develop greater sophistication about language, dialect, and register issues and are in a position to critique what they hear and read. They become conscious of the complexity of language diversity in their communities, and their attitudes toward language differences exhibit greater understanding, sensitivity, and respect.

The language that people use to talk or write about language variation also reflects a language attitude. Students should explore the terms people use when they discuss language, dialects, and registers. Terms related to national languages (Spanish, Hebrew, English) are fairly consistent, whereas terms related to dialects and registers differ even among linguists. Students sometimes use popular culture terms such as *country, down-home, Tex-Mex, hillbilly,* or *Val talk.* It is important to help students interrogate the use of such terminology and realize that such terms are often controversial and considered offensive and stereotypical. The terms *nonstandard* or *substandard* are often used to refer to the language used by racial, ethnic, or linguistic groups who are not part of the middle or upper classes. Linguists, however, prefer *nonstandard* to *substandard,* and discussing these various terms and searching out how they are used helps students consider the controversies involved. The term *standard* is often ascribed to the language of people in power or who have highly valued educational or economic backgrounds. The students find that standard English is represented by the language used by anchor newscasters in the United States and on the British (BBC) or Canadian (CBC) Broadcasting Companies. Many books, position statements, and Web sites are helpful for the teacher in these discussions (Farb, 1974; Smitherman, 1977, 1995).

Language History and Development

Language history is both personal and social. The ways in which individuals learn to speak, listen, read, and write are closely tied to the ways in which humans developed language and literacy over the centuries. In this section, I discuss individual, family, and social language histories.

Autobiographies and Biographies

First-grade teacher Keith Pearce has each of his students fill a shoebox with a baby picture and favorite artifacts that represent who they are as a way of introducing themselves to the class at the beginning of the year. He asks them to include things they read, wrote, drew, or built at home. As students search for the artifacts that represent their identities, parents and other adults are eager to join in the hunt. They discover baby books that document first words or sentences and folders or scrapbooks of writings and drawings. Mr. Pearce sets up a language history bulletin board and individual posters that include the child's picture with samples of their language use circling the picture.

Mr. Pearce asks his students, "When did you start speaking? What language(s) did you learn at that time? When did you start to write and to read, and what do you remember about it? What kinds of reading and writing did you or do you do? Who reads and writes with you?" When the students begin to share what they remember, some have few memories associated with language acquisition, but during the discussions they begin to remember more. The students suggest interviewing their parents, grandparents, or caregivers to gather more information, and what they discover is written and added to their displays. Students explore why families love to tell these anecdotes and why and how the stories become part of family lore and history. They invite their parents to class, and parents are always willing to share amusing and sometimes even embarrassing family language stories.

Older children develop their literacy autobiographies in a similar way by participating in a literacy dig of their own reading and writing materials and organizing the material into a Museum of History of Our Language. Some teachers begin a related theme cycle by reading aloud Roald Dahl's *Boy* (1984), which he wrote after discovering that his mother had kept all the letters he had written to her when he was a student at a boarding school in England. The students use their artifacts to build a time line of their personal language history, identifying when they began to speak, read, listen, and write and who was involved in these events, and listing specific words or books involved. The students combine the information they have in order to develop a class time line, which allows them to discover general periods during which they learned to speak, read, and write. Students are invited to write their language autobiographies in either prose or poetry.

Students develop family language histories as a result of what they learn about their personal language development. As students or parents share family language stories, the students ask questions about the language used at home and what their parents and grandparents remember about their language use. They discuss what language they spoke and read and how they wrote their signatures. David Schwarzer (2001) involves students and family members in developing a family tree that focuses on the languages that parents, grandparents, and great-grandparents spoke, wrote, and read, a project that often means examining primary documents. Creating such a diagram can easily be integrated into a social studies theme cycle on My Family Tree or My Roots. As the class begins to document the different languages their ancestors used, the students come to value language diversity. If some students in the class have little information about the history of their families, they are encouraged to work with a buddy or document the language of the people with whom they are living.

Such explorations include gathering letters from relatives, greeting cards, passports, and business documents to examine changes in spelling, grammar, and meaning of language throughout the history of the family. As students prepare to make presentations of their learning, the teacher explores with the students the ethics of using personal data, what permissions they need, and whether they need to use pseudonyms.

Once students have explored their language autobiographies and family language biographies, they ask questions that lead them to make connections with global language history. They come to realize that language changes and grows over time for individuals as well as for society in general. It is important for students to understand that each of us is actively a part of the history of language. History is not merely the past; rather, each person is the result of his or her personal as well as social history.

Child Language Development

Language biographies are closely linked to theme cycles on the development of language in young children. The development of personal or family language biographies often leads students to ask questions about how individuals learn to talk, to read, and to write. They audio- or videotape the language of babies or preschoolers in their homes, families, or neighborhood, and collect language samples in different contexts, such as when babies are playing alone with toys or on a swing, interacting with the student collecting the data or an adult, or on a walk or riding in the car. Students also collect materials their younger siblings write or read. They interview parents and grandparents to explore similarities and differences in language development from one generation to another.

The teacher brings in professional books on language development and helps students read selected passages to discover whether what they are learning about language development is the same or different from what linguists or developmental psychologists have discovered. They categorize the words babies use according to types and sounds and discover patterns and why such patterns develop; they hypothesize, for example, about the kinds of words babies use first. They also make lists of words that babies invent or pronounce in unusual ways.

Additional child language development studies include discussing languages children make up with their siblings, twin, best friends, dolls, stuffed animals, or imaginary playmates. Such explorations help students become aware of aspects of the language culture of childhood that are not studied much by language scientists and not well remembered by adults.

Where Words Come From

Whenever my classes discussed family language history or specific vocabulary terms, some students always wanted to know about the origins of vocabulary terms and names. Therefore, when student interest focuses on words, I recommend that the history of words become a theme cycle study. Students are also interested in the influences of different languages on English or Spanish words. Because my students were most interested in etymology when they were discussing various terms, I would ask questions at such times that focused them on word origins, such as "Why do you think [the word] looks, sounds, or means that?" and "How can we find out?" Raising such questions often sent students off on word origin searches. It's helpful to have dictionaries of idioms and word origins written for children, adolescents, and adults available in classroom libraries so they are readily accessible when students are anxious to discover more information about the history of words. In addition, searching the Web under terms such as *word origins* or *etymology* provides many resources.

Etymology is the history of a linguistic form from its origins and earliest recorded occurrences, to its transmission from one language to another, to its current usage, through an analysis of its component parts such as its grammar, meaning, pattern of sounds, and printed forms. Etymology is especially helpful for students who want to understand scientific terminology that often has its origins in Greek and Latin words.

Language Form

Miles Kushner's middle-grade students explore the forms that language takes by first considering the rules in the games or sports they play. He asks the class to form small groups and for each group to choose a game or sport they enjoy playing, including computer games. They are to diagram or write the rules they use and to record their disagreements as well. When the students share the rules of the games with the whole class, they also share their arguments and any resolutions they've come to. They also explore the reasons that everyone involved needs to follow the same rules and, when there are disagreements, how they decide which rules to follow in order to be able to play the game or sport. The students also talk about when they do or do not follow the rules of games or sports, when and why they change the rules, and the results of such changes.

The major concept Mr. Kushner wants his students to understand is that rules are developed as social conventions and that such rules are sometimes different in different contexts. Although players can invent new rules, these rules have to become conventional in order for the group to be able to play the game. Mr. Kushner sometimes extends the conversation by having his students consider traffic rules or rules of dress, depending on how important these rule-governed systems are to his students.

Mr. Kushner then asks his students to consider the ways in which the systematic rules of language are similar to and different from the systems of rules they follow in other parts of their lives. They consider the ways in which language rules change depending on their context, in the same way that rules for games change depending on, for example, whether they are played by men or by women (e.g., rules for women's and men's baseball and basketball), which league they are played in (because of age or country of origin), or historical period (over time). He helps students consider that conventions are not really a matter of wrong or right but become established simply by being what people are used to doing. During these discussions, which initiate various theme cycles on language forms, Mr. Kushner sends his students into the community to discover what their peers and adults think about the relationship between language rules and the rules of games and sports.

For centuries paying careful attention to the conventions of language has been a major focus in the teaching of language and language arts, especially in transmission-model classrooms. Teachers have spent a great deal of class time prescribing "correct" forms in speaking, reading, and writing. Whole language teachers have come to understand that students learn the conventions of language rules best when they have important reasons to use language and have opportunities to talk about the reasons for the application of specific rules.

In this section, I suggest language study that involves students in thinking about the kind of language to use when talking about language, using the form of language to focus on meaning, and researching aspects of grammar, phonology, and orthography. Although talking and thinking about language is a rich part of critical-moment teaching and strategy lessons, students' interests often lead the teacher and other class members to plan for theme cycles that focus on the form language takes.

Language about Language

When I worked with middle-grade students, I usually involved them in a study of language terminology throughout the semester or the year. The students recorded the language about language they read or heard on sticky notes, which they could easily move around and rearrange in order to develop categories. We created posters with headings such as Root Words, Prefixes, Suffixes, and Synonyms, depending on which terms the students found. The sticky notes included the word, highlighted in the sentence where the word was found, as well as the meaning of the word. Because I wanted the students to explore multiple meanings and to expand their understanding of the terms, I encouraged them to select two or three of the terms to explore in greater depth in small groups. Each group became experts on certain terms and categories, and it was their responsibility to respond to questions other students asked about those terms. These questions often sent the experts off to do more in-depth research. Judith Lindfors (personal communication, 1999) suggests that once students believe they understand a term well, they should be encouraged to find examples that do not fit their understanding and discuss with the class how their concept changed by thinking about their terms in new ways. As a result, students become aware that definitions are not simple denotations of meaning but instead represent a range of meanings, sometimes even contradictory ones. Since many language terms are used on standardized tests, the more students develop in-depth concepts about language terminology, the more confidently they respond to them in testing situations.

I also wanted my students to become conscious of how language is used differently in science, math, music, or art. We took the list of terms and categories we were developing and explored how they were used in different subject matter areas, often generating a class book called Language about Science or Language about Music. The books were revisited and updated regularly. We discussed our language study with the other subject matter teachers and encouraged them to send any language terminology issues back to my class for further discussion and record keeping.

Meaning across a Text

A number of middle school teachers use a story titled "Poison" by Roald Dahl (1953) to have students explore the form of a text. The story repeats the word *krait* many times. Although the students are usually concerned about the pronunciation of the word, we want them to become aware that pronouncing a term correctly is not as important as trying to discover its meaning, and that when a term is important, the author often provides many textual clues to facilitate readers' understanding. The purpose of this lesson is to help students consider how to search for such clues and to precipitate an in-depth study of texts' cohesive ties.

First, teachers photocopy the story and make small sticky notes available. Working in groups, the students circle the word *krait* or mark it with a sticky note. They then examine the text that comes just before and just after the word and draw lines on the photocopy with a different colored pencil or mark them with a different colored sticky note to the various phrases that help explain the word. In this way, students discover how meanings are developed across a text and how the context of the language surrounding an unfamiliar term provides cohesive ties between meaning and labels that help readers make sense across the text. Students become aware that as they follow cohesive ties, they often are able to develop the meaning of unfamiliar terms. As they apply this technique to other texts, they begin to examine the different ways authors use cohesive ties and how these strategies are the same or different in fiction and in other genres.

A similar examination can take place when one concept is represented by synonyms, a common occurrence in English. In one story, for example, the words *craft, canoe,* and *outrigger* all referred to the same boat being used by a boatman. The students were surprised to learn that these words all referred to the same object. In order to plan for such theme cycles, teachers need to find stories that include such language features. After their initial introductions to such language forms, students can continue their discoveries in all kinds of texts and report their findings to the class.

Students can also examine the forms that texts take by re-writing into play format stories that make extensive use of dialogue. After reading and examining the ways in which plays are formatted to represent dialogue, students develop a comparison chart to show the differences between stories with dialogue and stories with play formats. This also helps them understand the purpose of quotation marks and direct dialogue in narrative formats. Students then take some of the short plays they have been reading and turn them into narratives. This experience helps students discover why and how narrative involves greater use of description and characterization than plays do. They also explore the relationship between the role of oral language as used by an actor to express meaning and the different forms language takes to provide such meanings in written stories.

Grammar/Syntax

As I've said before, grammar is best understood within the context of its use. Any aspect of grammar the students raise for discussion during critical-moment teaching or strategy lessons can be expanded into theme cycles. Questions about issues such as the use of prepositions at the ends of sentences, the limited use or overuse of adjectives, the use of subjective and objective pronouns, or where to place independent clauses are best researched by students through (1) examining their own writing to see when and how they use a particular grammatical form; (2) reading favorite authors to see how and when they use the particular form; (3) reading scholarly books on language to discover the ways in which linguists and other language researchers talk about the form; (4) examining dictionaries and thesauruses to note the rules and exceptions; and (5) interviewing English teachers, businesspeople, linguists, journalists, and other adults to ask them their opinions about the form under examination. After the class decides on the particular form they want to research, they organize into groups, and each group selects one or two ways to research the form.

Puns and jokes are another avenue through which to explore grammatical issues. Marion Edman, my favorite language arts professor, loved to start us thinking about conventions of language use by telling us about a first grader who raised his hand and asked the teacher, "Can I go to the terlit [toilet]?" The teacher, in a somewhat severe tone, said, "Did you say *can?*," to which the child replied, "No, I said *terlit.*" Students love to collect puns and jokes and make books out of them that become wonderful sources for continuous study of language form.

Phonology and Orthography

Mindy comes up to her teacher and asks, "How come double *o* in words is so complicated? It makes so many different sounds." Don Howard, Mindy's third-grade teacher, asks her to bring her question to a class meeting the next day. Mindy tells the class that words such as *foot* and *boot* confuse her. Mr. Howard invites the class to list any rules they think they already know about how the pattern of two *o*'s in a word is represented in the sounds of English. The students then go on a double-*o* safari to verify the rules they have listed and to discover other complexities about related letter and sound patterns. Mr. Howard says that not only do his students become aware of the spelling patterns of English in this way, but also he sometimes discovers rules he didn't know about. Over the years, his students have participated in quotation mark, comma, cursive, and capitalization safaris, among others.

A safari search for exceptions to conventional rules of spelling and punctuation in environmental print easily develops into a theme cycle to research conventions and inventions of orthography. Collecting lists of unusual spellings and punctuation on signs (Likkur), billboards, t-shirts (Fonics wrks fur mi), and stores (Mays Department Store) helps students explore the reasons for exceptions or inventions. Likewise, examining old documents and cemetery markings helps students understand that spelling, punctuation, and the sounds of language change over time. Discovering the patterns of these unusual or invented spellings provides students with information about the systematic ways in which sound patterns map onto letter patterns.

Concepts that emerge from theme cycles on language form include:

- ◆ Students come to understand that the form language takes depends on the social conventions of such forms for communication purposes.

- ◆ They learn that conventions vary depending on the purpose of language use, and that language conventions are culture and context bound and relate to socioeconomic issues that often mark a reader, writer, or speaker's social status.

- ◆ They realize that conventional language forms develop over time as a way of easing communication within specific language communities by building on the inventions of previous communities.

- ◆ They become aware of how the language inventions of individuals or groups enrich communication and provide new forms through which to explore new ideas and establish new knowledge.

CHAPTER SIX

Focus on Language and Literature

Beverly Cleary explores letter writing and story writing in *Dear Mr. Henshaw* (1983); Louise Fitzhugh scouts out the problems that budding authors have keeping journals in *Harriet the Spy* (1964); Jean Fritz invites her readers to predict what happens next in her historical fiction (e.g., *And Then What Happened, Paul Revere?* [1996]); Aliki (1986) crafts a book about how to make books; and Mark Twain (1985) admonishes his readers in the frontispiece of *Adventures of Huckleberry Finn*:

> Notice. Persons attempting to find a motive in this narrative will be prosecuted; persons attempting to find a moral in it will be banished; persons attempting to find a plot in it will be shot.

Narratives, information, illustrations, and characters in books written for children and adolescents reveal the fascination that authors and illustrators have with ideas about and issues of language use, language learning, and language teaching. Well-written and well-illustrated books are rich resources for teachers to use as an impetus for language study theme cycles. The areas I develop for theme cycle language studies through literature include:

- ◆ Publishing
- ◆ Format and Font Variation
- ◆ Genre Variation
- ◆ A Study of Schooling

Publishing

I begin with a section on publishing because as students talk about books (Short & Pierce, 1990) they should have many opportunities to write and publish in response to their reading, which allows them to develop as authors and illustrators and discover the important relation between reading and writing. They will become selective about what they want to publish and consider the kinds of writing they like to do. A classroom or schoolwide publishing center that involves students in making books, magazines, online newsletters, and videos easily satisfies the presenting phase of learning. Students take great pride in their publications, especially when they are added to the school library collection and displayed prominently. In some schools, one grade level, such as all the fifth graders, handles the publishing center, which becomes a school tradition that the younger kids look forward to. In other schools, a teacher maintains the publishing center with representatives from each class, or individual teachers organize a publishing center within their classrooms.

The students should be involved in all aspects of the publication process, evaluate how it's working, and discuss how to maintain and improve it. A literature study examining how authors and illustrators work and how written materials are published provides opportunities for students to realize the power of authoring their own work. Working with a representative group of students from each classroom, the teacher introduces the perceiving phase of a theme cycle on publishing by saying to the kids, "How would you like to publish a magazine [or a newspaper or a book]?" (Wigginton, 1972), or "What can we do to continue the publication of our school literary magazine?"

Depending on the kinds of materials to be published and the age of the students, the teacher displays commercial as well as student-published materials. Commercially published student-authored works are available, as well as books for adults and children on bookmaking and publishing. *How a Book Is Made* by Aliki (1986) helps students realize they are capable of organizing a publishing center. Online at www.harperchildrens.com/hch/picture/features/aliki/howabook/book1.asp, Aliki takes students through the steps of bookmaking. Other online resources are found under topics such as children's bookmaking or publishing.

Professional works about the language experience approach to learning to read make reference to publishing and bookmaking processes (Van Allen, 1976; Van Allen & Van Allen, 1982).

In this approach, the significant learning activities in which students engage are highlighted through reading and writing opportunities that result in publication. Some professional books focus on the development of classroom and school publishing (e.g., Baskwill & Whitman, 1986), and TreeTop Publishing creates bare books to facilitate book publication (P.O. Box 085567, Racine, Wisconsin 53404-5567). Primary grade teacher Vera Milz recruits parent volunteers willing to sew blank books to facilitate bookmaking. In many schools, the art teacher supports the illustration and publication of books and magazines. Wallpaper stores and other businesses often provide materials to teachers who know how to scrounge. At the Keeling Publishing Company, which schoolwide reading resource teacher Debra Jacobson organized, the students published their writing as individual books or in the *Keeling Magazine,* which was printed twice a year (Jacobson, 1991, pp. 160–61). With $1,000 a year collected from the PTA and from proposals she wrote for district funds, Dr. Jacobson was able to buy cardboard and other equipment to enhance the bookmaking process. She often invited a local author (or illustrator) to be an author-in-residence—sometimes supported by the Arizona Humanities Council—who explored with the students the craft of writing and helped them with the publishing process.

During brainstorming about publishing their work, students discuss what they already know and what they want to know about publishing such as organizing, using the computer, printing, selecting what to publish, the roles of people needed in the publishing process, the functions of various publications, the audiences they serve, and of course the composing process itself, including revision and editing. Space is set aside and the classroom organized to actively involve students in all aspects of publishing. A table or desk with shelves and drawers with appropriate labels is reserved for the publishing center, and a filing cabinet in the publishing center houses different kinds of paper, pens, inks, artwork, cardboard, and so forth. Labeled bins on the desk reflect the kinds of jobs that are needed for publication purposes. One bin marked "To Be Considered for Publication," for example, is reserved for the drafts students believe are ready for consideration. The class has established procedures for publishing the writing that is selected by an elected publication committee headed by an editor, a position rotated among the students at regular intervals. The editor takes a leadership role and with the committee makes suggestions about additional revising and editing and returns the piece to the author. The author revises again and places the article or book manuscript into a bin labeled "Ready for Conference." The editor and the classroom teacher meet with the author, first discussing the content and then making editing suggestions. Grammar and spelling become a focus during the copyediting process, which involves checking out ambiguous sentences, run-ons, and other grammatical features that interfere with comprehension. The copy goes back to the author for a final revision and editing and is then placed in a bin labeled "Ready for Publication."

As they participate in revising and editing their own work as well as the work of their peers, the students examine language conventions. They learn appropriate terms for editing marks and how to use them in editing the work of others. Students have many opportunities to discuss appropriate uses of conventional grammar and spelling depending on the purpose of a piece of writing, and they examine changes in spelling and grammar over time as they relate what they are writing to their reading. The students develop lists of conventions to remind themselves to check specific features of their work before placing it in the "Ready for Publication" bin. The class also lists the grammatical and spelling features editors are most concerned with and compare those with the kinds of grammatical and spelling issues they are faced with in each other's writing. The teacher plans strategy lessons (see Chapter 4) to help the students understand the grammatical and spelling issues that crop up most often as conference topics and during class discussions and that reflect her own understanding of the linguistic knowledge that will be most helpful to the students. In addition, the class explores the inventions and unique styles of professional authors and illustrators and the freedom they exercise in relation to language conventions. The students expand their own writing styles as they become familiar with the styles of authors and illustrators. They discuss sensitive ways to help each other revise and edit and how to make suggestions without interfering with the author's meaning.

Additional roles for students in the publishing center include printer, paper cutter, and cover designer or artist. The ways in which illustrators, translators, and coauthors are listed on the title page are negotiated. The author's biography and picture are placed on the book jacket after students study the various ways such displays are presented in commercial publications. Schedules are posted for students to do final printing and formatting at the computer stations.

The variety of final products is limitless. Young children make books of their own writing that they have edited or that have been written from their dictation. Older students make books to read to younger children, or they write reports about what they are learning as part of social studies, math, or science theme cycles. Some books are written by the whole class, and sometimes pamphlets, brochures, magazines, and journals represent the research results of various members of the class.

To support language study, discussions also focus on the power of the press and related publishing issues. Students explore who has control of what gets edited and published and who decides on the topics, illustrations, diagrams, and photographs that are selected for publication. Through their reading and through discussions with reporters and authors, students discover the constraints on language in commercial publication, the limits placed on their own writing as a result of genre differences and the age or abilities of their readers, as well as the control that adults try to exercise over students' work (see the section on censorship in Chapter 7). Discussions about publishing include considering how authors choose their topics and keep track of what they want to write. With the teacher's encouragement, one third-grade class kept a running list of ideas they wanted to write about. Older students often keep a writer's notebook to keep track of ideas and events that lend themselves to writing, especially when their teacher shares her or his own writer's notebook with them.

Jeff LaBenz (1991, p. 316) discusses how his middle-grade students examined newspapers in the classroom and at home to start thinking about questions they would need to answer in order to publish a classroom newspaper. He encouraged his students to discuss with their parents different parts of the newspaper, such as which parts they read and why. The students brainstormed questions related to the organization and publication of a newspaper: How many people write the newspaper and what roles do they serve? Why are there so many different sections in the newspaper? What are they called? Do they do different things? The students then decided which sections were most relevant to their lives and what kind of news would be most interesting to their readers. The students developed eleven columns for their newspaper: Current Events, TV and Movie Reviews, Travel, Sports, Food, Book Reviews, Art and Leisure, Features and Interviews, Science and Technology, Want Ads, and Weather. I would also consider starting a theme cycle study that leads to the publication of a classroom newspaper by reading aloud Avi's *Nothing but the Truth* (1991), Nancy Garden's *The Year They Burned the Books* (1999), or more recent books that focus on newspaper publications in school settings.

Author/Illustrator Study

A number of times during a semester, a set of books by a specific author/illustrator is placed on display for browsing, including photographs, artwork, and biographical pamphlets. The display is often a response to an author or illustrator's name coming up spontaneously at some point during the semester or when an author who is a classroom favorite writes a new book or has a book serialized in the local newspaper. Librarians can provide lists of appropriate books and materials, and publishers are often willing to provide biographies of their authors/illustrators who often have Web sites that provide interactive opportunities for students. Many authors/illustrators are available for school visits that are supported by publishers or monies raised by parent-teacher groups. State or local humanities councils also sometimes support author visits or conferences. Publishers such as Richard C. Owen offer books about authors/illustrators, and students can always find book collections by and Web sites about authors/illustrators.

Author/illustrator studies provide opportunities for students to learn about and discuss the literacy and literary histories of authors/illustrators they know well through their reading. Students can explore how commercially published writers and artists develop their craft, how they work, and what they believe about writing, drawing, and the use of language, as well as their commitment to specific language issues such as literacy, censorship, and the kinds of support emerging readers and writers need. As a result, students compare the problems of authors/illustrators with their own struggles as developing readers, writers, and artists. They diagram or chart the ways in which styles, themes, and language are similar and different from book to book by the same author/illustrator, or compare one author/illustrator to another. The students choose their favorite author, illustrator, or poet and read as many of their books as they can. They engage with text sets, shared books, or read-alouds, and even young children recognize and can discuss the style, language use, and artistic features of specific authors and artists.

In *The Girl with the Brown Crayon,* Vivian Paley (1997) describes an author study of Leo Lionni she conducted with her kindergartners, and she documents the sophistication with which young children are able to seriously analyze Lionni's use of style, language, color, lines, and characterization. Through explorations of the lives and dreams of authors/illustrators, students and teachers can adapt their publishing centers to reflect some of the ideas they have learned about the crafts of writing and drawing from their literature studies.

Additional books that explore the roles of authors and illustrators include:

Pat Brisson, *Your Best Friend, Kate* (1992)

Tomie dePaola, *The Art Lesson* (1989)

Jules Feiffer, *The Man in the Ceiling* (1993)

Joan Lowery Nixon, *If You Were a Writer* (1995)

Bill Peet, *Bill Peet: An Autobiography* (1989)

Mark Strand, *Rembrandt Takes a Walk* (1986)

Wendy Thomas, ed., *A Farley Mowat Reader* (1997)

Elizabeth Borton de Treviño, *I, Juan de Pareja* (1965)

Jeanette Winter, *Emily Dickinson's Letters to the World* (2002)

Questions in an author/illustrator study focus on general issues about the lives of the authors and illustrators but also on language study: How do authors use language in different ways to respond to the same issue? How does the author grab your interest at the beginning of the piece? What role do illustrations play in encouraging reader interest? What language in the text is interesting, difficult, or unusual? What devices does the author use to help you understand new or unfamiliar language? In what ways does the author let you know that different characters are talking? How do illustrations relate to the language of the text?

Format and Font Variation

Why are books or pages formatted the way they are? As students immerse themselves in publishing experiences, examine the diversity of print in their environment, and explore the many ways authors and illustrators make use of print variations, they begin to raise questions about the many purposes this diversity serves. They become aware that authors, illustrators, and editors take great care with the images of a published text in order to appeal aesthetically to the eye of the reader as well as to enhance meaning. These features include the visible aspects or physical appearance of written language: the size, shape, form, and organization of designs, fonts, pages, paragraphs, letters, words, phrases, and sentences. Artists use a variety of formats such as pop-up pages, cutout forms, and use of artwork on covers, front pages, and page edges to extend the meaning of the text. Authors develop their characters by formatting their books as diaries or letters (see Scholastic's Dear America series). Sometimes they have different characters write separate chapters, viewing the same events from different perspectives. Poets sometimes use concrete poetry to parallel the look of the poem with its meaning. Young students show their awareness of the importance of how a text looks when they use all capital letters or fractured print to represent emotions or actions such as FEAR or **POW**. Exploring format and font variation through language study theme cycles heightens students' interest in writing and the publication of their own writing.

As with other theme cycles, making available collections of theme-related books and materials for browsing purposes is helpful, especially for initiating the perceiving phase of the cycle. It is acceptable to start with a small collection because students often add books themselves, and the theme study is sustained over time as the students add materials they find.

In the following discussions of theme cycles, I suggest exploring books and other written materials that use unique and innovative font and format variations to represent meaning, books that use print variations to represent language differences, and books that use nonalphabetic writing systems. Students can examine the differences between signs in alphabetic languages such as English or Spanish and signs in nonalphabetic languages such as Chinese or Japanese. They examine signs in horizontal and vertical orientations and realize that languages can be written in different orientations. Even before they go to school, children's writing in the United States is usually horizontal, while Japanese children tend to write vertically. Children who live in biliterate societies often demonstrate characteristics of more than one written language system in their early writing. In societies with alphabetic writing systems, children write capital letters even after they have been instructed to use both capital and small letters, because capital letters dominate the print available in their environments (Y. Goodman, 1980).

Variations Related to Meaning

Depending on student interest or teacher enthusiasm, the focus of a font and format study can take different directions. Teachers may decide to explore books that use letter or diary formats to help students write using similar formats. Or the students may notice during an illustrator study that the artist uses fonts in unique ways and thus decide to study such innovations in other illustrators' works and other books. In either case, the teacher follows up by reading an appropriately selected book aloud to the students and then making available a related collection of books for browsing. Or the theme cycle starts with a browsing table of related book formats. I do both at different times in order to vary the ways in which theme cycles are introduced. Bill Martin's

Sounds of Language series (1966–1967) and his Little Owl series let students explore how print is used as readers follow the print as it spirals, moves, and circles across the page or two-page spread. Although these series are out of print, teachers sometimes find old copies in school book rooms. Bill Martin Jr.'s Web site, www.michaelsampson.com/bill.htm, lists the books still in publication and new similar ones.

Authors and illustrators such as Eric Carle, Joanna Cole, Ed Young, Jorge Díaz, Janet Ahlberg and Allen Ahlberg, Bill Martin Jr., Peter Sis, and David Wisniewski, among many others, use format and font variations in their books. Both Avi and Jules Feiffer use cartoons with format variations. Searching these authors' Web sites or searching the Web using key words such as *children's books, literature with cartoons,* or *pop-up books* provides helpful lists for teachers and students. Walter Dean Myers's book *Monster* (1999) uses a movie script format written for adolescent students exploring the life in prison of a young person.

As students discover and explore these kinds of books, they raise questions about why authors and illustrators use such variation and explore the purposes of these innovative explorations. Students share what they like about the differences in style and how the variations expand and embellish the books' meanings. They list the conventional ways in which books are organized and format is used and then consider the careful ways in which authors/illustrators innovate. They chart the similarities and differences or make posters to illustrate different ways in which authors and illustrators work. Students explore their own writing to see if their pieces are good candidates for innovative formats and fonts, and then write unique manuscripts to explore particular styles.

Such comparisons highlight language study as students examine how different authors format chapters, dialogue, letters, and diaries. Punctuation and spelling become a focus of such study since some authors choose not to use punctuation at all or use it and different spellings in unconventional ways (see Zolotow's *My Grandson Lew* [1974]). Students discover that they know a lot about conventional use of print, spelling, and punctuation as they compare the conventional with the inventive forms they begin to notice. Their discussions provide the setting in which students are able to inquire into conventional font and format use and through such exploration become more confident in their own inventive uses of visible language features. Given such discoveries, class discussions often turn to considering why some teachers, parents, newspaper editors, and publishers insist on conventional language formats. Although for language study purposes the focus of the theme cycle is on orthography and format variation, the integration of illustration and other artistic styles helps students explore a range of ways in which meaning can be conveyed through symbols other than the alphabetic writing system.

Concrete poetry is another innovative practice that extends the conventional limits of fonts and formats. Students eagerly read and write such poetry, which relates form to meaning. The students, for example, consider a concept or word they want to explore, such as *icicle*. They list words or short phrases that are synonyms for the word and then organize them so that they visibly represent the word meaning. For *icicle* they would place the words in a long list with each word in the list shorter than the one above it so that when the poem is complete the overall look of the list is the shape of an icicle. Students are encouraged to look for books with concrete poetry and to think about the ways in which the look of a poem, a page, or an entire book extends the meaning of the work. Barbara Esbensen, for example, uses font variations to highlight her animal poems in *Words with Wrinkled Knees* (1997). Students work individually or in small groups to produce a list of words or phrases they think of when they hear words such as *fear, happiness, danger,* or *tragedy.* They are encouraged to change the word so it means different things. *Sun,* for example, might change to *sunshine, sunny, sunlight,* or *sunburst,* or *night* might change to *tonight* or *stormy night.* After they explore the word changes, the students are encouraged to draw the words or phrases so that the shape of it adds to their meaning.

Language and Cultural Variation

Font variations provide opportunities for students to explore language variation when they examine the ways in which authors represent the language of their characters in relation to second language, dialect, age, or register differences. Authors often use unique spellings, punctuation, and fonts to represent language that doesn't conform to conventional spelling and punctuation. Such variations are called *eye dialect* because they visibly represent a character's pronunciation.

The study of dialect representations in books, magazines, and cartoons involves students in an exploration of when, why, and how authors use eye dialect to represent the multiple ways in which languages are pronounced. In Chapter 7, I discuss dialect in terms of power relations in society. Some dialects are considered high status and are referred to in the popular press and sometimes in school settings as "standard" or "correct" forms, while other dialects are considered inappropriate for school use. I discuss representations of language variation here as well because authors often use font variations to represent the multiple ways in which their characters speak. Students can search for eye dialect in books, magazines, and cartoons. It is important for teachers and students to be aware that some authors are knowledgeable about language variation, and their representations of language variation are fairly accurate. Some authors, however, use representations of dialect in stereotypic and inaccurate ways. Such inconsistencies provide rich opportunities for teachers to help students read oral language representations with a critical eye.

In addition to the many books that include language variation, cartoons are also a good resource. *Snuffy Smith* by Fred Lasswell uses spellings such as "Yo're holdin' up th' dadburn game!!" to represent the speech of some who live in the Appalachian Mountains. *The Ryatts* by Jack Elrod uses spellings such as "'llowance time" and "He wuz happy" to represent the speech of very young children. The speech of people involved in certain occupations, such as truckers and disk jockeys, are often represented with eye dialect, which allows students to critique authors who represent differences among characters but use such representations only with certain populations. Although almost every speaker of English says, for example, *you are* as *yo're* or *was* as *wuz* in the context of oral speech, some cartoonists and authors use such spelling only with specific populations. Examining eye dialect use leads to critical analysis of the decisions authors make about character representation. In addition, comparing the different spellings authors use lets students see whether different authors use the same eye dialect spellings for the same pronunciations or whether authors use unique spellings. The teacher and students inquire into standardization of spelling across dialects and which issues authors need to address when they create characters who speak different dialects or languages. These uses of written language provide opportunities to explore grammatical, phonological, and orthographic issues. Students can find a lot of information on the Internet about these issues through a search of terms such as *cartoons, dialects,* and *eye dialect.*

Issues of language variation to explore with students include (1) how does the characters' language use affect my understanding and my feelings about them? and (2) why does the author use eye dialect in different ways for different characters?

A related theme cycle involves students in exploring font and format variation in writing systems other than English. I maintain a collection of children's and adolescent books in a range of languages such as Japanese, Chinese, Spanish, Russian, Arabic, Apache, and Navajo. Whenever I travel abroad or visit American Indian or Native Canadian schools, I add to my collection. Most libraries in large cities and at universities have collections of books for all ages in languages other than English, as well as magazines and newspapers, that can be checked out and brought into the classroom. In order to add to my collection, I have students search the print in their environment, including food, health, and cleaning products at home, to notice what messages are written in languages other than English. The Internet is another place to search for information in and about multiple languages. The theme study focuses on at least two goals: to make students aware of the multitude of written languages in the world, and to build respect for the languages and the people who speak them. Even when they can't read the language, students can examine newspapers in languages other than English to discover which features are similar to or different from those of English newspapers. Weather, sports scores, stock market information, and advertisements, for example, are usually easy to spot despite language differences. Eventually students become more comfortable with languages other than English, and they begin to find other instances of multiple language use, such as medicine information sheets and directions for games and toy assembly instruction.

Another theme cycle for studying language and cultural variations helps students read and comprehend unfamiliar languages in English texts as they explore the role of context and the significance of multiple language use in certain texts. *The Day of Ahmed's Secret* by Florence Perry Heide and Judith Heide Gilliland (1990), for example, introduces young English-speaking children to Arabic; *Here Comes the Cat!/Siuda idet kot!* by Frank Asch and Vladimir Vagin (1989) includes Russian. Some of these books have glossaries and others don't. Through such study, students explore the purpose of glossaries, how to use context to understand the meanings of other languages in texts, what authors do to make sure the reader comprehends, and why the author uses other languages that only some readers can understand.

Whenever possible I include in my book collections the same book in two languages, such as *Crow Boy* by Taro Yashima (1955) and *Faithful Elephants: A True Story of Animals, People, and War* by Yukio Tsuchiya (1988), both of which are available in Japanese and English editions. I read the book to the students in English the first day and then invite a speaker of Japanese to come in a few days later to read the book in the second language. We wonder why the lengths of the books are different. Sometimes the same book has different illustrators, and we discuss the similarities and differences in how the artists represent the same page of text.

Language study through literature can also focus on the role of translation in literature. I make every effort to have books available for my bilingual and multilingual students in their other languages and to include books that incorporate more than one language. Students explore books that have translations and raise questions about how two or three languages are displayed and whether each language is treated equally. It is not unusual, for example, for students to discover that when both English and Spanish are included in one book, English is often placed in the dominant position, such as on the left-hand page or at the top of the page. Students can undertake an important critique of the publication of literature by examining the degree to which authors and publishers take such issues into consideration.

I would encourage bilingual and multilingual students to translate if they choose to do so, but this encouragement needs to be approached with sensitivity. Many students are not aware that they are able to translate, so the teacher needs to move cautiously toward supporting students' translation opportunities. At the same time, however, monolingual students discover just how adept their bilingual and multilingual peers are with language when the latter are allowed to demonstrate their translation abilities.

Theme cycles related to these kinds of written language variations can begin in many different ways. In addition to browsing the books and other materials on display, students can brainstorm questions they have about their ability to read eye dialect and other language variations represented in print. Students often like to explore the use of italics, boldface, and single or double quotation marks. Rules found in publishing and other manuals such as those developed by the American Psychological Association or the Modern Language Association can be reprinted on posters, allowing students to compare the rules against their own work, peers' writing, and that of published authors. Other times such language study theme cycles emerge spontaneously when students are reading and encounter eye dialect or languages other than the ones they know and have trouble reading through them. Exploring the strategies that the teacher, other adults, and proficient readers use in such contexts helps students realize they don't always have to be able to pronounce or even know all the words in order to understand their reading.

Often in our ever-growing multilingual schools, students who do not speak English join the class. This is an opportune time for the teacher to explore with students written language variations. The students or their parents are invited to share written artifacts (books, magazines, letters, posters, etc.) from their homes that represent a language other than English read or spoken in the home. Parents may be asked to read a children's book written in their home language or share a poem or song with the class. Students whose native language is English are encouraged to interview their parents to discover whether they or other family members read languages other than English and have materials in those languages available to share as part of the literature study groups.

Inquiry expands into an exploration of the construction of meaning as students ask questions about texts and the uses of fonts and formats. It is perhaps even more important for students who have little contact with the range of rich languages and dialects in the world to have books in the classroom that represent multiple languages and dialects. All students have the right to know about the diversity of language and dialects and the global issues that relate to that diversity.

Nonalphabetic Writing Systems

Language study theme cycles are enhanced when students explore the ways in which meaning is expressed in writing systems that are not alphabetic. In the previous section, I discussed exploring languages such as Chinese and Japanese that are not based on alphabetic writing. In addition, symbols that express meaning nonalphabetically are used in a variety of ways. Books by authors and illustrators such as Anno help students explore math as a symbol system and the ways in which the number system is different from the alphabet.

Computers highlight the use of icons and other symbolic forms of meaning, so many students are already familiar with this kind of representation. Students also love to play with codes in order to make up their own secret messages. Nancy Garden (1981) has a book on codes and ciphers, *The Kids' Code and Cipher Book*, and teachers and students can find a number of more recent books on codes by searching the Web. The focus on codes easily leads to discussions about the Navajo code talkers of World War II and the books for adults and children on the code talkers' life-saving contribution to the war effort. Through explorations of the range of ways in which meaning is expressed through sign systems, students become more aware of the function of alphabetic writing specifically and the complexity of writing systems in general.

Other books involving dialect, second languages, and nonalphabetic language variation include:

◆ Mitsumasa Anno & Tsuyoshi Mori, *Socrates and the Three Little Pigs* (1986)

- Aliana Brodmann & Hans Poppel, *Que ruido! Cuento tradicional judío* (1990)

- Christopher Paul Curtis, *The Watsons Go to Birmingham—1963* (1995)

- Christopher Paul Curtis, *Bud, Not Buddy* (1999)

- Paula Danziger, *United Tates of America* (2002)

- Donald Davis, *Listening for the Crack of Dawn* (1990)

- Muriel Feelings, *Moja Means One: Swahili Counting Book* (1971)

- Muriel Feelings, *Jambo Means Hello: Swahili Alphabet Book* (1974)

- Leonard Everett Fisher, *Symbol Art* (1985)

- Lorenz Graham, *How God Fix Jonah* (2000)

- Sara Hunter, *The Unbreakable Code* (1996)

- Lynn Joseph, *The Color of My Words* (2000)

- Julius Lester, *The Tales of Uncle Remus: The Adventures of Brer Rabbit* (1987)

- Ellen Levine, *I Hate English!* (1989)

- Gay Matthaei & Jewel H. Grutman, *The Ledgerbook of Thomas Blue Eagle* (1994)

- Patricia C. McKissack, *Flossie and the Fox* (1986)

- Patricia C. McKissack, *Mirandy and Brother Wind* (1988)

- Margaret Musgove, *Ashanti to Zulu: African Traditions* (1976)

- Walter Dean Myers, *The Dragon Takes a Wife* (1995)

- Walter Dean Myers, *Monster* (1999)

- James Rumford, *There's a Monster in the Alphabet* (2002)

- Robert D. San Souci, *Callie Ann and Mistah Bear* (2000)

- Jon Scieszka, *It's All Greek to Me* (2001)

- Jon Scieszka, *The True Story of the 3 Little Pigs (by A. Wolf)* (1989)

- Leyla Torres, *Subway Sparrow* (1993)

- Nancy Van Laan, *Possum Come a-Knockin'* (1990)
- Mildred Pitts Walter, *Ray and the Best Family Reunion Ever* (2002)
- Ed Young, *Mouse Match* (1997)
- Ed Young, *Voice of the Heart* (1997)

Genre Variation

Genre variation is tied to font and format variation. Students raise questions about the relation between print form and genre and discover that differences in font and format often occur because of differences in content, author style, and the structure of language. Poetry is written differently than prose. Realistic fiction follows different formats from those of fantasy, and both are different from the writing about science and math. I use *genre* as the general term for the different ways in which written texts are categorized to talk about differences in style, content, and form. Even young children recognize similarities and differences among the works of authors and illustrators. When I read aloud a new book by an author or illustrator whose work primary grade students know, they quickly call out, "That's by Tomie dePaola" or "Is that an Eric Carle book?" Such spontaneous responses present critical teaching moments during which students can explore the characteristics that allow them to recognize their favorite authors and illustrators.

In the next section, I suggest organizing the classroom library as a way of exploring genre differences. Following that, the sections focus on theme studies such as exploring the characteristics of fiction, nonfiction, and multiple genres within a single text.

The Classroom Library

One way I often encouraged students to explore different genres was to involve them in organizing and maintaining our classroom library. A well-stocked classroom library is as important as a well-stocked school library. The classroom library provides important and readily accessible resources for inquiry studies. I planned for classroom library reorganization early each year and invited the students to organize the library to suit their own purposes. Over the years, students established different categories and procedures that ensured everyone understood the organization of the library and its uses. As part of the study, we planned a field trip to the local public library to discuss with librarians how and why they organize books the way they do and to address other issues the students might need to consider in organizing our classroom library. The school librarian (when we had one) also talked with my class to help with library organization. As a result, students learned about alphabetizing, ways to control for circulation, and what librarians take into consideration as they categorize different books. As part of the process, my students applied for library cards and wrote letters to their parents to encourage them to set aside time for regular family visits to the library. The letters, written in English or Spanish as appropriate, included directions to the library and information about its hours and services. Students also interviewed bookstore owners, who answered students' questions about ways to organize and display books.

The students took field notes during the field trips and interviews and used them to report back to the class. We discussed ways to organize, label, and display books that best suited our classroom setting. The students began to understand aspects of major library systems such as the Dewey decimal system and the Library of Congress classification and adapted the systems to fit our unique classroom library organization. They began to consider the importance of making book finding easy and managing access to and circulation of books. These discussions included a focus on genre differences since the students generally categorized the books according to the genres they were most interested in. Categories such as adventure, mystery, teen topics, slavery, cooking, sports, animals, and so forth were common over the years. Sometimes, if an author was particularly popular, such as Irene Hunt or Lloyd Alexander, the students decided to keep his or her books separated from the other categories. Within each genre they designated, my students organized the books alphabetically according to author. Inevitably, as we interviewed people who worked with books and discussed different categories, the students discovered that the conventional genres such as fiction and nonfiction are not always easy to establish. The students would list their questions about categorization and then revisit librarians and others who might be able to help them work through their newfound understandings.

When she organized her classroom library with her first graders, Vera Milz found that students remembered book titles better than authors' names, so they organized their books alphabetically according to title. When Dr. Milz was involved in a science or social studies theme cycle, the class would help her select the books to display for browsing. This led to discussions about what criteria they used to choose the books set aside for specific study. In addition, Dr. Milz's first graders and my middle school students were responsible for keeping track of book circulation, the shelving and care of books, and rules about how to maintain the library in good order. We elected librarians and other assistants on a rotating basis throughout the year and regularly set aside time during class meetings to discuss concerns related to library use.

Teachers have reported other ways their students organize books. Second-grade teacher Sue Martin, for example, helped her students realize they were all readers by discussing the importance of choosing books that are "just right" for them, and they classified books based on the purposes books served for them. The students decided they enjoyed different kinds of books at different times and came up with categories of books such as:

Vacation books: These are good to review for fun, but we put them aside for when we have more time to read. We take these books on trips in the car.

Just Right books: These are just right because they seem to fit. They are easy to read but at the same time there are new things to learn.

Dream books: These are books we would love to read but we need help to read. They are pretty challenging and sometimes uncomfortable to read alone, but we dream that we can read them independently one day.

Because the kids concluded that one text could be a vacation book for one person and a dream book for another, they often drew up their own personal lists. Often students kept their lists, especially of their dream books, to see if they could read more difficult books by themselves later in the year. In this way, they evaluated their own reading development. Many classroom libraries also include technology and organize CDs, videos, DVDs, and program disks according to genre.

Fiction and Nonfiction

It is important not to oversimplify differences between genres by focusing on narrow definitions of *fiction* and *nonfiction*. Early in my teaching, I realized that the differences between fact and fiction are not always clearly distinguishable. Even adults argue about the distinctions. Young students often have their own views about the differences between fantasy and truth. And older students often wonder why realistic fiction and narrative describe real events yet are not categorized as nonfiction. The best time to explore genre variation with students is when they raise questions during activities such as organizing the library, publishing their own texts, and discussing literature in study groups.

E. L. Doctorow, an American novelist who explores the boundaries between fiction, nonfiction, and other genres, has written a number of essays about the problems in distinguishing fact from fiction: "I am . . . led to the proposition that there is no fiction or nonfiction as we commonly understand the distinction: there is only narrative" (1983, p. 23), and "history is a kind of fiction in which we live and hope and survive, and fiction is a kind of speculative history" (p. 25). He supports his conclusions:

> We all know examples of history that don't exist. We used to laugh at the Russians who in their encyclopedias attributed every major industrial invention to themselves. . . . [O]ur own school and university historians had done just the same thing to whole peoples who lived and died in this country but were seriously absent from our texts: black people, Indians, Chinese. There is no history except as it is composed. (p. 24)

In order to establish the perceiving phase of exploring fiction and nonfiction and their subcategories, I often read statements such as Doctorow's aloud to students to help them think critically about conventional fiction subcategories such as fairy tales, folktales, drama, novels, and biographies, and nonfiction or expository subcategories such as history, geography, physics, human development, math, and music. I write the statement in large print, place it in the classroom, and invite students to collect similar statements to add to our collection of quotations. Sometimes I use a poem such as Nikki Giovanni's "communication" (1973, p. 35) to start students thinking about differences between fiction and nonfiction.

> if music is the universal language
> think of me as one whole note
>   if science has the most perfect language
> just think of me as Mc2
> since mathematics can speak to the infinite
> picture me as 1 to the first power
> What i mean is one day
> I'm gonna grab our love
> And you'll be satisfied

Poetry helps students discover the flexibility of genre, showing how content can be written in many forms in addition to fiction and nonfiction. Carl Sandburg (1920) writes about real-world phenomena.

Paper I

Paper is two kinds, to write on,
      to wrap with.
If you like to write, you write.
If you like to wrap, you wrap.
Some papers like writers, some
      like wrappers.
Are you a writer or a wrapper?

Pencils

Pencils
telling where the wind comes from
open a story.
Pencils
telling where the wind goes
end a story.
There eager pencils
come to a stop
... only ... when the stars high over
come to a stop.

As a result of the teacher's read-alouds, students' reading, and information they gather from test preparations and literature textbooks, the class lists different genres under columns labeled Fiction and Nonfiction, adding other columns as the students find the two categories limiting. The students examine the categories, comparing them to categories used by librarians and others, and corroborate those that work for them. They question other categories and add their own as needed. A major aspect of reading instruction is helping students be skeptical of what they read by examining and critiquing conventional categories. As students explore the variety of ways in which fiction and nonfiction are categorized, they begin to discuss concepts such as truth, fantasy, reality, and imagination, and they come to understand these concepts through intense discussion and thoughtful questioning. These opportunities affect their writing of various genres and help them explore their own flexibility and options as readers and writers. Through their brainstorming and discussions, students often wonder:

What different kinds of written stories are there?

Can you tell what kind of writing a piece is from the first sentence?

Do authors use different kinds of language in fiction than in nonfiction?

What sort of ending do you expect from a particular kind of story?

Are events always placed in order according to date?

After the students brainstorm, list their questions, and do further research, they often find ways to chart their discoveries in order to compare genres over time. The chart in Figure 9 is an adaptation of one used by Mellor and Raleigh (1984) to help students categorize different kinds of stories.

The students develop the headings for these kinds of comparison charts so they can relate them to their inquiry questions and how they want to present their ideas to others in the class.

Another way to explore the relationship between genres involves students in a theme cycle literature study of fiction and nonfiction by selecting a topic the students are interested in and exploring that topic through books written about the same topic but in different genres. In a theme cycle on schooling suggested at the end of this chapter are lists of fiction and nonfiction books about schools. The students can compare the language differences used to talk about school, teachers, and pupils. They can

Kind of Story	Typical Beginnings/ Endings	Typical Events	Typical Settings	Typical Characters
Mystery				
Fairy Tale				
Realistic Fiction				

FIGURE 9. *Comparison story chart.*

also examine and discuss reasons for the ways in which illustrations or diagrams are selected or displayed in each kind of text. They make posters and bulletin boards to illustrate their new learnings and chart their discoveries, and make graphs to document the different categories of books they collected about the schooling experience.

The use of nonfiction is important to such theme studies. Some readers prefer expository texts to fiction. Involving nonfiction also provides opportunities for students to explore the ways in which the writing of science is different from math or social studies writing. Students, for example, examine the different kinds of language the authors use to state their concepts, and the order in which they present information. Students become aware of the ways in which experts in different fields write about their craft. They also critique the authors' expertise in relation to the veracity of the content. In this way, students explore the kinds of research authors must do in order to make their writing believable. Such analysis raises these differences to a conscious level and helps students write their own reports as well as use such information to help them read nonfiction texts. They become more aware of how the organization of material, graphs, time lines, and diagrams help readers.

Through well-written picture books, upper elementary and middle school students learn a great deal about various concepts in different content areas and how people write in these areas.

Support from a teacher or librarian who knows the range of non-fiction picture books in the various content areas enriches theme cycle studies (Tiedt, 2000). I discovered a Web site of lists of illustrated books to use with ESL students and adults by searching for the words *picture books, middle schools,* and *adults.*

Some fiction books also lend themselves to the exploration of science and social studies issues. *La calle es libre* (Kurusa, 1981), available in both Spanish and English editions, is about a group of kids living in a crowded, poverty-ridden section of Caracas, Venezuela, who need a place to play. They are shooed away from their sports and games by adults who find them in the way as the kids play in the streets. Through the help of a sensitive and helpful librarian, the group finds ways to petition the government for a place to play. They have to solve all sorts of problems before they get a place of their own. This is a book that helps readers think about ways to actively make changes in their own lives by writing letters to government agencies, appealing for newspaper support, making demands, and having the determination to follow up. The book fits into the perceiving phase of a theme cycle on environmental issues and participating in government as an active citizen, and shows students the rich place literacy plays in problem-solving situations.

The book *My Place* by Nadia Wheatley and Donna Rawlins (1989) provides a view of the history of Sydney, Australia. The book focuses on children of different ethnic backgrounds who lived at the same site at different times over thousands of years of history. In each case, the ten-year-olds make references to their cultures, aspects of their lifestyles, and families. The authors make the point that history in Australia did not begin with European settlement. This book lends itself to theme cycle study about immigration, the environment, language, naming practices, and social justice. Books like *My Place* help students explore the use of first-person writing, personal narrative, and how young people can solve their own problems through language and literacy. They invite students to write about their own problems or communities in similar ways.

As mentioned earlier, there are many ways to amass books for the theme cycles suggested in these chapters. Teachers should look for authors who regularly write nonfiction as a place to start. When the teacher and students know the names of such authors, they easily find their books on Web sites. Both Vicki Cobb and Gail Gibbons, for example, often write about science concepts for very young students. Patricia Lauber writes about science topics for older students. Jean Fritz writes historical information, such as *And Then What Happened, Paul Revere?* (1996), and Anno often explores math concepts. Milton Meltzer (Saul, 1994) has produced many books in the field of social studies and has written a text about the uses of nonfiction for children and adolescents. HarperCollins (www.harperchildrens. com) lists Let's-Read-and-Find-Out! science books for first and second graders. These books were developed years ago by Roma Gans and Franklin Brantley and now are written by different authors. The National Science Teachers Association (www.nsta. org), National Council for the Social Studies (www.socialstudies. org), and the National Council of Teachers of Mathematics (www.nctm.org) publish journals for elementary and middle school teachers that list the outstanding childrens and adolescent books for each year in their fields of study. The lists include both expository genres and well-researched fiction.

The Same Story—or Is It?

Many teachers keep collections of books and short stories that lend themselves to examinations of not only fiction and nonfiction but also the ways in which authors use the same story in different ways (Sierra, 2002). I use a number of collections to explore such variations. I especially enjoy sharing my text set of stories related to an old Yiddish folksong/story I learned as a child about the history of a child's overcoat. There are many versions of this story/song, including one I wrote (Y. Goodman, 1998). What a wonderful surprise when I found out that the 2000 Caldecott Award winner was *Joseph Had a Little Overcoat* by Simms Taback (1999), which he originally published in 1977. There is also a version set in Hawaii (Indie, 1998). One possible theme cycle starts with involving students in singing and reading a number of the different versions and then comparing them. As they respond to their findings, students examine the legitimacy of retellings and multiple interpretations by storytellers, songwriters, and illustrators. Examining the different languages used to establish cultural validity, the ways in which the story/song changes, and how the illustrations tell a related and similar story all lead to considerations of literary quality. Students often use the publication dates of these books to explore which version is the original and whether thinking about the origins is important. The focus on intertextuality is another result of such study, as students explore the universality of narrative. Students share these stories at home with people of all ages to discover the degree to which the stories are part of their own histories. As with the little overcoat tale, there are many illustrated books of the same song, such as "There Was an Old Lady Who Swallowed a Fly," "Old MacDonald Had a Farm," and so forth. Songbooks broaden students' reading experiences beyond the texts they are most familiar with. With the introduction of songbooks, teachers and students explore a new symbol system to consider the multiple ways in which words and musical notation are related and how reading music is the same or different from reading written language.

Teachers can also gather the many books that allow students to examine the intertextual ties of stories around the world. La Llorona tales are common in the Hispanic culture, and students can explore both Spanish and English versions. The *pourquoi* tales that explore the origins of special animals are fun for students, especially when students get to compose their own. Origin tales of the Earth and its people, folktales, and fairy tales often have similar themes, event chains, and characters. In the study of these genres, it is easy for students to explore language and its use by people of different languages and cultures.

As I suggested for literature theme cycles in previous sections, I introduce the books during the presenting phase by displaying them for a few days before students read them. Sometimes I read one of the books aloud and then organize literature study groups so students can read and explore the stories they choose. If the students are very young, the teacher sometimes reads each of the books aloud, giving students time to examine the books between readings and to reread them by themselves or in pairs. Teachers who have sets of audio- or videotapes that go with the books make them available at a listening or viewing center.

	Language of Beginning and Ending	Description of Main Characters	Who Is Speaking	Unique Illustrations
Book Story 1				
Book Story 2				
Book Story 3				

FIGURE 10. *Comparing different versions of the same story.*

After the reading and discussion, students fill in a chart with column headings identifying features they want to explore (see Figure 10). These charts are maintained over time so that groups of students can add to them as they discover new issues to consider. More traditional charts list categories such as characters, settings, events, themes, and plots. This particular chart was developed as students focused specifically on the language of the texts.

Multiple Genres within a Text

There is no end to the ways that teachers can engage students in examining the different ways in which authors and illustrators create. Such an examination evolves from the categorization of different genres. Many books include characters who are actively engaged in using a range of genres such as diaries, journals, books, letters, and even motion pictures (Myers, 1999). Many of these books are in first person, which allows students to explore the uses of first-person and third-person narratives in both reading and writing. In *Dear Mr. Henshaw* (Cleary, 1983), main character Leigh Botts helps readers explore the ways in which letter and diary writing become personal for him even though originally these genres had been assigned by his teacher. Lucy Maud Montgomery, author of *Anne of Green Gables,* wrote in a journal she called her grumble book. As students experience such books as part of literature study or read-alouds, they are able to use the books as models to develop their own writing, discovering the range of genres they can experiment with as young authors.

The Magic School Bus series uses a complicated genre form that students enjoy analyzing. The author/illustrator team of Joanna Cole and Bruce Degen incorporate narrative, speech balloons, environmental print, signs, posters, and various other art forms to provide students with scientific information (see, for instance, Cole [1994]). Given these rich settings, teachers can have students consider the innovations authors come up with to engage their readers in complex material.

The Ahlbergs interweave multiple genres in their innovative *The Jolly Postman, or, Other People's Letters* (1986) to encourage students to consider the many different ways people use the mail. This book often prompts students to explore letter writing and to establish a class or schoolwide post office.

Other books that students enjoy and that help them inquire into multiple genres include L. Fitzhugh's *Harriet the Spy* (1964) and R. Klein's *Penny Pollard's Letters* (1987). Scholastic's Dear America series, originally written for adolescents, now includes a diary series for eight-to-ten-year-olds.

Language Play: Sense and Nonsense

Some genres of books lend themselves to a variety of non-narrative and nonexpository language forms such as poetry, verse, rap, puns, jokes, riddles, language play and nonsense, play party games, and songs. These often represent the literary culture of childhood common to every community (Y. Goodman, 1971).

A popular theme cycle I often developed with elementary and middle school students was the study of play party games and songs, riddles, puns, and jokes. This activity helps students explore their own culture of childhood or adolescence. As the students begin to collect examples of language play, their discussions lead to a number of data collection procedures. The students interview family members and study their own examples to see how the ones they collect are similar to or different from the games, jokes, songs, and chants members of their families remember. This provides a historical perspective on language play. When I provide historical collections of play party games and songs, the students become aware that adults are interested in such collections as well. They explore the important functions that play party games serve young children in a culture and the role of play in language development (Opie & Opie, 1992). The 1992 edition of *I Saw Esau* (first published in 1947) is illustrated by Maurice Sendak with helpful notes about the history of children's insults, riddles, tongue twisters, jeers, jump rope rhymes, and more, some of the references dating as far back as the 1600s. I suggest initiating such a theme cycle by reading selections from a book of play party games—such as Joanna Cole and Stephanie Calmenson's *Miss Mary Mack and Other Children's Street Rhymes* (1989), Joanna Cole's *Anna Banana: 101 Jump-Rope Rhymes* (1989), or Jane Yolen's *Street Rhymes around the World* (1992)—to the students and involving them in reading and chanting the verses. The students are invited to add verses they know and explain how they use them in their games (hide-'n-seek, choosing up sides, jump rope chants, etc.). Then the students brainstorm ways of collecting additional chants. These are published in class books or individual books or magazines. Family members are invited to add their own versions with information about dates, places, and the games that accompany the chants. These explorations sometimes culminate in presentations to other classes and families that involve demonstrating the physical movements of the accompanying dance or play routines. Local newspaper or TV news programs are often interested in publishing or broadcasting such events, especially when the students write or contact the papers or stations themselves.

Theme cycles about the culture of childhood consider language variation in relation to regional settings and the age and gender of the students. Students learn how the cultural experiences they participate in during their play are influenced by historical and political events and eventually develop the concept that each of them is part of history—that history is relevant to their lives. Adolescents are able to conduct similar studies in relation to the systems of tagging in their neighborhoods and the ways in which they are part of adolescent literary forms even as some adult critics reject them.

Many authors play with language and verse and thus can be included in this theme cycle. A few of my favorites include Dr. Seuss books, Fred Gwynne's *The King Who Rained* (1970) and *A Chocolate Moose for Dinner* (1989), "The Jabberwocky" by Lewis Carroll, and many poems by Shel Silverstein and Michael Rosen.

Storytelling and Writing Stories

The examination of genre through theme cycle study is a good way for students to learn from authors in order to write themselves. I end this section by exploring ways of encouraging students to think about the relationship between storytelling and story writing. During discussions of narrative genre, the teacher poses questions that invite students to think about themselves as authors or storytellers: What's the difference between telling a story orally and writing down a story? What choices do you have to make when you write a story? What changes do you need to make when you write a story compared to when you tell it?

The students are encouraged to keep a list of titles of or ideas from stories they remember, including who told them the stories. They compare their lists with those of others in the class and think about similarities and unique story forms. They explore whether the stories actually happened to them or to someone they know. Do their stories come from films, videos, or books they know well? Are they stories someone told them as children? Did they make up the stories themselves?

Students explore different ways to tell their stories or to write them. They explore concepts of past and present as they think about how the story would be different if they told it or wrote it as if it were happening now or had happened before. Students are encouraged to experiment with different approaches. They consider whether to use first person or third person; what language to use for each of the characters; how to start and end the story; and what events to include and in what order. They work with a buddy or in groups of three and discuss the changes they made each time they revised their story. The whole class then comes together to discuss what they learned through making those changes. Many of the issues the students explore while thinking about themselves as authors are aspects of literature they have already discussed in their literature groups. Thus, the students come to a greater understanding of how their reading and writing are related.

A Study of Schooling

I end this chapter by looking at a theme cycle on schooling that I have developed over the years with graduates, undergraduates, and middle school students. The importance of a theme cycle on schooling has ideological as well as educational ramifications. The general public has minimal knowledge about how beliefs about teaching, learning, and democratic processes affect the decisions teachers make about curriculum development. I believe that a study on schooling helps students understand that what teachers do in school is carefully thought out and planned. The theme cycle also provides a more specific picture of how a theme cycle develops.

The objectives of a schooling theme cycle revolve around getting students to think about how schools are organized, their purposes, and the kinds of learning experiences that are most effective. They consider the environments that best support learning, discover how teachers make decisions about curriculum in the classroom, and contemplate how they can be part of negotiating curriculum. They learn about who has decision-making power in schools and consider the ways in which political issues influence the lives of students and teachers in classrooms.

The perceiving phase of learning can be initiated in a number of ways. Books such as those listed at the end of this section can be displayed with historical artifacts such as old textbooks, a typewriter, old-fashioned writing implements, schoolbags, a school bell, old school lunch boxes, and so forth. Some teachers have old school desks they use for display purposes. Poems about schooling are photocopied so each student has a personal copy, or they are displayed on posters so the class reads them together at regular intervals.

I introduce a theme cycle on schooling by reading aloud *My Great-Aunt Arizona* by Gloria Houston (1992) if I want students to consider the kinds of experiences they have in school, or I read *Crow Boy* by Taro Yashima (1955) if I decide I want students to think about how they learn. In Donald Davis's *Listening for the Crack of Dawn* (1990), the short story "Miss Daisy" is a great read-aloud over a few days for older students exploring teaching methodology.

I have a large collection of books for children and adolescents on schools and their organization, literacy issues, students who struggle in schools, and teaching methodology, all of which readily stimulate discussion among students. Such collections should be available for browsing, and the teacher also introduces books through book talks, suggesting that students choose text sets or shared books that relate to issues most relevant to them. The students browse the books over the next few days, brainstorm the questions and concerns they have about the readings, and then indicate their first or second choices for the literature group they want to join. As they read together, they decide how many pages they want to read before they report back to the group at the next designated group meeting. Throughout their reading and discussion, students have time to ideate and list the issues or questions they want to know more about. They list their inquiry questions in their literature groups and begin their research to answer these questions as they continue their reading.

The teacher extends the students' thinking about schooling by reading aloud additional illustrated books such as the ones listed at the end of this section. The ideating phase continues as students respond to their experiences in their literature study groups and in whole class discussions following the read-aloud. Open-ended questions help connect students' school experiences with those they are reading about: Did you ever have such an experience?; Why do you think teachers (or other adults) in this story act the way they do?; Can you compare the school experiences in the books with your school experiences? Such conversations provide opportunities for students to present their own ideas and questions as part of the discussion.

Based on the literature discussions, the theme cycle can go in various directions. Questions and issues are discussed in the class and categorized. One class organized into five groups to explore:

(1) the rights students have in relation to extracurricular activities if they have problems in school; (2) the impact of censorship on the kinds of books kids can read in school; (3) the different ways that teachers teach kids; (4) who has more power—the teacher or the principal; and (5) do boys or do girls get into more trouble in school and why. In one of my undergraduate classes, we studied: (1) the role of controversial issues; (2) the impact of legal mandates on curricula; (3) the teaching about religion in elementary classrooms; (4) mainstreaming special education students; and (5) teachers' unions.

The students research their topics in libraries, on the Internet, through interviews of people from all ages, and through visits to institutions related to schooling. They continually discover new questions and ideas to explore. They develop projects; present final oral presentations, written reports for a class book, or a mural of an ideal school or a historical school they develop from interviewing grandparents; and write letters to various agencies to gather information or thank their visitors.

At some point early in the theme cycle, I ask students to list the experiences they have had in school that helped them learn the most and the experiences that were disruptive to their learning. When they come up with the two lists, we explore the elements that make learning easy or difficult. These lists can easily be made specific to learning to read or write or to content area learning if a teacher wants to focus on specific aspects of learning. After such a discussion, the students brainstorm a list of questions that their grandparents might answer in order to discover how learning and teaching were different two generations earlier. The lists are also useful for personal interviews with family members: Questions from such lists include:

What did you like best about school?

What did you like least about school?

Did you like your teacher(s)?

What kind of teacher(s) did you have?

What subjects did you have to study?

How did you get to school?

What did you learn about spelling and grammar in school?

How many kids were in your classes and how old were they?

When they write or talk to their grandparents and share the answers with the class, students discover new questions that lead to additional research, lots more reading, and continued written communication with their grandparents. Many grandparents have kept their own school notebooks, old textbooks, or report cards that they are willing to pass on to their grandchildren. Grandparents tend to be impressed with the seriousness of their grandchildren's interests. Janine Archey, a Detroit area fourth-grade teacher, encourages her students to write their grandparents at least once a year to establish generational relationships as well as to explore various historical events.

My Great-Aunt Arizona (Houston, 1992) stimulates a number of different theme cycles on school. Author Gloria Houston mentions William Matrimmatoe, a game played by the children in Aunt Arizona's school near Benson Creek, South Carolina. When I read this book to an audience of teachers in North Carolina about fifty miles from where the actual school was located, I got an immediate response from teachers, who recounted that members of their family had been in Aunt Arizona's classes and that they had heard about her most of their lives. The group was energized by the discussion, and everyone became involved in talk about this well-known teacher and her curriculum.

Class members called their parents and grandparents to interview them about what they knew about Aunt Arizona. Teresa Young reported that Arizona was her mom's fourth-grade teacher as well as that of all her aunts, uncles, and grandparents on her mom's side of the family; she had been their neighbor's teacher as well. Others went to the local library and unearthed books such as *Aunt Zona's Web* (1976), an autobiography by Arizona Hughes as told to Thomas C. Chapman, and learned a lot about the history of their local community. The interest in the William Matrimmatoe game led students to discover references to it in *Foxfire 5* (Wigginton, 1979, p. 69) and *Foxfire 6* (Wigginton, 1980, pp. 309–10) and in the Opies's book on children's play party games (1992). Another group interviewed their parents and gathered versions of William Matrimmatoe, which was reported by some to be a leapfrog game. The rhyming chant that accompanies the counting-out procedures starts with:

> William [or Willie] Matrimmatoe
> He's a good fisherman.
> Catches fishes, puts in dishes,
> Catches hens, puts in pans,
> Wire brier, limber lock,
> Three geese in a flock.
> One flew east, one flew west,
> One flew over the cuckoo's nest,
> Be gone home, Jack McLee.
> Ten o'clock in the night.
> The clock fell down,
> The rats ran 'round,
> Didn't they have a Yankee-doodle time?

Other groups focused on the various names, spelling, and origins of the game: William Tremmel Toe, William Tremble Toe, Willie Matrimmatoe.

We explored the various experiences Aunt Arizona planned for her students and related them to the principles of a whole language philosophy. Some students took the experiences Arizona used in her teaching and discussed what they would look like in a modern classroom.

Another aspect of the schooling study often includes students conceptualizing a philosophy of education. The teacher shares her or his philosophy and encourages the students to interview other teachers and the school administrators about what they believe about teaching and learning. The teacher adds questions to focus the students on language study: How important is it to be a good speller? Do you believe students need to know grammar and what does that mean to you? How do you think reading [or writing or spelling] should be taught? Students are encouraged to consider their own philosophy in terms of what kinds of teachers they would like to have.

After a schooling theme cycle with my middle school students about the development of middle schools in the district, we composed a cantata about the history of our middle schools. This was a formal presentation to the entire school in a morning performance and to parents in the evening. This group of students reported on the differences and similarities between middle schools and junior highs. We also organized our classroom to look like a one-room schoolhouse from the 1800s.

Other culminations of schooling studies have involved the display of photographs of early schoolhouses, including lists of rules for teachers and students. Some students come to conclusions about schooling by studying old spelling, grammar, reading, or language arts textbooks and comparing them to modern ones or to the use of authentic children's and adolescent literature. An eighth-grade teacher in Detroit told me that after reading aloud *Lyddie* by Katherine Paterson (1992) to her class, the students decided to explore teachers' strikes and find out whether they were legal in their state, if they had ever occurred, and if so, what the results were. They were surprised to discover that teachers in Lyddie's day often only had to graduate from high school before they could teach. Other middle school students explored the laws and results of the desegregation of schools and concerns about public education. These studies often culminated in students putting on mock trials.

I end this section with a very short selected list of books I often include in studies on schooling:

Children's and Adolescent Books Related to Schooling

Avi, *The Secret School* (2001)

Tom Birdseye, *Just Call Me Stupid* (1993)

Canadian Childhoods: A Tundra Anthology in Words and Art Showing Children of Many Backgrounds Growing Up in Many Parts of Canada (1989)

Miriam Cohen, *When Will I Read* (1977)

Miriam Cohen, *First Grade Takes a Test* (1980)

Roald Dahl, *Boy: Tales of Childhood* (1984)

Judy Finchler, *Testing Miss Malarky* (2000)

Leonard Everett Fisher, *The Schools* (1983)

Deborah Heiligman, *The New York Public Library Kid's Guide to Research* (1998)

Gloria Houston, *My Great-Aunt Arizona* (1992)

Irene Hunt, *Lottery Rose* (1978)

Ellen Levine, *I Hate English!* (1989)

Gay Matthaei & Jewel Grutman, *The Ledgerbook of Thomas Blue Eagle* (1994)

Katherine Paterson, *Lyddie* (1992)

Gary Paulsen, *Nightjohn* (1993)

Eve Merriam, *The Wise Woman and her Secret* (1991)

Leo Rosten, *The Education of Hyman Kaplan (by Leonard Q. Ross, pseud.).* (1937)

Elizabeth George Speare, *The Sign of the Beaver* (1983)

Jerry Stanley, *Children of the Dust Bowl: The True Story of the School at Weedpatch Camp* (1993)

Taro Yashima, *Crow Boy* (1955)

Ed Young, *Seven Blind Mice* (1992)

CHAPTER SEVEN

Focus on Language as Power

Opportunities to explore language as power and how language impacts each member of a democratic society within and outside the classroom are integral to the various studies of language discussed in previous chapters. In this chapter, I discuss language power issues that can be planned either as an independent learning theme cycle or as integral to other aspects of language study. Terms such as *ideology* or *political* are not often used during discussions of curricula in the United States. In fact, there are those who believe that teaching in schools can be objective and apolitical. Yet it is obvious that if curricula are to include "higher-order thinking skills" or "critical thinking," a component of most curriculum guides, then exploring the ideology and political nature of language and thinking in school settings is necessary. Critical inquiry engages students in highly reflective and serious thinking about the power and role of language. Through such inquiry and discussion, students discover themselves as critical thinkers and learners.

British education has a rich history of involving students of all ages in the critical analysis of language. An unauthored paper by a group of educators from Lancaster, England, states the importance of critical language knowledge:

> Language awareness programmes should help students not only with the operational and descriptive knowledge of the linguistic practices of their world, but also to build a critical awareness of how these practices are shaped by and shape social relationships and relationships of power. This critical awareness, in combination with purposeful discourse from children and others, can contribute to transforming existing literacy practices.

They conclude their discussion with a quote from Paulo Freire (1985), whose concept of liberatory pedagogy informs critical analysis:

Whether it be a raindrop that was about to fall but froze, giving birth to a beautiful icicle, be it a bird that sings, a bus that runs, a violent person on the street, be it a sentence in the newspaper, a political speech, a lover's rejection, be it anything, we must adopt a critical view, that of the person who questions, who doubts, who investigates and who wants to illuminate the very life we live. (pp. 198–99)

Examining in critical ways books, poems, magazine articles, TV sitcoms, news broadcasts, newspaper editorials, speeches by powerful members of the community, political cartoons, and the language of the poor and marginalized groups allows kids to become confident in their own ability, as Freire suggests, to question, doubt, investigate, and illuminate the life they lead. Teachers who encourage such explorations are courageous, taking the necessary risks to participate with students in controversial discussions about language and to take action together. Ira Shor (1991) calls such teachers dialogic, and describes the tensions of the teacher in such contexts:

The dialogic teacher has to be restrained and assertive *at the same time,* holding back from providing quick answers while posing challenging problems, intervening to present issues . . . while creating open space for student voices, not lecturing students on what to believe and not narrating passive scholastic information to memorize, yet leading the dialogue forward, . . . opening the classroom to student speech while integrating a critical study of standard usage (the language of power), . . . leading the class while inviting students to take the lead themselves. For the transforming teacher, this means being authoritative without being authoritarian, being expert without being arrogantly professional. This creative balance is learned in process over a span of years, as an experiment in remaking our teaching role. (p. 223)

The following topics include suggestions for critical language study:

◆ Power and Control

◆ Students' Right to Their Own Language

◆ Censorship

◆ Demystifying Language

Power and Control

As students become consciously aware that careful analysis of oral or written texts reveals power relationships, they attend more closely to language use and bring to class the results of their investigations. They observe and listen more carefully to language interactions that provide insight into power relationships whenever they encounter language issues that relate to race, ethnicity, language, class, or generational diversity. They continuously ask, Why does language take the form it does in these specific settings? Whose voices are heard? and Whose voices are silenced? The following theme cycles for studying the power of language, whether in the community, the home, or the school, are often initiated by discussion as the perceiving phase of students' learning.

Language Power in the Home and Community

Carol Crowell teaches bilingual primary grade students in Tucson, Arizona. She has her students take a sidewalk safari through their school neighborhood to explore the use of written English and Spanish in their community, which includes a majority of Spanish and bilingual Spanish-English language users. The children wondered whether Spanish or English was the most visible language in their community. With clipboards and cameras in hand, the students observed carefully. They noted the billboards, street signs, and notices on walls, storefronts, and market bulletin boards. The class photographers took photographs of the signs the students considered most important for their inquiry. Back in the classroom, the students categorized the English and Spanish signs and concluded that English is the privileged language in their community. The signs in English were official: the names of streets, traffic signals, directions, and construction sites. Most of the billboards were in English, although the children discovered two billboards in Spanish that advertised cigarettes and beer. Most of the signs in Spanish tended to be handwritten and stapled to bulletin boards in the supermarkets, on small businesses, or on homes. The students discussed the messages that such language use in the community sends about the value of Spanish. They decided that the Spanish billboards selling cigarettes and beer revealed advertisers' attitudes about the lifestyle of Hispanics. The students explored this and related issues for a few weeks with family members and kept adding to their data collection as they walked or took the school bus to and from home, or when they went shopping in other parts of the city. Some of Ms. Crowell's classes wrote to the billboard companies about the language issues they were discovering, and one class actually got a billboard company to put up a sign in Spanish in their community that reads, "Read to your children every day," similar to the one available in English.

Many teachers develop theme cycles to have students critically analyze the language of TV, radio, and newspaper commercials and ads that impact all members of society. Even very young children are able to explore truth in advertising and study the meanings of terms such as *always, never, 99 percent pure,* and so on, and to critically analyze how such terms influence their own (or their parents') buying practices. One first-grade teacher asks her students what food they want to buy based on an examination of ads, buys the food, and then prepares the food with the students, reads the small print on the package with them, and discusses whether the cooked product lives up to the advertisement. During these experiences, students begin to use terms such as *gullible, naive,* and *skeptical,* as well as *critical,* as they discover the vocabulary they need to name their ideas and concerns.

During such explorations, students become conscious of the role of fine print and warning labels in protecting the company or the consumer. They talk about fads and the impact of brand names and what happens to students who resist them or to those who become the consumers of what is most popular. The class organizes panel discussions that include students of different ages, parents, and store buyers in order to respond to questions the students have developed as a result of their research. I visited one class in a Detroit suburb when the children walked to a local supermarket to talk to the manager in charge of shelving goods. He showed the students a notebook that companies send to store managers telling them on which shelves they need to place certain goods so they are accessible to kids. Those specific items will be advertised on kids' television shows, so kids will be looking for them in stores. Discussions about product advertisement and placement are animated at any grade level because these issues are so relevant to the students' lives. In one case, discussions about shoe fads led another class to explore child labor used in the production of specific sports footwear. The magazine *Zillions: Consumer Reports for Kids,* also available online at www.zillions. com, is a helpful resource for such explorations.

Other possible studies concerning language power issues in the home and the community include:

What kinds of language do parents use with their children that children are not supposed to use with their parents?

Who talks most at the dinner table or during family discussions: men, boys, women, or girls? Does the topic of conversation make a difference?

What kind of language do some people use to silence other people, and how is such language used differently by men, women, adolescents, or children?

What kind of language makes you think someone is apologetic or angry, or feels superior or silly, etc.?

Language Power in the Classroom

Linda Christensen (1992–1993) often plans a testing study with her secondary students before periods of test taking by taking advantage of their anxieties—both those who do well in school and yet worry that they won't do well enough on the test and those who are not very successful and know they will not do well on the test. Christensen states, "I begin the unit by giving them a sample test, then exploring how they felt about it. Most felt humiliated. We explore why a test for college admission should make them feel like that. We ask why there should be tests to keep some people in and some people out of college" (p. 20).

Ms. Christensen encourages her students to gather statistics from FairTest (http://fairtest.org) that break down scores by race, class, and gender and to explore the ways in which statistics about tests are presented in government reports, newspapers, and other news broadcasts. She and the students explore essential questions such as: Are women less intelligent than men? Are rich people smarter than poor people? If not, how can we explain the differences in scores? Ms. Christensen explains the power of such inquiry: "The shift . . . from consumption of knowledge to the questioning and examining of assumptions moves students of diverse abilities away from the lock-step nature of a skills approach while at the same time challenging them with a rigorous, accessible curriculum" (p. 20).

Although Ms. Christensen is working with high school students, theme cycles about the powerful role that testing plays in curriculum development, learning, and teaching are helpful for students at any age. Books such as *First Grade Takes a Test* (Cohen, 1980) and *Testing Miss Malarkey* (Finchler, 2000) are appropriate for read-alouds or literacy study for elementary students because they result in animated follow-up discussions and provide opportunities for students to explore the power issues related to testing.

The controversies over using standardized tests to sort students have a long history. Teachers and students are caught in a dilemma. On the one hand, tests have long-range influences on students' academic histories, and teachers, administrators, and parents believe it is the schools' responsibility to prepare students to be successful test takers. On the other hand, tests affect the emotional well-being of students and place pressures on administrators, teachers, and students that interfere with curricular innovations. As students examine and critique various kinds of tests and the role of testing in schools and society, they become empowered because they become knowledgeable about how tests work, critical of their influences, and aware of test-taking procedures. *A Teacher's Guide to Standardized Reading Tests* by Calkins, Montgomery, and Santman (1998) provides many suggestions to help students demystify the test-taking process and consider tests as one specific genre that involves reading and response strategies that differ from those of other genres. In the process of inquiry into testing, students become more confident about taking tests.

Parents, family, and community members are eager to participate in discussions and studies about testing since there is a good deal of anxiety about testing in the community at specific times of the year. Reporting of tests scores and debates about high-stakes testing are available in newspapers and on television and radio. At times of heightened public awareness, it is most appropriate to involve students and their families in explorations of testing issues and to support students when they take action by participating in public debate, attending community meetings, writing letters to editors, or setting up panel discussions at the school. The students gather information about how and when older people took tests in order to build historical knowledge and gather information about other generations' attitudes toward test taking.

Another critical language study emerges from inquiry into how students label specific groups in school and leads to relevant and highly charged discussions. In a sixth-grade classroom in the Detroit suburbs, the students were exploring the labels students used in their middle school to designate the jocks, the eggheads, and other social groups the kids belonged to. The teacher involved the kids in such discussion during the first year of middle school so that they could learn to understand the social nature of the school community. The kids made a chart of the different groups, their labels, and their characteristics, and then examined the kinds of language the students used in relation to the groups. The students wrote plays, designed political cartoons, and held panel discussions to explore these terms and the issues that grew out of their use and how they affected their relationships with peers. They began to understand that the groups could include and provide a safety network for some students but at the same time could also establish cliques that excluded others. They interviewed friends and teachers in other middle schools and in high schools to discover and compare how different groups were labeled and treated. They also interviewed parents and other community members to find out whether such groups existed in previous generations and whether the labels and issues were the same.

Although social designations are common in all schools, rarely do students participate in open discussion that explores the consequences of such designations. These discussions are easily integrated with theme cycles that focus on collaborative community building, conflict resolution, and issues of racism and sexism.

The concepts students build about group designations within the school lead them to expand their studies. They examine, for example, ways in which the language on their favorite TV shows, CDs, and DVDs establishes positive or negative images of different racial, ethnic, religious, age, social class, or gender groups. Studies about the labels for groups of people start with those closest to the students, such as school groups, but expand to the use of labels that categorize groups in society and to an understanding of the power of such language to establish stereotypes and misinformation. Students discover and explore the reasons for specific labels and terms that are acceptable when used within a group but are considered offensive or taboo when used by outsiders.

These critical discussions and explorations should be part of language study whenever students raise questions about how language is used to hurt or exclude others. In Chapter 4, I discuss strategy lessons that allow students to evaluate their oral language interactions as they critique the language of others. Such sessions have students examine their own language behaviors such as wait time and turn taking and how such behaviors involve controlling or sharing discussion space with others. Self-evaluation is an important aspect of such discussions because students need to explore their responsibility for understanding the ways they use language to control others.

At the beginning of each semester in my classroom, I led such discussions. Since, however, these critical evaluations were taking place regularly, I was eventually able to turn the leadership of the discussions over to the students. We discussed the different language students used in leading discussions and the power of the discussion leader's position. We evaluated the language that was most respectful and successful in maintaining an animated discussion. We also tried to hold discussions without raising our hands or having someone call on the next speaker. The students concluded that this was easier in small groups than during whole class discussions. Because the students faced one another in small groups, they could tell from body movement when someone wanted to speak and could make sure that everyone had a turn.

During these discussions, students established rules about how to ensure the safety of expression of each member of the class and listed the strategies that help their discussions be more successful and democratic:

- ◆ Sit in a circle or a U shape so everyone can see everyone else.

- ◆ Make sure that others speak who want to before you speak a second or third time.

- ◆ If you want to change the direction of the discussion, ask whether anyone has something else to say about the current topic because you have an idea that will take the discussion in a different direction.

- ◆ If only a few people are talking all the time, someone should invite others into the conversation.

- ◆ Respect everyone's point of view but expect these positions to be open to respectful interrogation; this includes the teacher's position.

Through critical analysis of their own language use, students consider the different ways they use language during conversation, debate, and argument. The role of the teacher is crucial in such discussions. Teachers don't stand apart from discussions while suggesting politically correct ways for students to talk. Rather, teachers are part of the discussion. They share their own views but give the students the same opportunity to express their views. Teachers who find this kind of talk threatening may want to delay introducing such discussions until they know their students well or until they have observed colleagues in classrooms where successful discussions take place. It is helpful for teachers to discuss their concerns with the students by expressing their views about language power issues such as being respectful, listening carefully, and being open to diverse and unpopular opinions.

Questions such as "What knowledge and authority do teachers have?"; "Should teachers have the last say?"; "Do teachers always have the right answers?" help students know that the teacher is willing to share authority during discussions. To establish an effective environment for critical language study, teachers must be willing to critically analyze and be cognizant of their power in the classroom. When teachers demonstrate their willingness to share power, students are more willing to be respectful not only of the teacher's ideas but also of the ideas of other students. In such situations, I refer to Ira Shor's (1991) caution that the teacher is an authority without being authoritarian and an expert without being arrogantly professional.

Other possible studies concerning language power issues in the classroom include inquiry into (1) language interactions between male students and female students; between female teachers and male students; between male teachers and female students, and (2) language interactions between students and the principal and between the principal and teachers.

News Broadcasts and the Power of the Press

Roxana Morduchowicz (1991) describes a program in the public schools of Buenos Aires in which the sixth and seventh graders from different middle schools were responsible for a weekly radio program beamed to all city middle schools. The purpose was for the children to express themselves freely, to share research topics important to young adolescents, and to handle questions and comments from students from other schools. According to Ms. Morduchowicz, "They [the students] learned that to be responsible for a program means to inform with responsibility, to say the truth, not to censor the answers and to give everyone the right to express themselves freely" (p. 76). This and similar programs were established as Argentina was shifting from a military dictatorship to a democracy and the school districts were eager to have students read news critically and explore multiple viewpoints.

Understanding the role of news reporting and the power of the press is critical in democratic societies. Many schools have public address systems that tend to be used primarily by the school office or the principal. But these systems can also provide students with opportunities to lead news broadcasting and to explore the role of public radio and television in reporting news.

At Fair Oaks Elementary School in California, upper-grade students produced a school radio program in Spanish and English to explore the important issues of the day (Bird, 1989). On a rotating basis, a different classroom took responsibility for public address presentations. In other schools, the radio broadcasts become the responsibility of a specific grade level each year, with their teachers serving as advisors. Such opportunities give students legitimate and authentic reasons to explore ways of expressing their own ideas and to study the role of the press in radio, television, and newspapers in terms of who controls the news, how decisions are made about what is worth reporting, and the responsibility of the press to be objective and truthful.

Newspaper publishers and other news reporting agencies have guidelines for the kinds of language and topics that are permissible in reporting. In the November 1993 *Guidelines on Ethnic, Racial, Sexual and Other Identification* drafted by a newsroom committee of the *L.A. Times*, writers are told not to mention the racial and ethnic background of people in the news unless it is relevant. The guidelines state: "When deciding whether to mention someone's race, ask yourself:—Is the ethnic and racial identification needed? Is it important to the context of the story?—Is the story complete without reference to race or ethnic identification?" The guidelines deal with language related to Black and African Americans, Latinos, Native Americans, Whites, Illegal Immigrants, Jews, Arab Americans, and so on, including prescriptions about which terms should be used and which are considered offensive. Other guideline issues relate to names of holidays, gender identification, and other racial and ethnic identification issues (p. 1).

With their students, teachers gather guidelines and style manuals of various news agencies in order to analyze the purpose of such documents and to wonder: Who do the guidelines protect? Why is it in the interest of news agencies to have such guidelines available to their authors and broadcasters? Since such guidelines are updated every few years, teachers should send for them regularly. As they explore the different documents, students come to understand the reasons for them and to use the guidelines to critique and analyze the language of newspapers and broadcasts. As a result, students often write to news agencies or invite reporters and editors to their classrooms to discuss questions and issues they have with the ways the guidelines are used and the ways language is used by the press.

Students' Right to Their Own Language

In a democratic society, all people have rights, including young people. Exploring the democratic right students have to read, write, speak, and listen in their own language(s) and dialect(s) is integral to understanding language power issues. As teachers and students explore students' right to their language use and critique the ways in which this language right is often violated, they also come to understand their responsibilities as language users.

Language(s) and Dialects

In November 1972, the Executive Committee of the Conference on College Composition and Communication (CCCC) of the National Council of Teachers of English (NCTE) passed the following resolution, which was adopted as policy in a version that included explanatory background in April 1974:

> **Students' Right to Their Own Language**
> We affirm the students' right to their own patterns and varieties of language—the dialects of their nurture or whatever dialects in which they find their own identity and style. Language scholars long ago denied that the myth of a standard American dialect has any validity. The claim that any one dialect is unacceptable amounts to an attempt of one social group to exert its dominance over another. Such a claim leads to false advice for speakers and writers, and immoral advice for humans. A nation proud of its diverse heritage and its cultural and racial variety will preserve its heritage of dialects. We affirm strongly that teachers must have the experiences and training that will enable them to respect diversity and uphold the right of students to their own language.

I would initiate a theme cycle on students' right to their own language by displaying prominently in the classroom this resolution with other related quotes about language rights, reading them with the students, and providing lots of opportunity to ideate and revisit the ideas. A special issue of *College Composition and Communication (CCC)*, now available online from the National Council of Teachers of English at www.ncte.org/positions/language.shtml, includes the resolution that was adopted in the mid-1970s. In addition to a background statement explaining the rational of and support for the resolution, this position statement includes a bibliography and suggestions for further reading. Geneva Smitherman (1995) published an updated National

Language Policy adopted by CCCC that expands the focus on dialects to include a concern for maintaining students' heritage languages as well as second language learning. The article includes a retrospective on the history of and struggle for the adoption of the students' language rights document and reflects on recent debates, district and state laws, and educational policies regarding language diversity issues.

Quotes such as the following by Alice Walker (1988) might also be displayed in the classroom to highlight the discussion:

> For it is language more than anything else that reveals and validates one's existence, and if the language we actually speak is denied us, then it is inevitable that the form we are permitted to assume historically will be one of caricature, reflecting someone else's literary or social fantasy. (p. 102)

I would invite students to add their own meaningful quotations to our display of thoughtful quotes about language variation.

Issues of dialect and language variation are often prominent in both the popular and the professional press. In the late 1990s, the dialect issue became a national debate in response to the concept of Ebonics and African American English that was part of a resolution about language teaching and learning in California's Oakland Unified School District. An issue of *Rethinking Schools* (Perry & Delpit, 1997) provides the background on the Oakland schools resolution, the school district policy, and a Linguistics Society of America resolution on Ebonics, and gives teachers a range of points of view to share with students. The journal is guest-edited by Theresa Perry and Lisa Delpit and includes responses by many prominent language scholars; the articles and positions are ones students are able to consider and explore, especially in upper elementary grades and middle school.

By exploring position statements, newspaper articles, debates on television, and other related sources, students can document the values that different people hold about monolingualism or multilingualism and develop their own understandings about these issues. Students develop questions and list the complex issues that result from their brainstorming: Why are some languages or dialects valued more highly than others? How do I feel about the different ways people speak? What are the advantages and disadvantages of being monolingual, bilingual, or multilingual? How are dialects and language variations valued and accepted differently in speaking and in writing?

Students examine the Internet, download articles, analyze advertisements and comics, and take notes on TV shows and videos to document how language variation (dialects and second languages) is used in various resources as well as how language is used to designate speakers of other languages and dialects. Students interview or invite to class people who speak various languages and dialects in order to consider different points of view about language variation. They examine the language that writers and speakers use to discuss the issue and the people whose language is in question. Do they treat with respect the language variation of others, or do their comments reveal prejudices and stereotypes? At the same time, students examine their own language in their interviews and questionnaires, using the same criteria to reveal their own sensitivities and prejudices.

Reading aloud materials written in dialect or languages other than English is another way to explore and consider the power issues of language use. Students consider whether such reading shows respect for language variation and analyze the ways in which readers use dialects and international languages in their reading. As students examine language variation in their reading, they consider the appropriate ways they might use language variation in their writing. If teachers or students are not comfortable reading in a variety of language forms, they can listen to audiotapes of books that demonstrate language variations. In Chapter 6, I list books written for children and adolescents that include dialect and language variation. These should be part of book displays on language rights so that students can discuss authors' rights to represent the language of others and can critique the linguistic accuracy with which authors represent dialect and language variation.

The importance I place on inquiry into language variation for a language study curriculum is supported by Walt Wolfram, a linguistics professor at North Carolina State University:

Since nothing is more central to education and human behavior than language, dialect awareness programs should not be a tangential adjunct to so-called "core knowledge. . . . [I]t is essential to provide instruction specifically targeting language diversity at the local, regional and national levels. It is a curious and even dangerous omission when the unique sounds of a culture are silenced. (2000, p. 21–22)

Wolfram has developed dialect awareness programs for schools in which students conduct community dialect surveys. He suggests that students brainstorm to collect a list of ten words from the community that they know people use in different ways and then interview a range of community members by asking questions such as:

When people are hot and thirsty, they may get a _____ from the machine.

When you buy something from the store, the clerk puts it into a _____.

When you want counter food such as a sandwich with meat and vegetables in a large bun, you ask for _____.

The students avoid using the specific word and say "blank" instead when they read the sentences orally. Students then create a chart and tally the responses, and as they continue to read and talk about different dialects and other language variations and to interview family, friends, teachers, and linguists, they consider what kinds of trends they see in the use of the words. What does the survey show about the language use of different groups of people? In what ways does the community dialect seem to be changing?

The Web site of the North Carolina Language and Life Project (www.ncsu.edu/linguistics/code/research%20sites/ncllp2.htm) provides information about a number of dialect awareness projects. The Foxfire books, which document the language and culture of the Appalachian Mountain people, include information about collecting and transcribing their language and folklore. Information about Foxfire and related curriculum projects is available on the Web at www.foxfire.org/. Additional resources about language variation are available on the Web sites for the Center for Applied Linguistics (www.cal.org) and the National Clearinghouse for English Language Acquisition, formerly the National Clearinghouse for Bilingual Education (www.ncela. gwu.edu/). *American Tongues* is a video that helps high school and college teachers and students consider dialect issues (www.cnam.com/flash/index.html). As middle school students become interested in dialect issues, they also would benefit from watching this video with their teacher because it raises thoughtful questions and opportunities for further study.

Literacy

Students start to think seriously about their own right to literacy when they study the rights of humans to learn to read and write, to choose what they want to read and write, and to have personal opinions about their literacy. Theme studies related to the right to read and write follow explorations similar to those discussed in the previous section for considering the right to language use. Many different resources focus on the right of students to an education and literacy learning. The Universal Declaration of Human Rights is available from the United Nations Web site, www.un.org/rights, not only in English but also in Arabic, Chinese, French, Russian, and Spanish. NCTE publishes a pamphlet on "The Students' Right to Read" (also available online at www.ncte.org/positions/right-to-read.shtml), and the Legal Aid Society also offers students' rights pamphlets. As students search for the wide range of resources available on their rights to think, learn, and read, they could compile packets of material on students' rights that would be available in the school library for other students and teachers. Such packets could stimulate schoolwide discussions and actions related to students' right to their language and literacy.

A wealth of literature for young students provides opportunities for inquiry into the role of literacy and schooling in students' lives (see Chapter 6). Some books present the role of literacy in relation to oppressed peoples, such as Shirley Graham's *There Once Was a Slave . . .* (1947), which is about Frederick Douglass learning to read. Julius Lester's (1968) retellings of slave narratives include the risks to slaves when they initiated and participated in learning to read and write. *More Than Anything Else* by Marie Bradby (1995) explores Booker T. Washington's desire to read. Other books examine the role of students who struggle to learn to read, such as *Just Call Me Stupid* by Tom Birdseye (1993), or how children teach others to read, such as *A Wednesday Surprise* by Eve Bunting (1989). Discussions about literacy issues help students raise critical questions: Who counts as literate people in society? What language is used to designate people who are considered literate or those who are not? How are terms such as *illiterate* used and what is the purpose of such labels?

In response to such literature, which is often presented as read-alouds, a fourth-grade class of special education students decided that each of them would adopt one first-grade child in their school to read to each week and help them become excited about learning to read. These students realized that one reason they didn't feel good about reading was that they didn't know how relevant reading could be to their own lives. With their own teacher and the first-grade teacher, they planned an adoption theme cycle that involved procedures to read to their adopted first graders on a regular basis. They met with adoption officials, heard others' concerns about adoption, and filled out self-developed adoption forms. They got permission from their own parents and the parents of the first graders to go ahead with the adoption proceedings. Then they researched the backgrounds of the first graders to discover what they were interested in. They worked with the school librarian to find books suitable to read to the first graders, and they discussed with their teachers how to read to and with the younger students, setting up regular meetings with them. They selected books to read, planned follow-up activities, practiced reading aloud, and discussed with their teachers how to respond to the reading of the younger students. When they finally met with the younger students, the fourth graders read aloud to them and then participated with them in the interactive follow-up activities they had produced. Some examples included creating a board game of the story to play together; making a map of the story plot and leaving parts for the younger student to fill in; working together to turn the book into a play in order to perform for the two classes; and involving the first grader in writing or drawing a response to the book. After the initial reading and the follow-up experience, the fourth graders left the book with the first graders, whose responsibility was to read the book over the subsequent week, bring it back to the next session, and then read it aloud to their fourth-grade buddy. Over the year, the fourth graders also wrote and illustrated books with their younger adopted friends, took them to the school library, and helped them select additional books to read for the next reading session. In the process, the first and fourth graders not only learned a lot about adoptions and reading, but they also built respect for one another. Several of the first graders' parents reported that the fourth graders came over to their homes to invite the first graders to play sports or games at the local park after school and on the weekend. The principal and teachers reported that there was much less teasing from the younger children about the abilities of the older children and less bullying by the older students of the younger children.

Another class in this school, one that included a range of ethnic and racial minority students, became aware that the library lacked books about kids like themselves (Middle Eastern and Asian), so they examined anthologies, textbooks, and trade book materials available in the classroom and school libraries for portrayals of different ethnic, racial, and gender groups. The students wondered whether literacy was enhanced when the literature they read included the specific faces and voices of students like themselves. They analyzed magazines and newspapers in terms of the roles that women and people of color played to see which groups received the most space in advertisements, mention of achievements, stories, and articles, and how this might affect students' interest in reading. Some students examined sports pages for articles that addressed women and checked for food section articles of interest to men in order to examine stereotypes perpetuated in the popular press. When students shared what they were learning with family members, they then began to extend their study of stereotypes by examining the ways in which the different groups such as the elderly, mothers, teenagers, and teachers were represented in different literary materials.

Science, social studies, and math teachers broadened the theme cycle even more by encouraging the students to analyze the materials being used in the various subject matter areas. The students explored various questions: How are boys and girls represented in math texts? Who is seen involved in the experiments pictured in science texts? Who are listed as explorers and inventors in social studies materials? What language is used toward women, native peoples, or other minority groups? The students wrote to the publishers to share their research that provided evidence of particular biases. The replies they received often led to further critique and exploration.

Students can access many references to inquire into literacy related to racial, gender, ethnicity, and disability issues. One of the major organizations that has led the way in raising the consciousness of students and teachers to such issues is the Council on Interracial Books for Children, located at 1841 Broadway, New York, New York, 10023. Although I could not find a Web site when I searched for their name, I discovered a wealth of references to their work over the years the council has been active. Their "10 Quick Ways to Analyze Children's Books for Racism and Sexism" is listed on a number of Web sites, including http://birchlane.davis.ca.us/library/10quick.htm. This list raises questions that can be used as criteria to examine print material. Students adapt the list to their own inquiry as a way of critiquing the material they read. The Women in Literacy and Life Assembly of NCTE has guidelines for gender-balanced curricula in the English language arts that are available online from NCTE at www.ncte.org/positions/balanced-12.shtml. The guidelines include booklists for kids and teachers as well as information about issues and curricular ideas. Although the guidelines do not mention the study of language per se, the materials allow students and teachers to include critical language study in the curriculum. The National Association for the Teaching of English (NATE) in England publishes *Gender Issues in English Course Work*, which focuses on moving the issue of women's creativity and girls' needs into the whole curriculum. This publication is available from NATE at Publications, 50 Broadfield Road, Sheffield, England S8 OXJ.

Naming Practices

Names represent a significant aspect of an individual's or social group's identity. Naming practices are social conventions that relate to power issues both within and across cultural groups, and they often involve students' language rights. Through interviews, questionnaires, and an examination of naming practices in their reading and writing, students explore the power issues of naming practices in their families and communities.

Sandy Kaser's fifth-grade class was responding to a read-aloud of *Pueblo Boy: Growing Up in Two Worlds* (Keegan, 1991). The narrative follows the life of a Pueblo Indian boy and his family who are concerned about maintaining their ethnic heritage while at the same time contributing as members of the wider community. Most of the students in the class were of European American backgrounds. Andrew, one European American student, raised a question about the origin of names. In the book, the boy's Pueblo name had come to an elder during a deer dance. Andrew was interested in the fact that Pueblo Boy had both a Pueblo name and a second name that he used in public school.

Andrew then asked Erwin, a Pima Indian student in the class, if he had another name. "No," Erwin said, "but my grandfather had two names. I was just named after my grandfather." Other students wondered where their names came from. The class decided to set up an "I wonder" homework question: Where did my name come from? The next morning students gathered in the room before the bell, sharing their excitement about the results of their "I wonder" explorations with their families. One student was aghast to discover he had been named for a popular singer in the 1960s. One of the students said, "Nobody wants a weird name. You get made fun of. If you have a weird name, you go by a nickname or something." The students decided to continue to inquire into the origin of names as part of their theme cycle on self-identity. They discovered there were kids named Crystal Lake and Candy Cane, and one student reported hearing about a teenager named Shanda Lear. One of the language power issues they explored through their research was that the Indian tribes in southern Arizona had been given new names by their conquerors, but that various tribes were now returning to their original names. The students organized to do additional research and interviews to understand these kinds of practices.

Whenever naming practices became an issue in my classes, I would read aloud from books on anthropology for elementary-age students, such as *People Are Important* (Evans, 1951) and *All about Us* (Evans, 1968). Although these books are no longer in print, they can be found in libraries. They examine, in addition to other human practices, how naming occurs in social groups, and they stimulated my students to inquire into the origins and meanings of their names as well as to examine the similarities and differences of names and naming practices across and within the languages and cultures represented in our class. The students searched for the origins of their names in historical documents, folk stories, and the Bible and other religious documents, and they checked the names of relatives and important people in society. By interviewing parents and grandparents, they discovered how some of their names related to places or occupations. They found out that some parents pick a name because they like the way it sounds and that others choose names that represent important status in their culture. Students explored the use of nicknames among family and friends and often used the telephone directory as a resource to discover popular and unique names; they also researched why such patterns of popularity occurred. My class often raised questions with one another: How many different names do you have? When you were little, did someone choose a pet name or a nickname for you? Do you still use it now? Why or why not? Do different people call you different names?

Students also discovered cultural taboos or necessary conditions in some naming practices, multiple names for the same person that were used in different contexts, and names that represented religious, familial, or lineage practices. They explored the uses of diminutives such as Charlie (for Charles) and Junior that in some cases represented endearment and in other cases, such as for servants or slaves, were demeaning. We discussed the ways in which school personnel or immigration agents changed names to suit the sounds and spelling patterns of English when the names of students or immigrants seemed too difficult or foreign.

Students of all ages are interested in naming studies. Young children often build on the letters of their names when learning to read and write. They make a collage of their name with pictures cut from magazines that represent their personalities or members of their family. The browsing table organized for inquiry into naming practices includes, in addition to books on popular names, literature that focuses on naming issues:

Judy Blume, *Blubber* (1974)

Kevin Henkes, *Chrysanthemum* (1991)

Mabel Leigh Hunt, *Little Girl with Seven Names* (1936)

Kin Platt, *Hey, Dummy* (1971)

Teachers may find Eva Hoffman's (1989) *Lost in Translation* helpful for developing their own background on language power issues. This autobiography highlights the influences of naming practices as the major character moves from one culture to another. Selections from this book are good for read-alouds.

The *Arizona Daily Star* ran a viewpoint column with the headline "Don't Allow Kids to Call Adults by Their First Name" (Hart, 1999). The author believes that up to voting age, children and adolescents need to recognize the disparity between adults and children by calling adults by their last name prefaced with an appropriate title, such as "Mrs. Hart." Such articles help initiate the perceiving phase of a language study on naming practices, and because they often provoke letters to the editor, students end up with a range of views to consider.

During such discussions, I often added my personal experiences with naming, which helped students feel more comfortable sharing their own naming experiences and exploring how their experiences reveal the ways in which power relations are embedded in various naming practices. Because I wanted to establish a positive rapport with kids and counselors when I worked in summer camps, I introduced myself as Yetta. As a teacher, because of my philosophy of teaching and learning, I encouraged students to call me by my first name except in schools that had a policy of calling teachers by their last names. I continued this practice in my professorial role. I discovered over the years that although

Americans find it easy to call me Yetta, students who come from Asian, Arabic, or South American cultures are reluctant to call me by my first name no matter how well they know me. U.S. students are comfortable calling me Yetta long before they are comfortable calling my husband, the other Dr. Goodman, Ken.

Additional theme cycles related to naming issues include:

◆ Exploring the development of the various ways students use their written signatures and how their signatures developed over time.

◆ Collecting written signatures of parents and celebrities over time to examine how signatures change, and considering why such changes occur.

◆ Examining the spelling and pronunciation differences and the historical derivations of similar names such as Debra, Deborah, and Devora; Steven and Stephen; Sondra and Sandra; Rodriguez and Rodrigues; and Weis, Weiss, and Weitz.

Censorship

Studies related to censorship interest the students quite naturally when the community is caught up in an important case. Court cases concerned with the freedom of high school reporters are often reported in local newspapers. Recently the Supreme Court ruled on a law that constrains the freedom of the press for school newspapers, while the Michigan legislature passed a bill allowing greater freedom for high school reporters. The Student Press Law Center has a Web site at www/splc.org that includes information about censorship, speech in schools, and the language of student publications. It provides information about legal cases and guidelines that establish students' rights in publications.

A good time to initiate a theme study on censorship is during Banned Book Week, which is usually the last week in September. Libraries, bookstores, and newspapers often feature banned children's and adolescent books, and information is always available on the American Library Association (ALA) Web site at www.ala.org/bbooks. The ALA is one of the most active professional organizations concerned with censorship and supports a Freedom to Read Foundation. Rethinking Schools at www.

rethinkingschools.org has many resources for students and teachers on censorship issues. Jackdaws, which produces primary source historical materials such as reproductions of letters, diaries, and old newspapers and includes original quotations, vocabulary lists, and suggestions for stimulating critical thinking, has a number of collections that relate to censorship (see www.jackdaw.com). NCTE (www.ncte.org/censorship) and the International Reading Association (www.ira.org) have produced a joint Common Ground statement that provides resources, ideas for the study of censorship, strategies to respond to censorship, and lists of the groups involved in censorship issues. The opening statement to this document can be displayed in the classroom to generate ideating opportunities:

> All students in public school classrooms have the right to materials and educational experiences that promote open inquiry, critical thinking, diversity in thought and expression, and respect for others. Denial or restriction of this right is an infringement of intellectual freedom.

As with other theme cycle studies, developing and displaying a collection of relevant materials provides the opportunity for students to perceive the significance of censorship in their lives. Searching the Web using phrases such as *censorship and students, censorship and student newspapers,* and *censorship and children's literature* leads to a range of resources that students can use as part of their inquiries and that will help them expand their questions and concerns. Classroom displays might also include the First Amendment to the U.S. Constitution and Article 19 of the United Nations Declaration of Human Rights. A publication by Kathleen Krull (1999) focuses on students' rights and the U.S. Bill of Rights, including the topics of curfews and censorship. It includes addresses, Web sites, and lists of readings for students. Books that prompt kids to explore the issue of freedom of thought and its relationship to democracy include several by Avi such as *Nothing but the Truth* (1991); *Tinker vs. Des Moines: Student Rights on Trial,* part of the Be the Judge/Be the Jury series by Doreen Rappaport (1993); *The Rebellious Alphabet* by Jorge Díaz (1993); and *The Composition* by Antonio Skármeta (2000). Such books would be included in the browsing area and used as text sets or read-alouds to stimulate discussion and inquiry concerning censorship and students' rights.

Such materials and displays lead students to explore and discuss a broad range of issues and to examine the ways in which institutions and people control what students read and write; their access to magazines and newspapers; their right to express their views; dress codes; school searches; Internet access; and censorship of school newspapers. Teachers can involve students in an exploration of teachers' academic freedom in order to consider how decision making about curriculum affects or interferes with the students' right to know and learn. Students are encouraged to share their discussions with family members as they consider what they believe about students' rights and ways to protect those rights. They invite lawyers and other rights advocates representing various viewpoints to visit with them and help them in their deliberations. They organize panels and debates and adapt or write their own Declaration of Students' Rights. Throughout such discussions and follow-up activities, students explore their responsibility to gather evidence to support their views and to listen respectfully to others.

Teachers help the students discover whether their school district has written policies on censorship and the rights of students. Students interview administrators about any censorship cases that occurred in the district and how they were resolved. They critically examine the language people use when they talk or write about censorship, and they analyze the language of freedom fighters, civil rights advocates, and rock stars and rap artists, and the ways such language is criticized and sometimes censored. As a result, students become informed citizens who use their knowledge not only to become knowledgeable future voters in a democracy, but also to develop a keen interest and understanding of their rights, not as future adults but in the present.

Demystifying Language

It is unfortunate that learning about language is sometimes considered boring and uninteresting. When students respond with disinterest, chances are they are being taught about language prescriptively and that the teacher is not helping them to appreciate the relevance between language and their daily lives. One major role of critical language study is to help students understand that they already know a lot about language, that language is something they use daily, that they are capable of using language to control others, and that other people use language to control them. Raising these issues to a conscious level supports all students, but it is crucial for those who tend not to be successful in school and are not confident language users because they have internalized the notion that they are not capable language users. Helping students explore and reject the myths they have come to believe about themselves as language users and about language is an important part of demystifying language.

Doublespeak

Generally in language study in schools, teachers and students assume that language interactions are attempts by humans to communicate with clarity in order to make sure they are understood. But students also need to explore the notion that people often use language purposely to lie, to be sarcastic or ironic, or to distort the truth. Understanding the issues related to language and power includes being aware that people are capable of using language with deliberate malice in order to control others, and that such obfuscation is particularly problematic when used by people in power to hide or distort the truth for political or economic reasons. Critical language analysis leads students to critical thinking as they recognize language features that are used to control the thinking of others. Teachers can take advantage of many opportunities to explore with students such uses of language, especially when they relate to experiences relevant to students' daily lives.

NCTE gives a Doublespeak Award each year to highlight language used by government, business, and advertisers to deceive the public or evade the truth. The Doublespeak Award, in the words of the committee, "is an ironic 'tribute' to American public figures who have perpetuated language that is grossly deceptive, evasive, euphemistic, confusing, or self-contradictory" (NCTE, 1997, p. 8). The concept of public doublespeak is based on the term *newspeak* introduced by George Orwell in *1984*. William Lutz (1989) describes the concept of doublespeak in his book *Doublespeak: From "Revenue Enhancement" to "Terminal Living."* NCTE also gives a yearly Orwell Award to a published work that "most effectively treats the subject of public doublespeak" and has made outstanding contributions to the critical analysis of public discourse. Lutz received the Orwell Award for *The New Doublespeak: Why No One Knows What Anyone's Saying Anymore* (1996).

Teachers can use Lutz's works to inform their own studies of language used to control the behavior of the unsuspecting and then read appropriate sections to their students. Lutz, who provides examples of evasive language in law, business, and government, also includes suggestions about what people can do to combat doublespeak that teachers can adapt to the grade or age level they teach. As students discuss the language of international, national, and local leaders in the news, they list the features of clear language use and features of language used to confuse. These features become the criteria by which they nominate articles, broadcasts, CDs, advertisements, and other methods of communication that exhibit doublespeak or clear language use for their own doublespeak and clear language awards. A classroom committee is established to examine entries, which the students nominate (other classes may be involved), and then the whole class votes on them. The students send the results of their work to the people involved with accompanying documentation, and they also may send a news release to the local newspaper.

Encouraging students to observe the language of powerful leaders such as presidents and other national leaders provides opportunities to examine how language is used to maintain power and to express leadership in democratic or autocratic ways. The language of Bill Clinton and George W. Bush, for example, has been widely explored in the press and provides rich material for examination and critique.

Reading with a Critical Eye

Catherine Wallace (1988) at the London Institute of Education has her ESL students carefully analyze the daily newspapers to help them realize how the language of newspaper reporting influences public opinion. Dr. Wallace collects articles about the same issue from different papers, issues she knows her students are generally interested in. She might, for example, use reports about a troublesome sporting event or a rock concert and letters to the editor responding to such events, looking for articles that represent different points of view. She then photocopies the articles and letters and asks her students to read them carefully, noting words and phrases that represent negative and positive traits, and then discuss their results in small groups. Students list adjectives, nouns, and verbs that refer, in the case of the sporting event, to the members of each team, to the referees, and to the spectators. Dr. Wallace then asks students to explore the possible reasons a reporter would use particular words in the article and not others.

I witnessed a highly animated discussion in Dr. Wallace's class as students deconstructed an article with the headline "Women at War." The article begins: "The wild women of peace brought mayhem to Greeham Common missile base yesterday." Her students listed the adjectives in the article, which described the women as *wild* and *ugly;* the nouns included *war, mayhem, protesters, clashes,* and *hordes;* and the verbs included *tore down.* With her students, Dr. Wallace considered why a reporter would select wording such as *tore down* rather than *pulled down* and *hordes* rather than *crowds.* Such critical analyses help students understand that even newspaper articles are written by people with points of view and that their language choices represent their views or their newspapers' views. And as readers, it is our responsibility to be aware of and critical about the language use of all authors in all kinds of texts.

Dr. Wallace believes that critical analysis of written language provides second language learners with a sense of power over their new experiences. Such critical reading provides all students with that same sense of power. When a controversial issue is reported in newspapers and magazines, the students are encouraged to collect reports from a range of such publications, save them over a period of time, and then analyze them. Examples of such controversies might include immigration, water use, pollution, local and national elections, or the homeless. The teacher encourages students to place related articles on the bulletin board and asks them all to read the articles during the next few weeks, to add to the collection, and then to organize discussions that focus on critical language analysis.

After students have analyzed a number of writings, they examine a related set of articles in small groups and try to rewrite them without biased language. In a related writing activity, the teacher asks students to read about or view an action scene in a detective movie or book. The students write what they saw as if they were a court witness or a reporter and then compare their writings to each other's and with the original text. The purpose of this activity is for students to explicitly consider their language choices and the messages that language sends even when authors are trying to be objective in their presentation. Through such analytical experiences, students realize how difficult it is to write language objectively, and they can use such knowledge to become more critical readers.

I keep a collection of newspaper articles about language issues of interest to elementary and middle schools students; these articles can be displayed on bulletin boards or used as read-alouds to help stimulate critical language analysis. These articles also serve as proof that many authors, reporters, and other adults in the community argue about and debate language issues and often have concerns and insecurities about language and its use, all of which helps demystify language use.

Over the years, I've shared with students articles such as "Spanish Surnames as American as Salsa" (Galbadon, 2002), "It's Back in Style Again: 'Yiddish Spoken Here'" (Rourke, 2000), and "L.A. Schools Accommodate Ebonics" (Zernike, 1997). William Safire writes weekly articles on language for the *New York Times* that often deal with language controversies (search www.nytimes.com for Safire's column "On Language"). From newspapers around the country I've collected articles on commas and other punctuation, kids getting into trouble for using bad words in school, and the battle between dictionary publishers over certain words. I have advertisements by speech therapists who promise to change the seemingly inappropriate "twang" pronunciation (dialect) of people from Chicago to the more "appropriate" language sounds of professionals in L.A. in order to improve their employment opportunities. I share these examples to encourage teachers to search newspapers and other resources with their students for the latest language topics that provide insight into issues of language power and control.

With growing understanding of the role that language plays in society, students develop greater confidence in their ability to explore and act on language issues and to use language to express their meanings in appropriate ways—all of which allows them to participate in rather than be pawns of the power that language offers. Language study lets all students in on the possibilities of language use and analysis and allows them to understand their own power as language users in a democratic society.

References

Ahlberg, J., & Ahlberg, A. (1986). *The jolly postman, or, Other people's letters.* Boston: Little, Brown.

Aliki. (1986). *How a book is made.* New York: Harper & Row.

Altwerger, B., & Flores, B. (1994). Theme cycles: Creating communities of learners. *Primary Voices, 2*(1), 2–6.

Anders, P., & Guzzetti, B. (1996). *Literacy instruction in the content areas.* Fort Worth, TX: Harcourt Brace.

Anderson, C. (2000). *How's it going? A practical guide to conferring with student writers.* Portsmouth, NH: Heinemann.

Andersson, L.-G., & Trudgill, P. (1990). *Bad language.* Cambridge, MA: Basil Blackwell.

Anno, M., & Mori, T. (1986). *Socrates and the three little pigs.* New York: Philomel Books.

Asch, F., & Vagin, V. (1989). *Here comes the cat! Siuda idet kot!* New York: Scholastic.

Atwell, N. (1987). *In the middle: Writing, reading, and learning with adolescents.* Portsmouth, NH: Heinemann.

Atwell, N. (1998). *In the middle: New understandings about writing, reading and learning* (2nd ed.). Portsmouth, NH: Boynton/Cook.

Avi. (1991). *Nothing but the truth: A documentary novel.* New York: Orchard Books.

Avi. (2001). *The secret school.* San Diego: Harcourt Brace.

Bailey, M. (1967). The utility of phonic generalizations in grades one through six. *The Reading Teacher, 2,* 413–18.

Barnes, D. (1995). Talking and learning in classrooms: An introduction. *Primary Voices K–6, 3,* 2–7.

Baskwill, J., & Whitman, P. (1986). *A guide to classroom publishing.* New York: Scholastic.

Bettelheim, B. (1982). The unconscious at work in reading. In G. Hillocks Jr. (Ed.), *The English curriculum under fire: What are the real basics?* (pp. 73–86). Urbana, IL: National Council of Teachers of English.

Bird, L. (Ed.). (1989). *Becoming a whole language school: The Fair Oaks story.* Katonah, NY: R. C. Owen.

Bird, L. (1991). Literature study: Discovering real reading. In K. Goodman, L. Bird, & Y. Goodman (Eds.), *The whole language catalog* (p. 196). Santa Rosa, CA: American School.

Birdseye, T. (1993). *Just call me stupid.* New York: Holiday House.

Blachowicz, C., & Fisher, P. (1996). *Teaching vocabulary in all classrooms.* Englewood Cliffs, NJ: Merrill.

Blachowicz, C., & Fisher, P. (2001). *Teaching vocabulary in all classrooms* (2nd ed.). Upper Saddle River, NJ: Merrill/Prentice-Hall.

Blume, J. (1974). *Blubber.* New York: Dell.

Bradby, M. (1995). *More than anything else.* New York: Orchard Books.

Brisson, P. (1992). *Your best friend, Kate.* New York: Aladdin Books.

Britton, J. (1993). *Language and learning* (2nd ed.). Portsmouth, NH: Boynton/Cook. (Original work published 1970)

Brodmann, A., & Poppel, H. (1990). *Que ruido! Cuento tradicional judío.* Mexico: Consejo Nacional para la Cultura y las Artes.

Brown, H., & Cambourne, B. (1990). *Read and retell: A strategy for the whole-language/natural learning classroom.* Portsmouth, NH: Heinemann.

Bruner, J. (1966). *Toward a theory of instruction.* Cambridge, MA: Belknap Press.

Bruner, J. (1986). *Actual minds, possible worlds.* Cambridge MA: Harvard University Press.

Bunting, E. (1989). *The Wednesday surprise.* New York: Clarion Books.

Calkins, L. (1994). *The art of teaching writing.* Portsmouth, NH: Heinemann.

Calkins, L., Montgomery, K., & Santman, D., with Falk, B. (1998). *A teacher's guide to standardized reading tests: Knowledge is power.* Portsmouth, NH: Heinemann.

Cambourne, B. (1988). *The whole story: Natural learning and the acquisition of literacy in the classroom.* New York: Ashton Scholastic.

Canadian childhoods: A Tundra anthology in words and art showing children of many backgrounds growing up in many parts of Canada. Montreal, Quebec: Tundra Books.

Chandler, K., & Mapleton Teacher-Research Group. (1999). *Spelling inquiry: How one elementary school caught the mnemonic plague.* York, ME: Stenhouse.

Christensen, L. (1992–1993). Tales from an untracked class. *Rethinking Schools, 7*(1), 19–21.

Clay, M. (1979). *Reading: The patterning of complex behavior* (2nd ed.). Auckland, NZ: Heinemann.

Cleary, B. (1983). *Dear Mr. Henshaw.* New York: Morrow.

Clements, A. (1998). *Frindle.* New York: Aladdin.

Clymer, T. (1963). The utility of phonic generalizations in the primary grades. *The Reading Teacher, 23,* 252–58.

Cohen, M. (1977). *When will I read?* New York: Greenwillow Books.

Cohen, M. (1980). *First grade takes a test.* New York: Greenwillow Books.

Cole, J. (1989). *Anna Banana: 101 Jump-rope rhymes.* New York: Morrow Books.

Cole, J. (1994). *The magic school bus: In the time of the dinosaurs.* New York: Scholastic.

Cole, J., & Calmenson, S. (1990). *Miss Mary Mack and other children's street rhymes.* New York: Morrow Junior Books.

Collier, J. L., & Collier, C. (1974). *My brother Sam is dead.* New York: Scholastic.

Conference on College Composition and Communication. (1974). Students' right to their own language [Special issue]. *College Composition and Communication 25*(3), 1–32.

Cullum, A. (1971). *The geranium on the window sill just died, but teacher you went right on*. New York: Harlin Quist.

Curtis, C. P. (1995). *The Watsons go to Birmingham—1963*. New York: Delacorte Press.

Curtis, C. P. (1999). *Bud, not Buddy*. New York: Delacorte Press.

Dahl, R. (1953). Poison. In R. Dahl, *Someone like you* (pp. 150–66). New York: Knopf.

Dahl, R. (1984). *Boy: Tales of childhood*. New York: Farrar, Straus & Giroux.

Danziger, P. (2002). *United Tates of America*. New York: Scholastic.

Darling-Hammond, L. (1998). Education for democracy. In W. Ayers & J. L. Miller (Eds.), *A light in dark times: Maxine Greene and the unfinished conversation* (pp. 78–91). New York: Teachers College Press.

Davis, D. (1990). *Listening for the crack of dawn*. Little Rock, AR: August House.

dePaola, T. (1980). *The knight and the dragon*. New York: Putnam.

dePaola, T. (1989). *The art lesson*. New York: Putnam.

Dewey, J. (1925). *Experience and nature*. Chicago: Open Court.

Díaz, J. (1993). *The rebellious alphabet* (G. Fox, Trans). New York: Henry Holt.

Dickinson, E. (1944). *The poems of Emily Dickinson* (M. Dickinson Bianchi & A. Leete Hampson, Eds.). Boston: Little, Brown.

Doctorow, E. L. (1983). False documents. In R. Trenner (Ed.), *E. L. Doctorow: Essays and conversations* (pp. 16–27). Princeton, NJ: Ontario Review Press.

Dornan, R., Rosen, L., & Wilson, M. (1997). *Multiple voices, multiple texts: Reading in the secondary content areas*. Portsmouth, NH: Boynton/Cook.

Duckworth, E. (1987). *"The having of wonderful ideas" and other essays on teaching and learning*. New York: Teachers College Press.

Edelsky, C. (1994). Education for democracy. *Language Arts, 71*, 252–57.

Edelsky, C., & Smith, K. (1984). Is that writing or are those marks a figment of your curriculum? *Language Arts, 61,* 1, 24–32.

Emans, R. (1967). The usefulness of phonic generalizations above the primary grades. *The Reading Teacher, 25,* 419–25.

Esbensen, B. (1997). *Words with wrinkled knees: Animal poems.* Honesdale, PA: Boyds Mills Press.

Evans, E. (1951). *People are important.* New York: Golden Press.

Evans, E. (1968). *All about us.* New York: Golden Press.

Farb, P. (1974). *Word play: What happens when people talk.* New York: Knopf.

Feelings, M. (1971). *Moja means one: Swahili counting book.* New York: Dial Press.

Feelings, M. (1974). *Jambo means hello: Swahili alphabet book.* New York: Dial Press.

Feiffer, J. (1993). *The man in the ceiling.* New York: HarperCollins.

Finchler, J. (2000). *Testing Miss Malarkey.* New York: Walker.

Fisher, L. (1983). *The schools.* New York: Holiday House.

Fisher, L. (1985). *Symbol art: Thirteen [square]s, [circle]s, [triangle]s from around the world.* New York: Four Winds Press.

Fitzhugh, L. (1964). *Harriet the spy.* New York: Harper & Row.

Fleming, C. (2000). *The hatmaker's sign: A story by Benjamin Franklin.* New York: Orchard Books.

Fountas, I., & Pinnell, G. (1996). *Guided reading: Good first teaching for all children.* Portsmouth, NH: Heinemann.

Fountas, I., & Pinnell, G. (2001). *Guiding readers and writers, grades 3–6: Teaching comprehension, genre, and content literacy.* Portsmouth, NH: Heinemann.

Fox, M. (2001). *Reading magic: Why reading aloud to our children will change their lives forever.* New York: Harcourt.

Freeman, D., & Freeman, Y. (2000). *Teaching reading in multilingual classrooms.* Portsmouth, NH: Heinemann.

Freeman, Y., & Freeman, D. (1997). *Teaching, reading, and writing in Spanish in the bilingual classroom.* Portsmouth, NH: Heinemann.

Freeman, Y., & Goodman, Y. (1993). Revaluing the bilingual learner through a literature reading program. *Reading & Writing Quarterly: Overcoming Learning Difficulties, 9*(2), 163–82.

Freire, P. (1985). *The politics of education: Culture, power, and liberation.* South Hadley, MA: Bergin & Garvey.

Fritz, J. (1992). *Surprising myself.* Katonah, NY: R. C. Owen.

Fritz, J. (1996). *And then what happened, Paul Revere?* New York: Putnam & Grosset.

Galbadon, S. (2002, July 8). Spanish surnames as American as salsa. *Arizona Daily Star,* p. 11.

Garden, N. (1981). *The kids' code and cipher book.* New York: Holt, Rinehart, & Winston.

Garden, N. (1999). *The year they burned the books.* New York: Farrar, Straus & Giroux.

Gilles, C., et al. (Eds.) (1988). *Whole langauge strategies for secondary students.* New York: R. C. Owen.

Giovanni, N. (1973). *Ego-tripping and other poems for young people.* New York: Lawrence Hill Books.

Glazer, S. M. (1998). *Phonics, spelling, and word study: A sensible approach.* Norwood, MA: Christopher-Gordon.

Goodman, D. (1991). Planning and evaluation: Involving students and parents right from the start. In K. S. Goodman, L. B. Bird, & Y. M. Goodman (Eds.), *The whole language catalog* (pp. 254–55). Santa Rosa, CA: American School.

Goodman, D. (1999). *The Reading Detective Club: Solving the mysteries of reading.* Portsmouth, NH: Heinemann.

Goodman, K. (1965). Cues and miscues in reading: A linguistic study." *Elementary English, 42*(6), 635–42.

Goodman, K. (1986). *What's whole in whole language?* Portsmouth, NH: Heinemann.

Goodman, K. (1993). *Phonics phacts.* Richmond Hill, Ontario: Scholastic Canada.

Goodman, K. (1996a). *On reading*. Portsmouth, NH: Heinemann.

Goodman, K. (1996b). Principles of revaluing. In Y. Goodman & A. Marek (Eds.), *Retrospective miscue analysis: Revaluing readers and reading* (pp. 13–20). Katonah, NY: R. C. Owen.

Goodman, K., Bird, L., & Goodman, Y. (1992). *The whole language catalog: Supplement on authentic assessment*. Macmillan-McGraw Hill.

Goodman, K., Goodman, Y., & Hood, W. (Eds.) (1989). *The whole language evaluation book*. Portsmouth, NH: Heinemann.

Goodman, K., Smith, E., Meredith, R., & Goodman, Y. (1987). *Language and thinking in school: A whole-language curriculum* (3rd ed.). New York: R. C. Owen.

Goodman, Y. (1971). The culture of the culturally deprived. *Elementary School Journal, 71*(7), 376–83.

Goodman, Y. (1978). Kidwatching: An alternative to testing. *National Elementary School Principal, 57*(4), 41–45.

Goodman, Y. (1979). Letters. *Language Arts, 56*(5), 482.

Goodman, Y. (1980). The roots of literacy. In M. Douglas (Ed.), *Forty-fourth yearbook of the Claremont Reading Conference* (pp. 1–32). Claremont, CA: Claremont Reading Conference.

Goodman, Y. (1985). Kidwatching: Observing children in the classroom. In A. Jagger & M. Smith-Burke (Eds.), *Observing the language learner* (pp. 9–18). Newark, DE: International Reading Association, and Urbana, IL: National Council of Teachers of English.

Goodman, Y. (1996a). Retrospective miscue analysis in the classroom. In Y. Goodman & A. Marek (Eds.), *Retrospective miscue analysis: Revaluing readers and reading* (pp. 198–99). Katonah, NY: R. C. Owen.

Goodman, Y. (1996b). Revaluing readers while readers revalue themselves: Retrospective miscue analysis. *The Reading Teacher, 49*, 600–609.

Goodman, Y. (1998). *The little overcoat: Traditional folksong*. Greenvale, NY: Mondo.

Goodman, Y. (1999). Retrospective miscue analysis: Illuminating the voice of the reader. In A. Marek & C. Edelsky (Eds.), *Reflections and connections: Essays in honor of Kenneth S. Goodman's influence on language education* (pp. 311–31). Cresskill, NJ: Hampton Press.

Goodman, Y., Burke, C., & Sherman, B. (1980). *Reading strategies: Focus on comprehension.* New York: Holt, Rinehart, & Winston.

Goodman, Y., & Goodman, K. (1994). To err is human. In R. Ruddell, M. Rapp Ruddell, & H. Singer (Eds.), *Theoretical models and processes of reading.* Newark, DE: International Reading Association.

Goodman, Y., & Marek, A. (Eds.). (1996). *Retrospective miscue analysis: Revaluing readers and reading.* Katonah, NY: R. C. Owen.

Goodman, Y., Watson, D., & Burke, C. (1987). *Reading miscue inventory: Alternative procedures.* New York: R. C. Owen.

Goodman, Y., Watson, D., & Burke, C. (1996). *Reading strategies: Focus on comprehension* (2nd ed.). Katonah, NY: R. C. Owen.

Goodman, Y., & Wilde, S. (Eds.) (1992). *Literacy events in a community of young writers.* New York: Teachers College Press.

Goor, R., & Goor, N. (1983). *Signs.* New York: Crowell.

Gove, P. (Ed.). (1967). *Webster's third international dictionary of the English language.* Springfiled, MA: G. & C. Merriam.

Graham, L. (2000). *How god fix Jonah.* Honesdale, PA: Boyds Mill Press. (Original work published 1946)

Graham, S. (1947). *There once was a slave . . . : The heroic story of Frederick Douglass.* New York: J. Messner.

Graves, D. (1983). *Writing: Teachers and children at work.* Exeter, NH: Heinemann.

Greene, A. (1969). *Pullet surprises.* Glenview, IL: Scott, Foresman.

Gutiérrez, K., Baquedano-López, P., & Turner, M. (1997). Putting language back into language arts: When the radical middle meets the third space. *Language Arts, 74*(5), 368–78.

Gwynne, F. (1970). *The king who rained.* New York: Aladdin.

Gwynne, F. (1989). *A chocolate moose for dinner.* New York: Simon & Schuster.

Halliday, M. (1975). *Learning how to mean: Explorations in the development of language.* London: Edward Arnold.

References

Halliday, M. (1979). Three aspects of children's language development: Learning language, learning through language, learning about language. In Y. M. Goodman, M. M. Haussler, & D. S. Strickland (Eds.), *Oral and written language development research: Impact on the schools* (pp. 7–19). Proceedings from the 1979 and 1980 IMPACT Conferences, sponsored by International Reading Association (Newark, DE) and National Council of Teachers of English (Urbana, IL).

Hanson, G. (1991). Daydreaming. In K. Goodman, L. Bird, & Y. Goodman (Eds.), *The whole language catalog* (p. 22). Santa Rosa, CA: American School.

Harste, J., Woodward, V., & Burke, C. (1984). *Language stories and literacy lessons.* Portsmouth, NH: Heinemann.

Hart, B. (1999, September 15). Don't allow kids to call adults by their first name. *The Arizona Daily Star,* p. 15.

Harvey, S., & Goudvis, A. (2000). *Strategies that work: Teaching comprehension to enhance understanding.* Portland, ME: Stenhouse.

Harwayne, S. (1992). *Lasting impressions: Weaving literature into the writing workshop.* Portsmouth, NH: Heinemann.

Harwayne, S. (2001). *Writing through childhood: Rethinking process and product.* Portsmouth, NH: Heinemann.

Hasan, R. (1973). Children's conversation. *Nuffield Foreign Languages Teaching Materials Project.* London: Education Agency.

Heath, S. (1983). *Ways with words: Language, life, and work in communities and classrooms.* Cambridge, UK: Cambridge University Press.

Heide, F., & Gilliland, J. (1990). *The day of Ahmed's secret.* New York: Lothrop, Lee & Shepard Books.

Heiligman, D. (1998). *The New York public library kid's guide to research.* New York: Scholastic.

Henkes, K. (1991). *Chrysanthemum.* New York: Greenwillow Books.

Hillocks, G. (1982). *The English curriculum under fire: What are the real basics?* Urbana, IL: National Council of Teachers of English.

Hoban, T. (1983). *I read signs.* New York: Greenwillow Books.

Hoban, T. (1984). *I walk and read.* New York: Greenwillow Books.

Hoban, T. (1999). *I read symbols*. New York: Mulberry Books.

Hoffman, E. (1989). *Lost in translation: A life in a new language*. New York: Dutton.

Holdaway, D. (1979). *The foundations of literacy*. Sydney, Australia: Ashton Scholastic.

Houston, G. (1992). *My great-aunt Arizona*. New York: HarperCollins.

Hughes, A. (as told to Chapman, T. C.). (1976). *Aunt Zona's web*. Banner Elk, NC: Puddingstone Press.

Hughes, M., & Searle, D. (1997). *The violent E and other tricky sounds: Learning to spell from kindergarten through grade 6*. York, ME: Stenhouse.

Hunt, I. (1969). *Across five Aprils*. New York: Grosset and Dunlap.

Hunt, I. (1978). *Lottery Rose*. New York: Tempo Books.

Hunt, M. (1936). *Little girl with seven names*. New York: F. A. Stokes.

Hunter, S. Hoagland (1996). *The unbreakable code*. Flagstaff, AZ: Northland.

Indie, S. (1998). *Auntie*. Aiea, HI: Island Heritage.

Jacobson, D. (1991). The Keeling Publishing Company. In K. Goodman, L. Bird, & Y. Goodman (Eds.), *The whole language catalog* (p. 160). Santa Rosa, CA: American School.

Joos, M. (1962). *The five clocks*. Bloomington, IN: Publication 22 of the Indiana University Research Center in Anthropology, Folklore, and Linguistics.

Jorgensen, K., with Venable, J. (1993). *History workshop: Reconstructing the past with elementary students*. Portsmouth, NH: Heinemann.

Joseph, L. (2000). *The color of my words*. New York: Joanna Cotter Books.

Kasten, W. (1992). Speaking, searching and sharing in the community of writers. In Y. Goodman & S. Wilde (Ed.), *Literacy events in a community of young writers* (pp. 87–103). New York: Teachers College Press.

Keegan, M. (1991). *Pueblo boy: Growing up in two worlds*. New York: Cobblehill Books.

Kelley, E. (1955). Teaching current events in the schools. In R. Ellsworth & O. Sand (Eds.), *Improving the social studies curriculum* (pp. 59–70). Washington, DC: National Council for the Social Studies.

Kitagawa, M. (2000). *Enter teaching! The essential guide for teachers new to grades 3–6*. Portsmouth, NH: Heinemann.

Klein, R. (1987). *Penny Pollard's letters*. Melbourne, Australia: Oxford University Press.

Krull, K. (1999). *A kids' guide to America's Bill of Rights: Curfews, censorship, and the 100-pound giant*. New York: Avon Books.

Kucer, S., Silva, C., & Delgado-Larocco, E. (1995). *Curricular conversations: Themes in multilingual and monolingual classrooms*. York, ME: Stenhouse.

Kurusa. (1981). *La calle es libre*. Caracas, Venezuela: Ediciones Ekaré-Banco del Libro.

LaBenz, J. (1991). New ways to use the news? Tying your teaching together with a class newspaper? In K. Goodman, L. Bird, & Y. Goodman (Eds.), *The whole language catalog* (p. 316). Santa Rosa, CA: American School.

Ladson-Billings, G. (1994). *The dreamkeepers: Successful teachers of African American children*. San Francisco: Jossey-Bass.

Langer, S. (1957). *Philosophy in a new key: A study in the symbolism of reason, rite, and art* (3rd ed.). Cambridge, MA: Harvard University Press.

Larrick, N. (1982). *A parent's guide to children's reading* (5th ed). New York: Bantam Books.

Lasky, K. (1996). *True north: A novel of the Underground Railroad*. New York: Blue Sky Press.

Lester, J. (1968). *To be a slave*. New York: Scholastic.

Lester, J. (1987). *The tales of Uncle Remus: The adventures of Brer Rabbit*. New York: Dial Books.

Levine, E. (1989). *I hate English!* New York: Scholastic.

Lindfors, J. (1999). *Children's inquiry: Using language to make sense of the world*. New York: Teachers College Press.

Linkletter, A. (1957). *Kids say the darndest things!* Englewood Cliffs, NJ: Prentice-Hall.

Loughlin, C., & Martin, M. (1987). *Supporting literacy: Developing effective learning environments.* New York: Teachers College Press.

Lundsteen, S. (1979). *Listening: Its impact at all levels on reading and other language arts.* Urbana, IL: ERIC Clearinghouse and National Council of Teachers of English.

Lutz, W. (1989). *Doublespeak: From "revenue enhancement" to "terminal living": How government, business, advertisers, and others use language to deceive you.* New York: Harper & Row.

Lutz, W. (1996). *The new doublespeak: Why no one knows what anyone's saying anymore.* New York: HarperCollins.

Lyon, G. (1991). *Cecil's story.* New York: Orchard Books.

Lyon, G. (1998). *A sign.* New York: Orchard Books.

Manefield, T. (Producer), & McPhee, K. (Director). (1976). *Language at twelve* [Motion picture]. Film Australia. New York: Australian Information Service.

Manning, M., Manning, G., & Long, R. (1994). *Theme immersion: Inquiry-based curriculum in elementary and middle schools.* Portsmouth, NH: Heinemann.

Martin, B. Jr. (1966–1967). *Sounds of language readers* (teacher's ed.). New York: Holt, Rinehart & Winston.

Matthaei, G., & Grutman, J. (1994). *The ledgerbook of Thomas Blue Eagle.* Charlottesville, VA: Thomasson-Grant.

McKissack, P. (1986). *Flossie and the fox.* New York: Dial Books.

McKissack, P. (1988). *Mirandy and Brother Wind.* New York: Knopf.

Meek, M. (1988). How texts teach what readers learn. In M. Lightfoot & N. Martin (Eds.), *The word for teaching is learning: Language and learning today: Essays for James Britton* (pp. 82–106). Portsmouth, NH: Heinemann.

Mellor, B., & Raleigh, M. (with Ashton, P.). (1984). *Making stories.* London: ILEA English & Media Centre.

Merriam, E. (1991). *The wise woman and her secret.* New York: Simon & Schuster.

Moffett, J. (1968). *Teaching the universe of discourse.* Boston: Houghton Mifflin.

Moffett, J. (1983). *Teaching the universe of discourse.* Boston: Houghton Mifflin.

Moffett, J., & Wagner, B. (1983). *Student-centered language arts and reading, K–13: A handbook for teachers.* Boston: Houghton Mifflin.

Moffett, J., & Wagner, B. (1992). *Student-centered language arts, K–12: A handbook for teachers* (4th ed.). Portsmouth, NH: Boynton/Cook.

Moll, L., Amanti, C., Neff, D., & Gonzalez, N. (1992). Funds of knowledge for teaching: Using a qualitative approach to connect homes and classrooms. *Theory into Practice, 31*(2), 132–41.

Moll, L., & González, N. (1997). Teachers as social scientists: Learning about culture from household research. In P. M. Hall (Ed.), *Race, ethnicity, and multiculturalism: Policy and practice* (pp. 89–114). New York: Garland.

Mooney, M. E. (1990). *Reading to, with, and by children.* Katonah, NY: R. C. Owen.

Morduchowicz, R. (1991). Argentina: Teaching freedom of expression in a new democracy. In K. Goodman, L. Bird, & Y. Goodman (Eds.), *The whole language catalog* (pp. 76–77). Santa Rosa, CA: American School.

Morrisey, M. (1989). When "shut up" is a sign of growth. In K. Goodman, Y. Goodman, & W. Hood (Eds.), *The whole language evaluation book* (pp. 85–97). Portsmouth, NH: Heinemann.

Musgove, M. (1976). *Ashanti to Zulu: African traditions.* New York: Dial Press.

Myers, W. D. (1995). *The dragon takes a wife.* New York: Scholastic. (Original work published 1972)

Myers, W. D. (1999). *Monster.* New York: HarperCollins.

National Council of Teachers of English. (1997). The doublespeak award. *Quarterly Review of Doublespeak, 23*(2), 8–9.

Nixon, J. L. (1995). *If you were a writer.* New York: Aladdin.

Ogle, D. (1986). K-W-L: A teaching model that develops active reading of expository text. *The Reading Teacher, 39,* 564–70.

Opie, I., & Opie, P. (1992). *I saw Esau: The schoolchild's pocket book.* Cambridge, MA: Candlewick Press. (Original work published 1947)

Owocki, G. (1999). *Literacy through play.* Portsmouth, NH: Heinemann.

Owocki, G., & Goodman, Y. (2002). *Kidwatching: Documenting children's literacy development.* Portsmouth, NH: Heinemann.

Paley, V. (1981). *Wally's stories.* Cambridge, MA: Harvard University Press.

Paley, V. (1997). *The girl with the brown crayon.* Cambridge, MA: Harvard University Press.

Paterson, K. (1992). *Lyddie.* New York: Puffin Books.

Paulsen, G. (1993). *Nightjohn.* New York: Delacorte Press.

Peet, B. (1989). *Bill Peet: An autobiography.* Boston: Houghton Mifflin.

Perry, T., & Delpit, L. (1997). The real Ebonics debate. *Rethinking Schools, 12,* 1–36.

Peterson, R., & Eeds, M. (1990). *Grand conversations: Literature groups in action.* New York: Scholastic.

Peyton, J., & Staton, J. (1993). *Dialogue journals in the multilingual classroom: Building language fluency and writing skills through written interaction.* Norwood, NJ: Ablex.

Piaget, J. (1977). *The development of thought: Equilibration of cognitive structures.* New York: Viking Press.

Platt, K. (1971). *Hey, dummy.* Philadelphia: Chilton.

Portalupi, J., & Fletcher, R. (2001). *Nonfiction craft lessons: Teaching information writing K–8.* Portland, ME: Stenhouse.

Postman, N. (1966). *Exploring your language.* New York: Holt, Rinehart and Winston.

Postman, N., Morine, H., & Morine, G. (1963). *Discovering your language.* New York: Holt, Rinehart and Winston.

Raleigh, M. (1981). *The languages book.* London: ILEA English Centre.

Rappaport, D. (1993). *Tinker vs. Des Moines: Student rights on trial.* New York: HarperCollins.

Read, C. (1971). Pre-school children's knowledge of English phonology. *Harvard Educational Review, 41,* 1–34.

Read, C. (1974). *Research on children's categorizations of speech sounds in English.* Dept. of English, Programs in English Linguistics, University of Wisconsin.

Read, C. (1986). *Children's creative spelling.* London: Routledge & Kegan Paul.

Rigg, P. (1992). Environmental print: Promises and practices. In H. Wrigley & G. Guth (Eds.), *Bringing literacy to life: Issues and options in adult ESL literacy* (pp. 291–92). San Mateo, CA: Aguirre International.

Robert, H. (with Vixman, R.). (1977). *Robert's rules of order.* New York: Jove.

Roberts, J., Ross, C., & Boyd, J. (1970). *The Roberts English series: A linguistics program* (2nd ed.). New York: Harcourt, Brace & World.

Roney, R. (2001). *The story performance handbook.* Mahwah, NJ: Lawrence Erlbaum.

Rosen, H. (1998). *Speaking from memory: A guide to autobiographical acts and practices.* Stoke-on-Trent: Trentham Books.

Rosten, L.(1937). *The education of Hyman Kaplan (by Leonard Q. Ross, pseud.).* New York: Harcourt, Brace.

Rourke, M. (2000, July 7). It's back in style again: "Yiddish spoken here." *Tucson Citizen,* p. 7B.

Ruíz, R. (1988). Orientations in language planning. In S. McKay & S. Wong (Eds.), *Language diversity, problem or resource? A social and educational perspective on language minorities in the United States* (pp. 3–25). New York: Newbury House.

Rumford, J. (2002). *There's a monster in the alphabet.* Boston: Houghton Mifflin.

Safire, W. (2002, October 11). Language. *The Arizona Daily Star,* p.12.

Samoyault, T. (1997). *Give me a sign! What pictographs can tell us without words.* New York: Viking.

Sandburg, C. (1920). *Smoke and steel.* New York: Harcourt, Brace and Howe.

San Souci, R. D. (2000). *Callie Ann and Mistah Bear.* New York: Dial Books.

Saul, E. (1994). *Nonfiction for the classroom: Milton Meltzer on writing, history, and social responsibility.* New York: Teachers College Press.

Scieszka, J. (1989). *The true story of the 3 little pigs (by A. Wolf.).* New York: Scholastic.

Scieszka, J. (2001). *It's all Greek to me.* New York: Puffin Books.

Seeger, P. (1986) *Abiyoyo: Based on a South African lullaby and folk story.* New York, Macmillan.

Schwarzer, D. (2001). *Noa's ark: One child's voyage into multiliteracy.* Portsmouth, NH: Heinemann.

Shaughnessy, M. (1977). *Errors and expectations. A guide for the teacher of basic writing.* New York: Oxford University Press.

Shor, I. (1991). Overcoming teacher-talk and student silence: Freirean dialogue for critical education. In K. Goodman, L. Bird, & Y. Goodman (Eds.), *The whole language catalog* (p. 223). Santa Rosa, CA: American School.

Short, K., & Harste, J. (with Burke, C.). (1996). *Creating classrooms for authors and inquirers* (2nd ed.). Portsmouth, NH: Heinemann.

Short, K., & Pierce, K. (Eds.). (1990). *Talking about books: Creating literate communities.* Portsmouth, NH: Heinemann.

Sibley, C. (1993, August 9). Sometimes the wrong word can be absolutely right. *The Arizona Daily Star,* p. 11.

Sierra, J. (2002). *Can you guess my name? Traditional tales around the world.* New York: Clarion Books.

Skármeta, A. (2000). *The composition* (Trans. E. Amado). Toronto: Groundwood Books.

Smith, F. (1983). Demonstrations, engagement and sensitivity. In F. Smith (Ed.), *Essays into literacy: Selected papers and some afterthoughts* (pp. 95–106). Portsmouth, NH: Heinemann.

Smith, F. (1985). Does your writing send the wrong signals? *Personnel Journal, 64*(12), 28–30.

Smitherman, G. (1977). *Talkin and testifyin: The language of Black America.* Boston: Houghton Mifflin.

Smitherman, G. (1995). "Students' right to their own language": A retrospective. *English Journal, 84,* 21–27.

Speare, E. (1983). *The sign of the beaver.* Boston: Houghton Mifflin.

Stanley, J. (1993). *Children of the dust bowl: The true story of the school at Weedpatch Camp.* New York: Crown.

Staton, J. (1988). *Dialogue journal communication: Classroom, linguistic, social, and cognitive views.* Norwood, NJ: Ablex.

Strand, M. (1986). *Rembrandt takes a walk.* New York: C. N. Potter.

Sulzby, E., & Teale, W. (1991). Emergent literacy. In R. Barr, M. Kamil, P. Mosenthal, & D. Pearson (Eds.), *Handbook of reading research* (Vol. II, pp. 725–57). New York: Longman.

Taback, S. (1977). *Joseph had a little overcoat.* New York: Random House.

Taback, S. (1999). *Joseph had a little overcoat.* New York: Viking.

Tapia, E. (1999). "I wouldn't think nothin' of it": Teacher candidates survey public on nonstandard usage. *English Education, 31*(4), 295–309.

Taylor, D. (1993). *From the child's point of view.* Portsmouth, NH: Heinemann.

Taylor, D. (1998). *Family literacy: Young children learning to read and write.* Portsmouth, NH: Heinemann.

Taylor, D., & Dorsey-Gaines, C. (1988). *Growing up literate: Learning from inner-city families.* Portsmouth, NH: Heinemann.

Thomas, K. (2001, June 21). Instant messages are lasting. *USA Today,* p. 3D.

Thomas, L., & Tchudi, S. (1999). *The English language: An owner's manual.* Boston: Allyn & Bacon.

Thomas, W. (Ed.). (1997). *A Farley Mowat reader.* Niwot, CO: Roberts Rinehart.

Thomason, T. (1998). *Writer to writer: How to conference young authors.* Norwood, MA: Christopher-Gordon.

Tiedt, I. (2000). *Teaching with picture books in the middle school.* Newark, DE: International Reading Association.

Tierney, R., Readance, J., & Dishner, E. (1980). *Reading strategies and practices: A guide for improving instruction.* Boston: Allyn & Bacon.

Torres, L. (1993). *Subway sparrow.* New York: Farrar, Straus & Giroux.

Tovani, C. (2000). *I read it, but I don't get it: Comprehension strategies for adolescent reading.* Portland, ME: Stenhouse.

Trelease, J. (1982). *The read-aloud handbook.* New York: Penguin.

Treviño, E. de (1965). *I, Juan de Pareja.* New York: Bell Books.

Tsuchiya, Y. (1988). *Faithful elephants: A true story of animals, people, and war* (T. T. Dykes, Trans.). Boston: Houghton Mifflin.

Turbill, J. (Ed.). (1982). *No better way to teach writing.* Rozelle, New South Wales, Australia: Primary English Teaching Association.

Twain, M. (1985). *Adventures of Huckleberry Finn.* Berkeley: University of California Press.

Tyson, C., & Kenreich, T. (2001). Studying social action through children's literature. *Social Students and the Young Learner, 14,* 22–25.

Van Allen, R. (1976). *Language experiences in communication.* Boston: Houghton Mifflin.

Van Allen, R., & Van Allen, C. (1982). *Language experience activities* (2nd ed.). Boston: Houghton Mifflin.

Van Laan, N. (1990). *Possum come a-knockin'* (G. Booth, Illus.). New York: Knopf.

Vygotsky [Vygotskii], L. (1978). *Mind in society: The development of higher psychological processes.* Cambridge, MA: Harvard University Press.

Walker, A. (1988). *Living by the word: Selected writings, 1973–1987.* San Diego: Harcourt Brace Jovanovich.

Wallace, C. (1988). *Learning to read in a multicultural society: The social context of second language literacy.* New York: Prentice-Hall.

Walter, M. (2002). *Ray and the best family reunion ever.* New York: HarperCollins.

Watson, D. (Ed.). (1987). *Ideas and insights: Language arts in the elementary school.* Urbana, IL: National Council of Teachers of English.

Watson, D. (1996). Reader selected miscues. In Y. Goodman & A. Marek (Eds.), *Retrospective miscue analysis: Revaluing readers and reading.* Katonah, NY: R. C. Owen.

Watson, D., Burke, C., & Harste, J. (1989). *Whole language: Inquiring voices.* Richmond Hill, Ontario, Canada: Scholastic.

Weaver, C. (1979). *Grammar for teachers: Perspectives and definitions.* Urbana, IL: National Council of Teachers of English.

Weaver, C. (1996). *Teaching grammar in context.* Portsmouth, NH: Boynton Cook.

Weaver, C. (Ed.). (1998). *Practicing what we know: Informed reading instruction.* Urbana, IL: National Council of Teachers of English.

Wheatley, N., & Rawlins, D. (1989). *My place.* New York: Kane/Miller.

Whitmore, K., & Goodman, Y. (Eds.). (1996). *Whole language voices in teacher education.* York, ME: Stenhouse.

Wigginton, E. (Ed.). (1972). *The foxfire book.* Garden City, NY: Anchor Press.

Wigginton, E. (Ed.). (1979). *Foxfire 5.* Garden City, NY: Anchor Press.

Wigginton, E. (Ed.). (1980). *Foxfire 6.* Garden City, NY: Anchor Press.

Wilde, S. (1992). *You kan red this! Spelling and punctuation for whole language classrooms, k–6.* Portsmouth, NH: Heinemann.

Wilde, S. (Ed.) (1996). *Notes from a kidwatcher: Selected writings of Yetta M. Goodman.* Portsmouth, NH: Heinemann.

Winter, J. (2002). *Emily Dickinson's letters to the world.* New York: Frances Foster Books.

Wolfram, W. (2000). Everyone has an accent. *Teaching Tolerance, 18,* 20–23.

Wood, P. (Ed.). (1977). *The salt book.* Garden City, NY: Anchor Press.

Wortman, R. (1990). *Authenticity in the writing events of a whole language kindergarten/first grade classroom.* Unpublished doctoral dissertation, University of Arizona.

References

Wortman, R., & Matlin, M. (1995). *Leadership in whole language: The principal's role*. York, ME: Stenhouse.

Yashima, T. (1955). *Crow boy*. New York: Viking Press.

Yolen, J. (Ed.). (1992). *Street rhymes around the world*. Honesdale, PA: Boyds Mills Press.

Young, E. (1992). *Seven blind mice*. New York: Philomel Books.

Young, E. (1997). *Mouse match: A Chinese folktale*. San Diego: Silver Whistle.

Young, E. (1997). *Voices of the heart*. New York: Scholastic.

Your family language tree. (2000, April). *Kids Discover, 10,* 12–13.

Zernike, K. (1997, January 26). L.A. schools accommodate Ebonics. *The Arizona Daily Star,* pp. 1, 43.

Zolotow, C. (1974). *My grandson Lew*. New York: Harper & Row.

INDEX

AUTHOR

Yetta M. Goodman is Regents Professor in the Department of Language, Reading and Culture at the University of Arizona. She consults with education departments and speaks at conferences throughout the United States and in many nations of the world regarding issues of language, teaching, and learning, with implications for language arts curricula. In addition to her research in early literacy, miscue analysis, and the reading and writing processes, she has popularized the term *kidwatching* by encouraging teachers to be professional observers of the language and learning development of their students. Goodman is past president of NCTE and CELT, has served on NCTE and IRA boards of directors, and has been an active member of commissions and committees of numerous professional organizations. She was a principle force in the development of IRA-NCTE-cosponsored conferences that examined the impact of oral and written language development research on schools. She is a spokesperson for whole language philosophy and in her extensive writing is focused on classrooms, students, and teachers.

This book was typeset in Sabon by Electronic Imaging.
Typefaces used on the cover include Lithos and Frutiger.
The book was printed on 50-lb. Husky Offset paper
by IPC Communications.